# Vitali's Ireland

Time Travels in the Celtic Tiger

Also by Vitali Vitaliev:

# Vitali's Ireland

Time Travels in the Celtic Tiger

**Vitali Vitaliev**

*Gill & Macmillan*

*For Christine*

Gill & Macmillan Ltd
Hume Avenue, Park West, Dublin 12
with associated companies throughout the world
www.gillmacmillan.ie

© Vitali Vitaliev 2008
978 07171 4076 3

Typography design by Make Communication
Print origination by O'K Graphic Design, Dublin
Printed and bound in Great Britain by MPG Books Ltd,
Bodmin, Cornwall

This book is typeset in 10.5/13 pt Minion

The paper used in this book comes from the wood pulp of
managed forests. For every tree felled, at least one tree is
planted, thereby renewing natural resources.

A CIP catalogue record for this book is available from the
British Library.

5 4 3 2 1

The extract from 'Squarings' by Seamus Heaney (on page 217)
is reproduced by kind permission of Faber and Faber Ltd.

# Contents

'To write a good book about a country, one has to leave it first'

VISSARION BELINSKY

'Ireland—frustrating, friendly, infuriating, unforgettable and forever fascinating'

CHRISTOPHER WINN

# Acknowledgments

My heartfelt thanks to:

Royal Literary Fund, Northern Ireland Tourism Board (and personally to Pauline Gormley), Ireland West Tourism (and personally to Ciara O'Mahony), Connemara Tourism, Baedeker Verlag, John Murray Publishers, the *Rough Guide* and *Village* Magazine.

I am also grateful to Fergal Tobin, Jerry O'Callaghan, Michael Manning, Tommy Carlin, Tom Galvin, Dylan Scammel, Eimear Bruen, Jenny MacDonald, Orla Hasson, Charlotte Cox, John Reilly, Colin Murphy, Dmitri Vitaliev and Vincent Browne.

Special credits to Mary Sellen.

# Introduction

*'Ireland is a little Russia.'*
(GEORGE MOORE, 1911)

*The stretch of black, oil-like water between the pier and the ferry was widening slowly, almost reluctantly, as the Rotterdam-registered* Norbank, *with me on deck, left Liverpool Docks.*

*Having a water-filled gap between one's future and one's past—with no bridges in sight—is helpful when trying to make a new start.*

*It was the evening of 18 September 2004. I was heading for Dublin to take up a new job and to recover after a painful divorce—in short, to begin a new life, although as a writer who had always regarded his own being as a literary device, I would rather call it a new book.*

*My old Honda jalopy was one of three private vehicles squeezed in by enormous long-distance lorries on the car deck of the cargo ferry.*

*I spent the evening in the passenger lounge surrounded by beer-swilling and chain-smoking truckers. For them, this journey was an ordinary commute, with no metaphorical meaning involved.*

*Inside my cabin, I browsed a couple of Irish dailies, bought the day before in a WH Smith outlet at London's Charing Cross station. The moribund gloom and doom emanating from their pages was such that I felt like opening the porthole to get some fresh air. The weather in Ireland was beastly and likely to get worse. The whole country was but a rip-off and had become a burial ground for unfinished EU-subsidised projects. The death toll on the roads was growing by the minute. Irish writers were miserable and lonely. And to cap it all, some mysterious 'Dublin grave-digging row' was nowhere near to being resolved. Even one potentially good-news item ended on a despondent note: 'Identity of capital's lucky lotto winner still a mystery'.*

*I was reminded of the old Soviet joke: Optimist and Pessimist bump into each other in a Moscow street. 'You know what,' says Pessimist, 'life is so awful that it cannot possibly get any worse!'*

*'But it can! It can!!!', Optimist exclaims cheerfully.*

*Could it all be really so glum in Ireland, my newly adopted country, that had recently made it to the exclusive club of the twelve wealthiest nations of the globe and whose capital, Dublin, came second (after Sydney) in the world's friendliest city category of BA's annual travel awards?*

*I was about to find out for myself, I thought, while lullaby-ed by the muffled and strangely soothing buzz of the ship's engine.*

*I was woken up by a loud intercom announcement at 4.30 a.m. The Norbank was approaching the port of Dublin. In the lounge, the sullen-faced truckers were hastily munching their breakfasts. I tried to light up, but was told off by one of the crew: 'We are now in Irish territorial waters, and smoking in public places is not allowed.'*

*I looked around: as if by magic, all the ashtrays had disappeared from the tables overnight.*

*I went out onto the deck. It was windy, and lighting up a match was like trying to catch a bird with bare hands...*

*The first rays of the morning sun were peeping timidly from behind the clouds, lighting up the grim and fairly eclectic silhouettes of the sleeping Irish capital. From the sea, it looked as if Dublin was greeting me with a wry, gap-toothed smile.*

———

Ireland was familiar to me from my childhood days of vicarious map-assisted island-hopping. In my teens I was attracted to a dog-eared collection of Irish short stories that I spotted at our local library. Lovingly translated into Russian, the stories were tight, neatly structured and reminiscent—in their poetic melancholy—of the Russian prose of the early 20th century, the so-called 'silver age of Russian literature'. The similarity of the mood and the issues—social and emotional—was striking, and that couldn't fail but trigger my interest in the country.

Then, from a history book, I learned with trepidation that in Celtic Ireland poets were at the very summit of the social hierarchy —alongside druids and (somewhat disappointingly) lawyers. It was reassuring for a young poet like myself, who by the age of 17 had already published lots of separate verses, but not a collection that required a so-called 'steam engine'—a poem, that is, glorifying Lenin, the Communist Party and our happy Soviet existence.

By then, we were living in the Soviet Ukraine, in the eastern part of it, bordering on Russia, and I soon discovered the amazing parallels in Irish and Ukrainian history. Like Ireland, Ukraine was forced into an Act of Union with her much bigger neighbour in 1654—the agreement masterminded by the treacherous Ukrainian 'het'man' (Cossack military commander) Bohdan Khmelnitskiy. Like Gaelic in Ireland, Ukrainian language and culture had been subjected to merciless russification. In the Ukrainian university where I studied, all subjects were taught in Russian, and several of my fellow-students were expelled for talking Ukrainian to each other in the interval between lectures.

Even the Potato Famine had its analogue in Ukrainian history— the massive starvation of peasants in the early 1930s caused by Stalin's ruthless 'collectivisation'. An old Ukrainian peasant woman once told me how famished villagers went to towns in search of bread only to be met by machine-gun fire on approach.

And just as Ireland is still unable to come to grips with its long-awaited independence and sudden wealth, 'free' modern Ukraine cannot quite shake off the all-permeating influence of its weakened, yet still powerful, oppressor.

George Moore was wrong: Ireland is not a little Russia. It is rather a little Ukraine.

Another reason for my fascination with Ireland stems from a seemingly insignificant episode much later in my life and career. In the year 2000, when I was working as a columnist for the travel section of the *Daily Telegraph* in London, I wrote a feature about Venice, where, among other things, I compared it to an ageing, yet still graceful, woman suffering from insomnia and dragging restlessly around the house in her worn-out, loose-fitting slippers in the night. To me, the soft splashes of canal water against the ancient Venetian stones sounded like the shuffling of slippers across the floor…Later, I used this comparison in one of my books.

This metaphor was picked up and pounced upon by some kill-joy literary critics who laughed at it acerbically, considering it too graphic and far-fetched. I got an unexpected defence from my Irish readers and from a couple of Irish newspapers who claimed that the metaphor actually worked and was relevant.

That episode had greatly enhanced my perception of Ireland as the land of refined literary tastes and well-developed imaginations…

I did try to immigrate to Ireland once before, in January 1990, when—as a result of my journalistic investigations into the burgeoning Soviet Mafia—I was faced with death threats from the Mafiosi and with increasing harassment by their friends in the KGB. The situation became unbearable, and I had no choice but to defect from the USSR with my family.

We found ourselves first in London, but did not feel safe there and wanted to move on. Knowing that Ireland was always willing to accept writers, I arranged a meeting with a Third Secretary of the Irish Embassy—a lanky loose-jointed fellow. 'Yes, we like writers,' said he, 'but we actually hate journalists.'

We ended up in Australia instead, thus following in the footsteps of so many exiles of the past. I will never forget the St Patrick's Day celebrations in Melbourne in 1991. The whole city was painted green, and tongue-in-cheek signs of the type PARKING FOR THE IRISH ONLY were all over the place. I couldn't help the feeling, however, that the festivities were somewhat strained and artificial. Fourteen years later, as a Ukrainian-born Russian carrying British and Australian passports, I thought that with time I would be honoured to add a touch of 'Irishness' to my already extremely muddled identity.

For that, I needed to explore the country, to criss-cross it in search of that elusive and volatile substance—the Irish spirit as I knew it (or thought I knew it) from childhood.

But what was the best way of doing so?

Travelling back in time has always been one of humankind's most cherished dreams. This explains the preoccupation of science-fiction writers with time machines or any other device which allows us to peep behind the curtain of our own past.

Science fiction aside, I have discovered real vehicles capable of taking me many decades back into the past. I mean old guide-books—Baedekers, Murrays, Bradshaws, Cooks.

For me, these pocket-size tattered volumes are full of time-travel magic, especially when I find an old London Tube map (with a curtailed pink Northern Line ending at Highgate), a faded landing card, or just a dried-out, hundred-year-old flower in between their tattered pages. Touching such books is like touching eternity itself, for bygone realities and small practicalities of the distant past come to life in their estranged, meticulous and matter-of-fact style. In this respect, old guide-books are preferable to fiction: they provide me with an ossified time carcass, which I am free to fill with the contents of today's reality, or with that of my own imagination.

A casual pencil mark, left by a long-deceased anonymous traveller of yesteryear on the margins of 1873's *Murray's Handbook to France*, opposite one particular ferry route from Dover to Calais; or a tick next to the cheapest horse carriage rate from the railway station to the city centre in my native Kharkiv (*Baedeker's Russia*, 1914); or the underlined exact departure time of a train from Sienna to Milan in *Bradshaw's Continental Railway Guide to Europe*, do more for my imagination (and therefore—for my time-travels) than heaps of post-Victorian novels. When I see (and touch) these faint, yet curiously assertive, marks of time, I—for a fleeting moment—become a turn-of-the-19th-century traveller myself.

No matter how busy I am, I make sure I open an old guide-book every day thus (literally) staying in touch not only with eternity, but also with reality.

When I arrived in Ireland on that September day, I resolved that the best way to discover my new country would be to follow in the footsteps of the venerable Baedeker in the late 19th and early 20th centuries—that is, by travelling with one eye on the past, or time-travelling, if you wish…

Baedeker Handbooks, or 'Baedekers', are the most famous guide-books in the world. Started by an Essen-born and Heidelberg-educated publisher Karl Baedeker in 1839, they remain unsurpassed in their authority and precision of detail.

Baedeker's advice was always based on first-hand experience. Even when saying—somewhat peremptorily—that 'Europeans as a rule should never inquire after the wives of a Muslim' (I like this overcautious 'as a rule') in the early editions of his Egypt Handbook, he sounded as if he knew exactly what he was talking about, and the reader was led to believe that Baedeker himself had made numerous 'inquiries' after Muslims' wives before coming to the conclusion that they should be best avoided.

It was very seldom that Baedeker allowed his personality (having travelled so much, he should have been a clandestine romantic) to come through. In one of his Handbooks to Paris, he calls the French capital 'a temptress of a city which no one leaves without regret.'

Baedeker was simultaneously a scholar and a sportsman, a *bon-vivant* and a botanist, an archaeologist and a theatre-goer, an artist and a historian. He never minced his words: 'The Sweizerhaus…is an inn built ten years ago, which however provokes complaints because of the landlord's lack of politeness,' he wrote in the 1846 edition of *A Handbook for Travellers in Germany and the Austrian Empire*. Or take the following tip from his 1904 *Central Italy*: 'Iron bedsteads should if possible be selected as being less likely to harbour the enemies of repose.'

Likewise, Baedeker never went into raptures and was very sparing with the 'stars' he himself invented to award to the best (in his opinion) hotels, churches, towns/cities and even views. All later guide-book writers simply 'borrowed' this simple method of evaluation. Had it not been for Baedeker, clichés like 'a five-star hotel' or a 'three-star restaurant' would not have existed.

The best Baedeker guide-books came out between 1897 and 1909—the years known as the Golden Age of Baedeker. Among them, were annual editions of *Baedeker's Great Britain* and *Baedeker's London and Its Environs*—the pride of my ever-growing collection. However, having ventured as far as Scotland and the Hebrides, having covered all the main travel destinations of the globe (except for China, Japan, Australia and New Zealand), Baedeker[1] did not cover Ireland until the late 1960s.

Without Baedeker, my idea of time-travelling in Ireland with a comprehensive old guide-book was under threat and would have had to be buried, had I not come across John Murray's[2] superb *Handbook for Travellers in Ireland*, the first edition going back to the 1850s. I was lucky to get hold of a copy of its rather rare (like most pre- World War I guide-books) 1912 edition and decided that—in the absence of a Baedeker—it would be the best available time-travelling companion.

Armed with the 1912 guide-book—as well as with J.G. Bartholomew's 1914 *Survey Gazetteer of the British Isles*, based on the 1911 Census reports, the substantial *Imperial Gazetteer* edited by W.G. Blackie (1855) and a number of other antiquated sources—I tried (as much as possible) to stick to the general advice of good old Baedeker which, in certain cases, was not a problem: 'when the traveller is in a hurry, and his route does not coincide with that of an omnibus, he had better at once engage a cab...' Wherever possible, during my journeys throughout Ireland, I boarded at Murray-recommended hotels, and also tried to test the verdict of the undeservedly forgotten Irish writer, journalist, poet, composer and passionate 'motorist' Filson Young, whose book *Ireland at the Crossroads*, published in 1903, when the author was only twenty-seven, was yet another time-travel companion of mine: 'Ireland, that land of comfortless hotels...'

My journeys through Ireland were journeys into posterity—and through the past into the present and the future—not just with one antiquarian guide-book, but with a number of old folios from my collection, including (for the sake of balance to Murray's scholarship and precision) an incredibly naff, stereotype-laden volume, *Near Home or Europe Described*, published by Longmans, Green and Co in 1910 and targeting, as it seems, some dumb and hooray-patriotic Edwardian English teenagers. One of the book's

lengthier chapters is on Ireland—the country that the authors
benevolently refer to as England's 'little sister': 'Many English
people know very little about Ireland. Some of them seem to think
that the Irish are half-savages, who live in mud cabins with their
pigs, and eat hardly anything but potatoes... I have heard of a
family who kept a horse in their room! This family lived in a dark
cellar in a town...' And on the next page: 'The poorest of the Irish
do not care much about mending their clothes, and often wear
them in rags', and—to cap it all—'The Irish children are rosy,
merry little creatures.'

The undisputed 'gem' from the lengthy Ireland chapter of *Near
Home* is: 'Limerick, on the river Shannon, is the fourth city. Have
you ever heard of Limerick gloves? They are made of the skins of
Irish kids.'

'One cannot embrace the unembraceable,' in the words of Kozma
Prutkov, a spoof pseudo-omniscient 'author' created in jest by a
group of 19th-century Russian writers. I realised from the start that
covering the whole of Ireland, small as it was, would have been
impossible and unnecessary. The routes of my travels in the South,
therefore, were rather arbitrary and were largely defined by
journalistic assignments and/or by the kindness of local tourism
authorities who were interested in my time-travelling project and
offered to help. My Southern adventure took the form of a number
of separate journeys from Dublin, where I was living and working
at the time. As for the North, I tried to stick as much as possible to
one of Murray's 'Skeleton Routes', a suggested itinerary in his
*Handbook*. Having secured the enthusiastic support of the
Northern Ireland Tourism Board for the duration of the trip, I was
able to complete it in one stretch of twelve revealing, impression-
packed days (see Part III).

Having put on the imaginary Dom Pedro waterproof boots of
the early-20th-century traveller and donning a no-less-imaginary
Octagon Crown tourist cap (as opposed to the impractical bowler
hat of *Near Home*-style stereotypes which could be easily blown
away by the sweeping winds of West Cork and Connemara), I
looked out for the spirit of old Ireland, the Baedeker-forsaken land

of poets and druids, of rebels and chieftains, of early motor-cars and steam trains—straight out of my childhood dreams.

The result of that search is in front of you now.

# Part I

'A Tour through the South'[3]

# Chapter 1
# Irish for a Day

'Other people have a nationality. The Irish have a psychosis,' said Brendan Behan. From what little I knew about Ireland—a small, long-suffering country with a huge Diaspora, a history of extreme poverty and disproportionate artistic achievement, I dared to assume that being Irish was neither a 'nationality' nor a 'psychosis', but a destiny.

'Stereotypes about the Irish and those of Irish heritage are so pervasive that sometimes they are not even recognised as generalisations or considered offensive, as they would be if they were directed at racial minority groups,' writes Pat Friend in his excellent website *www.allaboutirish.com*. He then gives an example: 'The other day I tripped over my shillelagh as I was watching a leprechaun swing at a fairy because he was drunk and fighting, having had too much Guinness on his way to find his pot of gold at the end of the rainbow.'

All those us-bred modern clichés, alongside their British precursors (e.g. 'The Irish *when* good are perfect'—Lord Byron), are but outrageous trivialisations of the important concept they are trying to represent. 'Cultural identities…were never monolithic and are becoming much less so,' in the words of Professor Paul Gifford, Director of the Institute of European and Cultural Identity Studies at St Andrews University.

Nonetheless, the Irish seem to be as preoccupied with pinning down their elusive national identity as the Australians, or, say, the Scots. And whereas the former keep fluctuating from declaring themselves European one day and Asian (or Aboriginal) the next, the latter still tend to define their identity first as 'un-English' and only then as Scottish—the trend that can be found in Ireland (particularly in the South), too.

So what is 'Irishness', after all?

'A logical place to start the exploration of the Irish question is in a dictionary,' according to Pat Friend. Let's follow his advice and consult my London-published 1990s' *Collins Concise Dictionary*: '*Irish*—1. Relating to, or characteristic of Ireland, its people, their Celtic language, or their dialect of English. 2. *Inf. offens.* Ludicrous or illogical'.

'*Inf.offens.*' bits aside, the dictionary's first definition of 'Irish' seems to be 'covering' only one part of the forcefully divided nation and has little to do with the Irish in the country's North, for whom, according to Edward Moxon Browne's *National Identity in Northern Ireland*: 'British national identity can be regarded as a primordial umbrella. In Northern Ireland', continues he, '…national identity is an exclusive and divisive concept (isn't this true about any other country of the globe?)…It is rooted in the colonisation of Ulster by Protestants; and, consequently, by opposing views of the legitimacy of the state and its boundaries.'

Indeed, how can we talk about one monolithic Irish identity when the nation itself is split between two different sovereign states that until recently were effectively at war with each other? The concept of 'an open national identity', suggested by Rutherford Mayne and Gerald MacNamara in the 2004 Spring-Summer issue of 'The Journal of Irish Studies', makes much more sense to me.

Before starting my journeys around Ireland, North and South, I thought it would be helpful to try and understand what 'Irishness' as such was about. Intrigued by the promise of a 'Be Irish for a Day' experience at Causey Farm near Kells (I had found the ad on the Internet), I went to the Royal County of Meath in search of an answer.

'More elbow grease!' Lily, the lively mother of the Murtagh family of ten, was commanding as I mixed flour, soda, salt, eggs and my own elbow grease in an attempt to make a loaf of Irish bread.

It was 11 a.m., and I already felt at home at the friendly family farm. And, indeed, more 'Irish' than ever before.

My frantic bread making was followed by a short *ceilí* dancing lesson in the former cowshed. For someone who had always had two left feet (possibly even three), it felt like a succession of pole vaults without a pole. Then came my turn at bodhrán-playing, which was similar to eating a bowl of Miso soup with one chopstick (at least, that was how it felt to me—both in terms of hand movements and of the sounds I managed to extract from my uncomplaining bodhrán).

Both classes were conducted by the delightful Deirdre Murtagh (learning to spell Irish names—first and last—could also be a part of the 'Irish for a Day' experience), one of Lily's seven daughters.

The family's 'Irish for a Day' venture, started in 2001, was booming. Bookings were coming from all over the world, from Finland to Saudi Arabia, and the feedback from the visitors was nothing short of ecstatic.

Among other typically 'Irish' activities, offered by the Murtaghs, were hurling, turf-cutting, rope-making and milking a cow. I was momentarily tempted to do the latter, but thought better of it, having remembered that while trying (unsuccessfully) to milk a cow for the first and last time in my life in Australia, the newspaper I was then writing for was taken over by Conrad Black. It seemed like a bad omen.

'We are trying to bring people together through Irishness,' Deirdre told me as I munched through the freshly baked loaf of soda bread that I myself made (well, almost).

'But what *is* Irishness?' I asked her eagerly.

Just like myself, she found this concept difficult to define.

I had to carry on searching.

———

*'Almost all the Irish speak English, though they have a language of their own…'*
('NEAR HOME OR EUROPE DESCRIBED', LONDON, 1910)

'Irish timing,' Olivia Duff, the helpful manager of the Headfort Arms Hotel in Kells—my pied-à-terre on my one-day quest for

Irishness—muttered sardonically, looking at her watch. My next contact, Tomás Ó Maonaile, was running late. As it turned out, he had got stuck in traffic. So dense was the traffic through the town that a bus recently even hit the town's famous market cross.

No one enjoys sitting in a traffic jam and breathing petrol fumes, but Tomás had reasons particularly to hate this unhealthy 'Irish' experience. A native Irish speaker and an aspiring property developer, he had two passions in his life: preservation of the Irish language and protection of the environment. His hope was to try and combine both in his new project—an eco-friendly housing estate, populated exclusively by gaelic speakers. This might sound like a rather drastic requirement, but Tomás believed that the dire state of Ireland's long-suffering native tongue justified it.

'There are not enough Irish schools in the country, and very few textbooks,' he was saying as we drove to Brugh na Mí—his prospective housing development four miles away from Kells.

A solitary 'show cottage' stood on the would-be estate, in the shadow of the historic Funghan Hill, but Tomás said that thirty families, willing to participate in his 'Irish for life' (as opposed to 'Irish for a day') experience, had already expressed interest in buying houses there.

'Here, there will be an organic vegetable garden and an Irish-language learning centre, and there—in the middle of the compound—a children's playground...' Tomás was pointing to empty patches of land and could be easily dismissed as yet another airy-fairy Irish dreamer, but his determination was such that I knew he was going to succeed.

'He who loses his language—loses his land,' runs an old Cornish proverb. And his identity too, I could add. A language dies somewhere in the world every week, according to UNESCO, and the ancient Irish—expressive, poetic and melodious—should not be allowed to become one of them. For with it the very concept of 'Irishness' would disappear too.

The wind was rustling through the grass, as if whispering something gently in Irish...

———

*'If it [the Irish language] keeps itself free from the intrusion of that plague of things Irish, politics, as it claims to do, its influence will have far-reaching effects in brightening the homes and enriching the lives of the peasantry...'*
('A HANDBOOK FOR TRAVELLERS IN IRELAND',
   MURRAY, 1912)

As part of my search for Irishness, Tomás took me to Ráth Cairn —a predominantly Irish-speaking settlement, or Gaeltacht, founded in 1935. Almost all signs in the town were in gaelic only. It was there that I learned (under duress) my first two Irish words: *mná* and *fir*—when looking for a toilet inside the local community centre. What can I say? There's no better way of mastering a foreign language than when confronted with everyday basic needs. To my great relief (in more than one sense), however, there was a lady's silhouette above the mysterious *mná* sign (there was none above the *fir* one, mind you).

In Ráth Cairn I met Nadya Genserovskaya—a nineteen-year-old Russian and a fluent speaker of Irish. Moscow-born Nadya had come to the town ten years previously with her Russian mother who had married an Irishman. She went to an English school, but—being linguistically alert—picked up Irish soon.

'At home we speak either Russian or Irish, but not English,' she told me with a smile. A student of German at Trinity College, this young polyglot assured me that she felt more at home in Ráth Cairn than in Moscow.

'Ireland is a kind country,' she said simply when I asked her what she thought 'Irishness' was about.

———

*'Kells...is most famous for what is not here.'*
(THE 'ROUGH GUIDE TO IRELAND', 2004)

Reluctant to leave Ráth Cairn, I was late for my next appointment.

Or was I simply getting 'Irish-ised' and, without realising it, adjusting to 'Irish timing'?

Having missed Brian Curran, the chairman of Kells town council, in his town hall offices, I was directed to his shop, called 'Shamrock'.

At first glance, 'Shamrock' looked like an ordinary souvenir shop-cum-hardware store: kettles, irons and kitchen utensils were displayed on the shelves alongside green-clad 'Irish' dolls and 'Irish Humour' socks (the humour of the latter item was totally lost on me). A toy 'singing monkey' called Charlie greeted customers at the entrance. If touched, Charlie would start twitching and chanting in high-pitch falsetto: 'Yippy-yah-yah, yippy-yippy-yah!'

It took me a while to spot the sign above the counter, behind which the owner himself—bespectacled and redheaded—was standing in state: BRIAN CURRAN. FUNERAL DIRECTOR. PERSONAL SERVICE. COMPLETE FUNERAL ARRANGEMENTS.

Numb with surprise, I noticed a couple of funeral wreaths discreetly tucked into a far corner, and all the regulation questions I was meaning to ask Mr Curran (about the composition of the town council, the redevelopment of Kells and so on) became irrelevant.

'Is this some sort of a joke?' was the only thing I could utter.

'Yes and no,' was the reply. 'I think every funeral director must have a gift shop as a façade...'

He took me to a side room, where half-a-dozen ready-to-use coffins were neatly stacked.

At least, they were not exhibited in the shop-window, next to the singing monkey and the mysterious 'Irish Humour' socks. From my reading of Pete McCarthy's book *McCarthy's Bar*, I knew it was not that unusual for an Irish country pub to sell bicycles as well as pints of Guinness, but I was still thoroughly unprepared for this funeral director's office, conveniently situated at one of Ireland's craziest road-crossings, complete with no fewer than nine approach roads, doubling as an unpretentious and down-to-earth (forgive my unintended pun) souvenir shop. I suddenly felt that I had come a step closer to understanding the true meaning of 'Irishness'.

'Say bye to Charlie,' suggested Mr Curran as I was leaving.

And so I did.

Chapter 2

# The Garden of Ireland

'...*in Wicklow, a pedestrian is understood.*'
('A HANDBOOK FOR TRAVELLERS IN IRELAND',
MURRAY, 1912)

'*The peasantry of Co Wicklow are quiet and
industrious, and are said to be generally
handsome, with Roman profiles.*'
(THE 'IMPERIAL GAZETTEER', W.G. BLACKIE, ED.,
1855)

YOU ARE ENTERING THE GARDEN OF IRELAND ran a cheerful
road sign near Bray. Having just negotiated the largely tree-
less streets of central Dublin, I was glad to be entering a
'Garden', even if a metaphorical one. As my second time-travelling
journey in search of Irishness, Co. Wicklow was an obvious choice,
being the closest to Dublin, where I was based.

Before the journey, I looked up Co. Wicklow in the appropriate
reference book—in this case in *Lippincott's New Gazetteer of the
World*—a 2,100-page, ten-kilo boulder of a tome (the weightiest
folio in my collection), published in London in 1906—a volume
that a 1912 traveller would have been likely to consult: 'Wicklow is
a mountainous district abounding in romantic scenery...It is
mainly a pastoral county. Pop. in 1851 98,978; in 1901—60, 284...'

This laconic entry on page 2001 of the matter-of-fact 'Gazetteer'
struck me as rather unusual. It was the only one in the whole of
that behemoth of a book where the word 'romantic' was used.

The fact that the county's population dwindled almost two-fold
between 1850 and 1901 reflected the massive emigration in the

aftermath of the Great Famine. Interestingly, according to the 2005 *Encyclopaedia of Ireland*, the population of modern Wicklow is only slightly above its 1850 mark at 114,719. The style of the Encyclopaedia's entry on Co. Wicklow, however, was somewhat different from that of the Gazetteer: 'Co Wicklow…comprises an extensive natural environment (*sic*) on the doorstep of a large city…' Little 'romanticism' here, I had to admit.

'There is a strange savage quality about the mountains and the sea that begins to deteriorate when you call it scenery (or—in modern terms—'environment'—vv),' the inimitable Filson Young wrote in *Ireland at the Crossroads* in 1903.

I thought that the politically correct term 'natural environment' had a much bigger deteriorative force than 'scenery'.

At least, the Wicklow Mountains were still there and seemingly intact.

Shortly after Bray,[4] formerly known as 'the Brighton of Ireland', and one of the most pleasant and best-situated watering places in the country' (Murray, 1912) now home to Ireland's largest MacDonald's, occupying the disembowelled and still graceful (from the outside) building of the former historic Town Hall— the Wicklow Mountains came into full view. They were neat, compact—as if freshly packaged—and not at all dramatic, with no steep cliffs, snow-capped peaks or gaping precipices. In all fairness, they were not even proper mountains, but—as it was aptly put by my down-to-earth 2004 *Rough Guide to Ireland*—'really round-topped hills, ground down by the Ice Ages, with the occasional freakish shape…'

'A tour through Wicklow is a favourite relaxation with all Dublin residents, who are, indeed, fortunate in having almost at their own doors a succession of changing scenery, in which mountains, sea, wood, and river are blended together, furnishing environs that no other city in the kingdom can boast,' Murray wrote in 1912. Judging by the sheer number of cars running in both directions on the N11 motorway ninety-three years later, it was still the case. My 'patriotically' green and 'unpatriotically' tiny Fiat Punto was blending nicely into this flow.

'One of the first things he [the motorist] will notice, is the almost universal habit of allowing domestic animals of all kinds to occupy and browse on the roadways. Care, and constant care, must be taken in regard to them, if the motorist is to avoid risk and unpleasantness,' noted Murray.

The distracting part played by domestic animals was now taken by ubiquitous road signs, pointing to 'heritage sites', 'scenic routes' and other local attractions and 'amenities'. DRUIDS' GOLF COURSE said one of them, and my imagination immediately conjured up the image of a bearded druid in a baseball cap lifting his golf club to the skies.

Near Enniskerry, a brown sign with POWERSCOURT GARDENS on it flashed past my window. To me, it was a reminder not so much of the magnificent country house of Lord Powerscourt as of Powerscourt waterfall. When, encouraged by Murray, I went to have a look at that 'very fine fall, though, like every other, dependent for scenic effect on the volume of water in the river', I was shocked to discover that one had to cough up €6 to admire the 'wonderfully fine? (JM) view. It was in a way even more shocking than nightly fireworks above Niagara Falls on the US-Canada border (to enhance the natural beauty?)—at least they didn't charge for staring at them.

While in Ireland, I saw only one worse example of Celtic Tiger greed: an old seafood shop in a Dublin suburb that used to give away fish heads to local angler boys, started charging the boys 50 cent per fish head in 2003!

Having to pay for seeing a waterfall sounded like yet another Ostap Bender scam. That fictitious smooth operator, hero of 1920s' novels such as *The Twelve Chairs* and the *Little Golden Calf*, created by a brilliant tandem of Soviet writers, Ilya Ilf and Evgeny Petrov,[5] once found himself terribly hard-up in the Russian town of Piatigorsk in the Northern Caucasus and came up with the idea of charging gullible tourists an entry fee to The Drop—a puddle of stinking malachite at the bottom of a mountain cavern. When questioned by an inquisitive militiaman for what purpose the money was being collected, Ostap quickly retorted: 'For general repairs to the Drop...So that it won't drop too much.'

I could envisage a dispassionate Powerscourt Waterfall park warden addressing a similar query: 'For the waterfall, not to fall too much.'

It has to be said that the resourceful Ostap only charged thirty kopecks for the view—a pittance compared to the six-euro Powerscourt viewing fee—probably due to the fact that any 'repairs' to a waterfall were bound to be much costlier than those to The Drop.

To be able to observe the surrounding landscape and to read directions, while maintaining my time-travelling 'double vision' (i.e. constantly measuring up realities against the 'ossified carcass of time' in my ninety-three-year-old guide-book), I had to stay in the 'slow' left lane, and as a result was constantly tailgated by other drivers which was annoying and felt similar to someone peeping over your shoulder trying to read your newspaper in a crowded train carriage.

I noticed that Irish motorists loved tailgating—much more than their British, Australian or even French counterparts. This is a significant change from 1912, the dawn of motoring, if we believe John Murray:

'Courtesy and consideration from others are as quickly responded to in Ireland as in any country in the world, and the motorist who exercises both will have no difficulty in travelling through Ireland in all its highways and byways.'

I thought that obsessive tailgating was probably part of the new 'Celtic Tiger' mentality, for some modern Irish drivers, indeed, behaved not like 'courteous' and 'considerate' motorists, but rather like tigers in pursuit of their prey. They—and not 'domestic animals of all kinds'—constituted the main 'unpleasantness' on the roads of Ireland in 2005.

No wonder Ireland was only one of three countries in Europe that saw an increase in the number of people killed on its roads in 2004. Among the most tragically ironic accidents was that of James Bohanna, a 21-year-old farmer, who was travelling home after spreading slurry on a field near Ballycullane in Co. Wexford. At some point, the spreader on his tractor became detached and blocked the road as he turned into the lane leading to his farm. It was already dark, so he jumped out of his cab to run down the road and warn passing motorists to slow down to avoid the danger. He was struck by an oncoming car almost straight away and died instantly.

I turned off the motorway to visit Wicklow Town, the county's capital, and followed numerous signposts to Wicklow Gaol—the town's main tourist attraction.

I crawled through the town centre for half an hour trying to find a parking spot and was reminded of Murray's description of the traffic in 1912 Ireland: 'At cottage doors, or in shops in villages and towns, horses and carts are left standing alone, and the rushing noise of a motor or sound of the horn is apt to cause a bolt.' No amount of honking on my part made any difference ninety-three years on: the cars, parked all over the place, simply refused to budge.

'Pedestrians' might still be 'understood' in 21st-century Wicklow, but motorists definitely weren't…

I had to drive up the hill away from the centre and finally squeezed my Punto into a narrow gap between cars in a 'School Set Down Only' car park. Descending on foot back to the town centre, I caught a view of the whole of Wicklow—a sight that corresponded almost exactly to Murray's 'quaint-looking town stretching in a semicircle round the bay, and, with the cliffs on the South, the few ruins of the Black Castle, and the distant promontories of Wicklow Head, makes up a very charming landscape.'

You can change the wallpaper and rearrange the furniture in the rooms of an old house, but you can't replace the view from its windows…

Walking down New Street, I came across 'The Forgotten Lady'—a shop specialising in huge garments for women. It was an obvious misnomer and should have been renamed 'The New Lady', the reason being that—due to a near-absence of junk-food and couch-potato culture—obese 'ladies' (as well as 'gentlemen') were much less common in the early 20th century than they are now. The world-famous Sears, Roebuck & Co. catalogue had to print a special note in its 1908 issue apologising for nor being able 'to furnish larger sizes' than the 28-inch-waist and 42-inch-bust in women's 'frocks'—rather average by modern standards!

The name of a barber's shop in Market Square—'The Rebel Barber'—was at a first glance even more puzzling, before I realised that it referred to the fact that Wicklow was at the margin of the 1798 rebellion, and the statue of Billy Byrne (or as it was put by Murray—in somewhat derogatory fashion—'Statue to "Billy" Byrne, the rebel leader of 1798', stood across the Square, near the town hall. It was surrounded by loitering teenagers.

I decided I would never use the services of 'The Rebel Barber' (even if the name of that shop had a proper historical explanation), for where was the guarantee that he wouldn't start 'rebelling' while cutting my hair? I didn't want to end up with my ears trimmed up—instead of my curls...

With that resolution firmly in mind, I entered the semi-dark lobby of 'Wicklow's Historic Gaol' now a museum, of course.

'Can I have a quick look at the Gaol?' I asked a black-clad female receptionist.

'Are you from Germany?' she asked me in return.

Although in Ireland I am often confronted with the question: 'Which part of Italy do you come from, Mr Vivaldi?', I have as much Italian blood in me as Pavarotti has Ukrainian. But interestingly, I have never been taken for a Ukrainian, simply because most people in Ireland do not seem to have a clue what Ukraine actually is—a vegetable, a mineral, or, indeed, a country. Psychologically speaking, the near-obsessive desire of the Irish to know where their accidental interlocutor comes from can probably be explained by not being quite certain of their own place in the modern world and by frantically trying to position themselves in it.

But to think that I was German—that had only happened to me once before—not in Ireland, but on the aptly monikered Scilly Islands. And it was not for your average beer-swilling German that I was mistaken, but for Herr Karl Baedeker, one of the pioneers of modern guide-book writing, himself!

In year 2000, I habitually travelled around the UK with a tattered copy of *Baedeker's Britain*, 1893. A staff member at the tourism office in Hugh Town, the Scillies' capital, who had been forewarned of my arrival and of the main tool of my research (the old Baedeker guide-book, of course), asked me whether I could read in English. I answered in the affirmative adding that I could write, too, and had just published my seventh book in that language. I was then asked when exactly I was going back to Germany.

'It is nice to meet you, Mr Baedeker,' the woman smiled. 'They have just phoned me from London and asked me to reserve a room for you...'

I realised that—in an amazing twist of fortune—I had been eclipsed by my own old guide-book and denials were useless.

'*Der Kutscher ist betrunken*,'⁶ I replied gravely, using the only complete German sentence I knew by heart. The 1886 edition of *Baedeker's Manual of Conversation*, another gem of my book collection, had for once proved helpful...

Having reassured the inquisitive receptionist at the gaol that I was not German, but a Ukrainian-born Russian, with British and Australian citizenships, temporarily living in Ireland (I could see her reaching for her handbag—probably in search of an aspirin), I proceeded to the first room of the gaol-cum-museum that was called the 'Education Room'.

On one of its walls, next to the old map of Tasman Peninsula, was a drawing of 'the Model Prison of Port Arthur', Tasmania's most horrific gaol, where many convicts, dispatched from Ireland (including 105 from Wicklow), ended their lives.

Port Arthur and the whole of 'Tasman Peninsula' were familiar to me. While living in Melbourne, I frequently travelled to Tasmania, for it reminded me of Europe. Indeed, the convicts of that 'secondary' British gulag (they were normally sent there for misdemeanours committed while already serving their terms in continental Australia), knowing there was no return, had planted numerous European trees, built Gothic churches for themselves and thatched cottages for their gaolers. The Model Prison of Port Arthur opened in 1830 and had a 'silent' or 'separate' policy. Its inmates lived and worked in solitary confinement, in complete silence and anonymity. They were called out by numbers only, just as in German and Soviet concentration camps a hundred years later.

The British 'experiments', however, went further. They made the convicts wear masks at all times, lest they be recognised by their fellow sufferers in 'airing yards'. It was only in the chapel, where each prisoner had his own 'praying box', allowing a view only of the priest and the altar, that he could remove his mask. Warders never spoke to prisoners and communicated solely by hand signals.

In the 1850s Port Arthur was frequently visited by inspectors from London who were very impressed by the colony's 'pioneering' methods. One thing they failed to understand, however, was why prisoners in Port Arthur were going insane in growing numbers. A special asylum had to be built in the prison grounds. In 1871, the number of mad convicts reached 111, exceeding Port Arthur's sane population, and soon afterwards The Model Prison had to close, since there were no 'normal' inmates left.

I am still of the opinion that punitive psychiatry as a method of suppressing dissent was attempted first not by the Russian Bolsheviks, but by the British in Port Arthur, still described as an achievement in some British history manuals.

I was brought back to reality by an obstreperous Irish toddler, happily knocking on the glass dome covering a model of Wicklow Gaol's gallows—complete with miniature freshly hanged prisoner, his tiny pink tongue falling out of his mouth. The little brat's young mother was telling him off: 'See, that man was very naughty—he was knocking on the glass, like you are, so you'd better stop…' The kid immediately calmed down. Dr Benjamin Spock would certainly have disapproved.

PLEASE WAIT TO BE SUMMONED BY A GAOLER! warned a sign at the prison's entrance. I waited and waited, but nothing happened, so I just went inside to be greeted by the hubbub of pre-recorded voices emanating from numerous mannequin sets. Everything —prisoners, gaolers, sailors, guards in Port Arthur (the exhibition followed the exiled convicts to Tasmania) and even a plate of thin prison gruel—was made of plastic. The convicts spoke (or rather moaned) with a distinct Irish drawl ('Oh, we shouldn't have started this mutiny[7]…Now I'll never see Wicklow again…'), whereas the warders had a feline Cockney accent ('I don't trust these Irish convict bastards…').

A man, dressed in black period costume of uncertain period,

suddenly materialised from nowhere and introduced himself as 'Richard Beeton, the gaoler'. I asked whether he was a relation of Mrs Beeton, but he ignored my question and said, with a bad English accent: 'If you get locked in one of the prison cells, just bang on the door—I'll come and get you out for a few bob...'

The café was firmly shut, 'for stock-taking', I was assured by a handwritten note stuck to the door. That was an obvious lie: there was not a single living soul inside the café, and all the chairs had been placed on table tops. 'Stock-taking' was a common excuse for closing down shops and restaurants indefinitely in the Soviet Union. The other popular pretext was a mysterious 'sanitary hour' that often lasted for days on end...

At the Museum exit, next to a tattered mannequin of a warden, clutching a rubber stamp in his plastic hands, freshly printed 'Wicklow County Gaol Release Forms' were neatly stacked on a table:

> This is to confirm the release of..........
> Who resides in the town of...................
> In the country of...............................
> CRIME COMMITTED:
> For the crime of stealing 127 dead rabbits being the property of Thomas Byrne, a sentence of four months' imprisonment.
> Having completed your sentence and the Gaoler being satisfied that you have reformed and therefore are fit to be discharged into society, you are hereby released from Wicklow County Gaol
>
> OFFICIAL RELEASE STAMP

Having visited a number of kitschy museums, I was nevertheless shocked by such a blatant trivialisation of gruesome Irish history. As someone who came close to being imprisoned himself for his views, dissenting from the official Soviet dogma, and who had visited a number of prisons and labour camps as a journalist, I was extremely sensitive (possibly, over-sensitive) to any belittling of human suffering—for reasons political or purely commercial.

And I hadn't endured the gift-shop yet. Many months of travel in the USA taught me to be wary of museum gift shops. I will never forget a porcelain salt-and-pepper grinder on sale (for $25) in the gift shop of the Seventh-Floor Museum in Dallas, Texas—the very building from where President Kennedy was so treacherously shot dead. The grinder was in the shape of JFK's head, and one could squeeze salt (or pepper) out of it by twisting the President's neck!

The stock of the Wicklow Gaol gift-shop was not that outrageously inconsiderate, yet still extremely insensitive. Among the items displayed were 'Die Cast Metal Handcuffs with Working (*sic*) Lock & Keys—not suitable for children under 3' (but clearly fine for playful four-year-olds—a tempting buy for the young mum of the toddler from the education room). And next to the handcuffs: 'whoopee cushions', fridge magnets, bottle openers, hair brushes, erasers, etc.—all proudly carrying the Wicklow Gaol logo on them.

It came as no surprise to learn from one of the museum brochures that 'Wicklow Gaol can be booked as a venue for business seminars'. As I read later in the *Wicklow People*, a local newspaper with headlines of the type, 'Heroic Bouncer Saves Drowning Woman', the county 'has been aggressively marketed for industry'. And the county's history, too, I could add.

I could not possibly leave Wicklow Town without 'inspecting' the only Murray-recommended hotel that was still there—The Grand. Indeed, it was still 'nestling in Wicklow Town' (to quote the hotel's glossy brochure), yet its once beautifully Victorian exterior and interior had been modernised beyond recognition. A couple of stained-glass windows and a mahogany reception stand in the lobby were the only reminders of the Grand's former grandeur—as testified by several old photos of the establishment displayed above the bar, next to a framed copy of the mystifying 'Tourist Menu of the Year 1995' (the food would have been a bit stale for my taste. Another genuine touch of bygone times was the old drawing of a man with a smoking pipe in his mouth on the door of the gents' toilet. Otherwise, cheap dusty rugs, plastic furniture and a terrible stench from the kitchen prevailed. The 'tea/coffee making facilities, television with access to hair dryer, iron and ironing boards', generously promised by the hotel's brochure, did little to enhance the non-existent ambience.

In the lobby, from where the now-defunct Grand Staircase—an essential feature of every Victorian hotel—must have originated, a poster advertising the WEDDING PACKAGE AT THE GRAND HOTEL included:

BRIDAL SUITE FOR BRIDE & GROOM
GLASS OF CHAMPAGNE ON ARRIVAL (just one?)
RED CARPET
WHITE LINEN FOR TABLES
PERSONALISED MENU CARDS—
and—last but not least—
CAKE STAND AND KNIFE

The munificent 'package'—we were warned by the small print at the bottom of the poster—was 'based on minimum numbers of 100'.

Next to this impressive example of the miserly Celtic Tiger epoch, was a photo of a lady inside one of the hotel's rooms (possibly, the very 'bridal suite for bride & groom'). She was looking at herself in the mirror, carefully wrapped in a white towel, another—smaller—towel bound around her head. It was plain she hadn't exercised her right to a hairdryer yet. I was reminded once more of Filson Young's comment in *Ireland at the Crossroads*: '... Ireland, that land of comfortless hotels...'

———

Thank God, shopping for souvenirs (or any kind of shopping, for that matter) was not on the agenda of the much less commercially minded travellers of yesteryear. The only time 'shopping' is ever mentioned in Baedeker's *Manual of Conversation*, 1886 is in the chapter on how 'to hire, or buy a horse':

'I wish to hire/buy a horse, to take a ride through the town and its environs; have you one to let out? If I like it, perhaps I may buy it.'

'Yes, Sir; I have chestnut horses, white-spotted, dapple-gray, bay, grey, spotted-grey, black, white, dun, spotted, piebald and cream-coloured. I have some of all kinds. What colour would you wish your horse to be?'

'I care little about his colour, provided he has not a bald face and is handsome and tractable... '

And so on, before it comes to haggling over the price:

'How much do you ask for him?'

'Fifty pounds have been offered for him more than once, which I have refused; you shall have him for sixty.'

'This is very dear. Such a price frightens me.'

'Examine the head, the chest, and the legs of this horse. He is faultless in all points. His mouth is so fine he could almost drink out of a glass...'

Unlike shopping, helping the traveller to choose a place to stay overnight was of utmost significance to both Murray and Baedeker. Their methods of research, however, differed substantially. Baedeker inspectors always travelled incognito and never accepted 'freebies', whereas Murray was much less autonomous and was prepared to run an ad for a hotel in return for hospitality. Since Baedeker, sadly, never ventured to Ireland, we have to rely on Murray for a general description of early-20th-century Irish hotels:

'Speaking generally, the hotels of Ireland are inferior to those of England, Scotland or the Continent,' he begins, only to add diplomatically: 'There are however, many exceptions to this general statement.'

Among those 'exceptions', by the way, he specifically names 'The Wicklow district', where 'good hotels have rapidly developed'.

'Many of the smaller hotels, 'Murray continues, 'are not so bad as they appear at first glance. Outward indications of characteristic

Irish free-and-easy carelessness (*sic*—vv) may be accompanied with substantial food and clean sleeping accommodation; almost invariably with good-humoured civility and attention.'

Talking about the quality of service, Murray seemed to favour so-called 'boots' (locally based servants with no special training) over the 'imported waiter'—'an exotic luxury often engaged for the season from Dublin or some other city'. This thought is echoed by Filson Young, who in *Ireland at the Crossroads*, speaks with derision about 'the little army of Swiss waiters, those half-witted creatures who only know the world of hotels, rush hither and thither in the discharge of their remorseless disobedience.'

My own observations of travelling in Ireland in 2004–6, show that the role of the noncompliant Swiss waiters of a hundred years ago has now been usurped by newcomers from Poland—often even more defiant and 'disobedient' than their notorious Swiss precursors.

Staying at Woodenbridge Hotel in Co. Wicklow (allegedly, the country's oldest hotel in existence) which was described by Murray as 'excellent' in 1912, I watched Polish kitchen workers monopolise the establishment's only public phone to conduct endless conversations with their homeland and totally ignore the paying hotel guests, hopping from one foot to another in the lobby in feeble (and largely futile) attempts to attract their attention.

When I had a problem with the electric lights in my room one evening, a Polish electrician, called Pan Fix-it-owsky (clearly, I've invented this name), turned up only to say that he spoke very little English and therefore I would have to wait until the morning (when the whole issue of electric lighting would become irrelevant in any case).

Whereas lighting inside my room was non-existent, the same could not be said about the hotel's own façade, brightly lit by two powerful searchlights. It would have been fine, had it not been for the fact that one of them was also lighting up my room—not to the extent to allow me to read and write, but well enough to stop me sleeping.

I called Reception at about midnight, asking them to switch the lights off and was told that they (the lights) would have to stay on 'until the last patrons leave the car park of the hotel's bar'.

Judging by boozy noise from downstairs, the party in the bar was still in full swing.

'When will that be?' I enquired.

'At one a.m.'

'For sure?'

'No…'

They were prepared to ignore the interests of the hotel's guests for the sake of a bunch of money-spending boozers.

When the lights were still on at 1-30 a.m., I called Reception again. The phone was answered by a Polish night porter who sounded exactly like my friend, Pan Fix-it-owsky.

'We can bring you a mattress to cover up the window,' he suggested.

I had to spend the night in the treacherous glow of the Celtic Tiger's predatory eyes…

Among other things, the Woodenbridge Hotel boasted a regulation 'De Valera Suite', where the former Irish President, allegedly, spent his honeymoon.

Looking back at my travels around Ireland, I have to admit that it was hard to find an Irish hotel that did not claim to have hosted the ubiquitous De Valera, even if for one night only. In England, the same could be said of Charles Dickens, and in Scotland, of Mary Queen of Scots.

A framed Victorian poster of the hotel *('First Class. Best views in Wicklow, if not in all Ireland. Sanitary work has been carried out on the finest and first scientific principles.')* hung on the Reception wall, next to a dubious, and clearly not Victorian, ad for 'Adult Dancing'.

'Well, at least the views are still stunning,' I was thinking at breakfast. The tables were unclean, the waiters—sullen, and the orange juice was off. The 'scientific sanitary principles' of yesteryear seemed to be well-forgotten.

———

*'Rathdrum is a place of no special interest in itself.'*
('A HANDBOOK FOR TRAVELLERS IN IRELAND',
MURRAY, 1912)

RATHDRUM—HOST TOWN TO BAHRAIN ran the road sign. I found it puzzling in the extreme. What was the connection between this small Wicklow town 'of no special interest' and the independent sheikdom on the Persian Gulf?

The only mental link I could draw was entirely of my own making. Several years ago, I wrote a spoof limerick for the 60th birthday of a Ukrainian friend of mine, now living in Melbourne, Australia. It went like this:

> There lived an old man in Ukraine
> Who once travelled to Melbourne by train.
> He returned in a week
> Feeling hungry and sick,
> For his train got stuck in Bahrain.

If we are to believe that limericks as a genre originated from the early-19th-century Irish-language satirical verses of the Poets of the Maige from Co. Limerick, then the association—no matter how flimsy and illogical—would be as follows: Bahrain was mentioned in my limerick; limericks come from Ireland; Rathdrum is a town in Ireland. Bingo!

I was on the way to my hotel in Woodenbridge and decided to stop in Rathdrum to withdraw some cash from the ATM. As I was walking towards it, my way was suddenly blocked by a black armoured van. Behind it, a khaki-coloured army truck suddenly screeched to a halt. Several dozen heavily armed soldiers in camouflage uniforms and flak jackets jumped out and surrounded the van, their submachine guns aimed at the doors of the Bank of Ireland.

It all happened so fast that I didn't have time to get scared or even surprised—I just stood there on the pavement, clutching my bank card and watching.

'What's going on?' I asked a passer-by—a podgy middle-aged man, most likely a local.

'Can't you see?' he chuckled. 'They are delivering afternoon tea to the bank...'

'No, seriously.'

'Seriously? They are worried about bank robberies by the IRA—hence all the fuss. That's how they deliver cash to banks in Ireland these days. Just gives the soldiers something to do, I guess.'

A couple of minutes later, the soldiers jumped back into the truck and it sped away, together with the van. The anti-hold-up operation, which itself looked like a carefully planned hold-up, was over.

'At least now we know that the money is there, so we can go and break in safely,' commented my facetious companion.

I decided I'd rather withdraw cash somewhere else.

On the way out of Rathdrum, I braked next to another HOST TOWN TO BAHRAIN sign and got out of the car. SPECIAL OLYMPICS, 2003 was written in the right-hand corner in small letters I hadn't been able to discern from behind the wheel.

Hosting the Bahrain Special Olympics team several years before should not have been recorded as Rathdrum's only claim to fame. It was, after all, 'home' not just to Bahrain, but also to Charles Stewart Parnell, one of Ireland's most important and interesting politicians. But, except for a modest road sign pointing towards Avondale House, where Parnell was born in 1846, there was no mention of the 'uncrowned king of Ireland' in Rathdrum. Unlike that of 'Thomas "Buck" Whaley', who, according to an impressive memorial plate in the town centre, 'walked to Jerusalem and played handball against the Walls of the Old City.'

———

To use one of Baedeker's (and Murray's) favourite epithets, Rathdrum was a 'quaint' town indeed! Just like the whole of Co. Wicklow that, over the two years in which I lived in Ireland, became one of my favourite destinations. Even now, living in London, I often return to the Wicklow Mountains in my meditations and dreams.

Enjoying the beauties of Co. Wicklow, however, did not stop me from noticing other—less attractive—details. Most of them, it has to be said, were fairly recent 'innovations'.

It is hard to imagine a spot more romantic and calming than The Meeting of the Waters 'at the confluence of the Avonmore and Avonbeg, which here unite.' (Murray). Even if these days it could be also called 'The Meeting of the Watering Holes' due to the two unremarkable pubs beside the visitor centre, with one of Ireland's tackiest gift-shops, straddling the place where the rivers merge. There, I could easily relate to the following observation of Murray's: '…it must be confessed that tourists often feel a certain amount of disappointment with it [The Meeting of the Waters], a necessary result when any place or thing has been exaggerated…', although what he meant in 1912 was the famous poetic description of the spot by Thomas Moore, 'Ireland's National Poet', carved in stone and replicated all over the place.

I also enjoyed passing through the picture-postcard village of Avoca (Murray used to spell its name and that of the surrounding valley as 'Ovoca'), alias 'Ballykissangel', with its graceful church and unlikely Greek wine bar, The Village Greek, on the river bank. Even a *Wicklow People* article claiming that some of the village houses were infested with 'rats as big as elephants' had failed to deter me from frequent purposeless detours to the village and to the near-by town of Aughrim ('a pretty village'—Murray)—charming and beautifully kept, with elegant crescent-shaped terraces, lined with gas lanterns; with the genuine Nana May's Coffee Shop, serving excellent espresso and a substantial Full Irish Breakfast for a mere €6.50—the price of a sandwich in Dublin. Aughrim was also home to one of the best-preserved small Victorian hotels in Ireland—Lawless's Hotel ('quiet quarters at the little hotel for cyclists and pedestrians'—Murray). Sadly, the Celtic Tiger had reached Aughrim, too: most houses at O'Neill & Flanagan Estate Agents were priced at over €600,000. And revisiting Aughrim shortly before leaving Ireland in December 2005, I was saddened to see that the whole Victorian quarter (which, ironically, included the offices of O'Neill & Flanagan), had been razed to the ground to vacate the space for a new housing development of rubber-stamp modern cottages.

Visiting Glendalough, I could not help remembering a wise 1903 pronouncement of Filson Young: 'There was never any more absurd idea than that prosperity could be brought to Ireland by opening it up as a tourist resort.'

The same disease which had taken hold of Wicklow Gaol also seemed to have infected Glendalough, starred by Murray in 1912 for its 'silent and deserted ruins' giving 'a singular impressiveness to the scene'. The sacred site has been nearly destroyed by rampant tourism: interpretation centres, re-enactments of all kinds and constantly wowing elderly American visitors. No longer 'silent and deserted'…

The unique monastic city itself, which, incidentally, could be also reached by St Kevin's Bus Services (!), was so well hidden behind flea markets, 'St Kevin's ice-cream' (!) stalls, gift shops and Internet cafés that it took a while to find it nestling behind the huge concrete visitor centre, charging a hefty entrance fee.

St Kevin would have to take a bus to get to his cave these days. To while away the time, he could have sucked on his own 'St Kevin's ice-cream' on the way!

No 'tiger'—Celtic or other—could, however, swallow up the striking views from the Wicklow Gap, one of the best natural vantage points in the country reached by driving up the historic British-built Great Military Road. The only slight distraction blocking the view was a large 'interpretation' sign, which announced: 'Deep inside the mountain is a 292 megawatt electricity generation station, managed by the Electricity Supply Board'. I was reminded of Filson Young's statement, 'Who would care to go on to the beach after having read the sign-post, "This way to the beach"? What has the great sea to offer for the entertainment of the frame of mind created by that sign-post? So much direction takes the heart out of curiosity…'

What a brilliant mind he had. I couldn't help thinking that all those unnecessary signposts not only spoiled the best sights, but also transformed any beautiful view into someone else's—boring and importunate—'point of view'.

Thankfully, there were few 'directions' to Greenan Farm near Rathdrum run by Jonathan and Will Wheeler—father and son, no interpretation signs or visitor centres. They were the only real farmers I met in Co. Wicklow. In full accordance with W.G.

Blackie's 1852 description of Wicklow people, they were both 'industrious' and 'handsome', albeit I had failed to notice whether their 'profiles' were 'Roman' or not, as Blackie suggested.

The farm was home to a set of lovely little museums of traditional farming tools, machinery and household items. It also possessed Ireland's largest collection of old bottles. Why not? Old bottles, with their peculiar shapes and faded labels, Midleton Whiskey (a rare Cork blend), Thwaites Mineral Water, Bovril, or Dr Nelson's Improved Inhaler, can be no less fascinating than old books.

The museums struck me as genuine. Unlike Glendalough or Wicklow Gaol, they were very much *alive*, probably because the collectors' main aim was not to make megabucks (the entry fee to the farm was symbolic), but to preserve the past. They were both equally concerned about the ongoing destruction of Ireland's old values.

'We began collecting in 1970, feeling it was a pity that the old ways were being forgotten,' said Wheeler Senior.

'We'll never make a fortune, but it is our way of life,' echoed his son. 'It's a shame they're building all these ugly houses on sacred sites, including here in Wicklow, for Ireland has such small and sensitive landscape. And reporting unlawful developments can be dangerous...Ireland is punch-drunk on its so-called economic boom...'

They were right, of course, and it seems apt to finish the chapter on the still-beautiful Co. Wicklow with a quote, not from an old, but from a bang up-to-date source, a piece in the London *Independent* newspaper from 11 April 2005: 'History [in Ireland] has taken second place to a sense of a country revelling in new-found prosperity...It is a country where materialism often prevails over old ways.'

Sad, but true...

Chapter 3
# A Short Way to Tipperary

'Tipperary is the most demoralised county in
Ireland, and has long been disgraced by every sort
of violence and outrage.'
(THE 'IMPERIAL GAZETTEER', W.G. BLACKIE, ED.,
1855)

'Made familiar to many by the World War I
marching song It's a Long Way to Tipperary, the
county was actually picked simply for the
rhythmic beat of its name. In fact, Tipperary isn't
particularly far from anywhere...'
(THE 'ROUGH GUIDE TO IRELAND', 2004)

Several weeks after my foray to Wicklow, I visited Tipperary
(both the county and the town) on my way to the Aran
Islands. I had arranged to film my trip, along with my good
friend Jerry O'Callaghan, a veteran Irish film director and TV
presenter, who wanted to make my impressions of Ireland into a
TV series for RTÉ. To have the series commissioned, a pilot was
needed, and that was precisely what Jerry and I were trying to put
together during our randomly chosen journey.

I was lucky to have Jerry as my travel companion and guide: his
knowledge of Ireland was second to none. Besides, he was still
widely (and fondly) remembered from numerous TV programmes
he had presented and was often recognised by strangers—a fact
that helped us overcome a number of (metaphorical) hurdles and
allowed me to bask in the shadow of his fame.

We left Dublin on a drab October morning, both properly

armed: Jerry with his ultra-modern, state-of-the-art digital camera and recording equipment; I with a small portable collection of mostly very old books and gazetteers, in which, of course, I included my *Handbook for Travellers in Ireland*.

Our first coffee stop was in Kildare, 'a neat little town' (Murray) and the capital of its namesake county. Or was it the other way around: the town was the county's namesake? A Dublin friend told me once that all Irish towns which share their names with their county are horrible. If true, then Kildare was definitely an exception: the town looked solid, leafy and still very 'neat'. A TIDY TOWN, the road sign at its entrance announced proudly.

Whereas Murray wouldn't have had a problem recognising Kildare's general appearance, he would have been stunned by the new noises in its streets: the English language was hard to hear, and most passers-by spoke a peculiar tongue that I initially took for gaelic.

'No, it is not gaelic,' Jerry told me authoritatively.

I pricked up my linguist's ears. Of course! I should have guessed: it was Lithuanian, occasionally interspersed with Polish—a direct result of the 2004 EU enlargement.

A Polish waitress at Macari's Diner spilled coffee onto my freshly washed jeans (I regularly become a receptacle for waitresses' and air hostesses' spillages) and apologised. In Polish, of course. The much-publicised EU enlargement had so far cost me a visit to the dry-cleaners. The Bank of Ireland money dispenser in the main square offered a choice of 'English' and 'Gaeilge' on its screen, but no Lithuanian or Polish. Not yet...

Every rubbish bin in Kildare was decorated with a spidery (somewhat swastika-like) cross of St Brigid which made me wonder whether religion in Ireland was being slowly but surely relegated to litter.

Our next stop—Roscrea, Co. Tipperary—would throw some light on the issue.

As we entered Co. Tipperary (The *Rough Guide* was right: it is not a long journey from Dublin), I was reading the 'Holy Ireland' chapter of Filson Young's *Ireland at the Crossroads*: 'The great unfading inheritance of Ireland is her religion. It has outlived her war-like traditions, it has stifled her romantic spirit, it has smothered her worldly ambitions; and to-day [I am keeping Filson Young's antiquated orthography here], the narrowest and least advanced form of Catholicism, it burns with a great nervous and wasting vitality in the frail body of the country...'

Living and working in Ireland, I was able to witness the tremendous popular backlash against the religious totalitarianism that had governed the country for centuries. In the small newsroom of the Dublin magazine, where I worked, my colleagues would start swearing and spitting every time the sound of church bells was broadcast over the radio.

'I hate the church so much for what it has done to our country,' one of them told me.

'Aren't you a Catholic?' I asked.

'Yes, of course,' she replied. 'But I don't believe in God.'

I had visited Roscrea once before when I stopped there to have a look at St Cronan's Roman Catholic church and to have a drink of water. On the outside wall of a public toilet right behind the church, there were two signs: DRINKING WATER, with no tap underneath, and HOLY WATER, with a tap firmly in place—a classic example of Hobson's choice. The holy water had a distinct after-taste of rust.

These two signs, with just one tap, could serve as a good metaphor for the state of religion in modern Ireland, I thought: the alternative was there, but only on paper. In reality, people have to use the only 'tap', made available to them by those in power and by their own prejudice—historically motivated and therefore deeply rooted in their psyche. The spiritual alternative for Ireland's declining religious zeal has yet to be found.

It was those two signs above the water tap that we wanted to film in Roscrea. It was pouring. Driving through the outskirts of the town, we saw half-a-dozen excavators and bulldozers, their headlights flashing, digging through an old street next to the ruins of St Cronan's Augustinian Priory. As we were passing by, the metallic Celtic Tiger beasts were biting through a lovely old pub, overgrown with ivy and already half-ruined, as if mauled by their insatiable jaws, to make space for some modern 'cottages' or bungalows, no doubt. Those nondescript structures were springing up all over Ireland like mushrooms after rain in an unprecedented 'bungalow blight', disfiguring the country's fragile landscape. Ireland was in the throes of an unanticipated property boom. Stories abounded of decrepit garden sheds somewhere in the Irish Midlands being snapped up for a quarter of a million euro…Had avarice and Mammon come to replace religion inside Ireland's tormented soul?

A discarded excavator's digging bucket was lying in the mud—like the skull of a dead (yet not extinct) sabre-toothed Celtic Tiger…

There is nothing as drab as an Irish small town on a rainy and dull autumn afternoon. We drove up the hill and made sure that both signs and the only tap were still there. Yet filming was out of the question due to the big funeral taking place inside the church. The black-clad congregation was spilling out onto the church grounds and we decided the mourners wouldn't quite approve of two strangers filming the wall of a public toilet beside them. So we drove off for a cup of coffee.

When we returned a couple of hours later, the funeral that we had witnessed was over, but another one—even bigger and plusher than the previous—was in full swing.

'Let's go and film the bulldozers near the priory,' suggested I, without realising that the town's cemetery was on the priory's grounds. By the time we reached the spot, the first funeral had relocated there, and two grave-looking grave-diggers in dirty bobble hats were gravely finishing their grave job.

I had noticed that the Irish loved funerals and did them with gusto. During my two years in Ireland, there was rarely a morning, going to work in Dublin and later in Sandycove, that I wouldn't bump into a long and lavish funeral procession, complete with limo-hearses and solemn, stone-faced undertakers. In Russia and Ukraine, bumping into a funeral procession first thing in the morning is thought to be a good omen for the day. Yet in all my years there, I had seen such processions only three or four times (not that people did not die there—they did like flies, it was just that the funerals were normally private and low-key). That was probably why my Russian/Ukrainian days were not particularly lucky…

It was getting dark and clearly we were not destined to do any filming that afternoon. And although we had been literally pursued by funerals, it was obvious that Russian superstitions did not apply to Ireland. We had to stay overnight in Roscrea and hope that the following morning would be relatively less mournful.

According to its own glossy brochure, Racket Hall Country House Hotel on the outskirts of Roscrea was an 18th-century 'Olde Worlde' Country House 'exquisitely refurbished in keeping with its true character'. In reality, that meant 'mutilated, disembowelled and painted bright yellow in keeping with the peculiar New Ireland taste, or rather total lack of it.' Several bits of the original 18th-century façade, spared by the jaws of the voracious beast, did well to highlight the atrocity. Inside, it was all cheap 'luxury': imitation pillars and lots of plastic.

The same brochure assured us that, 'each guest room overlooks one of the many spectacular views surrounding this prestigious Victorian dwelling'. We couldn't verify that last bit, for our rooms only 'overlooked the views' of heavy rain and cotton-wool-thick mist.

Racket Hall Country House Hotel was surrounded by golf courses (at least, that was what the brochure asserted), all thoroughly hidden by the fog, and doubled as a 'Golf & Conference Hotel'. I knew that golf had become a big industry in Celtic-Tiger Ireland—a process that must have started a long time ago, for, according to Murray in 1912, 'the game has taken a firm root in Ireland in recent years, and the interest is daily increasing'. The guide-book went on to explain that golf was played in Ireland, 'probably as far back as 1855, having been introduced by the officers of Highland regiments stationed there, but…was little known until 1881, when the Royal Belfast Club was founded.'

I had always been a bit suspicious of golf and particularly of golf-players. The reason was that, although the game did not exist and was never played in the Soviet Union, when I grew up, it had very negative connotations there. In Soviet films about the West, the 'baddies'—invariably decaying, yet cheerful capitalists plotting

against the USSR—were always playing golf. Playing and plotting…
Plotting and playing…Pok-pok…Plot-plot…Watching the
would-be golfers, driven inside by rain, in the lobby of Racket Hall
didn't entirely change that misconception of mine. From the look
and sound of them, it was obvious that golf in Ireland was played
exclusively by old and fat Americans. The democratic nature of the
game (forgetting the costs of the gear) must have lain in the fact
that it could be enjoyed by grossly overweight people as well as
slim ones. Looking at the Americans in the lobby, I decided I was
not old and fat enough to become a golf-player. Not quite.

There was one bright spot about the hotel though. It was in the
shape of a blue-eyed, open-faced girl behind the reception desk. I
thought she might be Russian and, possibly, from Siberia—only
Siberian girls, to my knowledge, had such aquamarine eyes,
reflecting the waters of the world's largest lake, Baikal (I had a
Siberian girlfriend many, many years ago).

My guess proved right: Masha, the receptionist, was indeed from
Siberia, and what's more from Irkutsk, the nearest city to Lake
Baikal. She had come to Ireland a year before and had already
acquired an Irish boyfriend, a student at the near-by garda training
college at Templemore.

To salvage the day's shoot, we decided to film an interview with
both of them. Masha proved eloquent and knowledgeable, if
somewhat camera-shy: she admired Ireland and Oscar Wilde. Her
Irish boyfriend was a bit disappointing: he had no idea who Oscar
Wilde was. It was obvious that Wilde's writings were not on the
garda training curriculum…

In the evening, we drove back to the town centre to check our e-
mails. Roscrea's only Internet café was on the top floor of a shop
selling cheap Irish souvenirs and Barbie dolls. I could not believe
my ears when they told me that the price of Internet access was €5
per hour—the highest I had ever come across. They also claimed
to have Broadband, whereas in fact they didn't: the computers
were extremely slow, and it took me minutes to download a small
attachment! To cap it all, their Microsoft Word was exclusively
in…Hungarian, one of the most obscure European tongues (to
make working on your PC as difficult and as slow—and hence as
pricey—as possible, no doubt). The Hungarian Microsoft

experience was even worse than the one I once had at a hotel in the Swiss town of Schaffhausen where the only PC available to the guests was stubbornly printing 'Z' instead of 'Y', and 'Y' instead of 'Z'. A friend of mine was rather puzzled to receive my message that ended with some Turkic-sounding interjection: 'Bze-bze'!

There were fewer funerals at St Cronan's Church the following morning, and we managed to successfully film both signs above the one and only water tap. I even had enough time to record in my notebook a great epitaph, spotted on a tombstone in the neat and picturesque Church cemetery:

> IN LOVING MEMORY OF PADDY O'CONNOR
> BORN INTO TIME, MAY 22 1900
> BORN INTO ETERNITY, DECEMBER 30 1980

The Irish, it appeared, not only loved funerals, but were rather fond of death, too.

We didn't have time to properly explore Cashel, 'though a city, but a poor place' (Murray). From a distance the stunning Rock reminded me of a ruined Moscow Kremlin (if one can imagine that). The resemblance got stronger when we came closer and saw clusters of ugly modern bungalows around the Rock. The aggressively omnipresent cottages blocked the view of Ireland's prime historic and architectural gem.

'The Cashel Rock' gift shop had the tackiest collection of 'souvenirs' I had ever come across—worse even than the souvenir kiosk in Dallas's 7th-Floor Museum. Most of the Cashel 'gifts' had anal connotations: postcards with bare bums, or towels with 'Bumming Around Ireland' printed on them in large letters. A number of 'items' had 'Kiss my ass' in Irish (as kindly translated by Jerry) written on them, too. Who were all those multiple bottoms targeting? Paedophile priests? Or unsuspecting 'ordinary' tourists?

'The tourist is at the mercy of every kind of ruffian...he is always looked upon as a low fellow, an inquisitive vulgar beggar, a loud-mouthed trot-about, a coarse eater, a foreigner,' Liam

O'Flaherty wrote in his highly ironic *A Tourist's Guide to Ireland* which came out in 1929. His words sounded extremely apt and up-to-date nearly eighty years later in modern Cashel.

Whatever economic developments and other welcome changes the Celtic Tiger might have brought to Ireland, refined (or plain good) taste was definitely not one of them. We found further proof of this on the outskirts of Cashel as we pulled over next to an ornate country cottage, introducing itself on the road sign as BLUE RIVER VILLA.

In Ireland in 1910, if we believe the idiotic *Near Home or Europe Described* guide for English brats, 'In many places the [Irish] cottages' had 'gardens in front, as pretty as English gardens'. There was, 'generally a little patch of potato-ground near the cottage, and a cow or some goats grazing about, and the pigsties are outside at the back...' This pastoral description finishes with a stunning statement: 'I have heard of a family who kept a horse in their room!'

Well, for better or for worse, the reality of 2005 rural Ireland was strikingly different. The cottage (sorry the 'villa') itself was hardly visible behind the countless garden gnomes, gazebos and pseudo-antique statues in its front garden. Further 'decorated' with imitation Doric pillars at the entrance, it was the epitome of unadulterated kitsch that testified not only to its owners' appalling taste, but also to the fact that they were awash with money and weren't quite sure what do with it.

There were unlikely to be any horses kept inside Blue River Villa, but I could bet it had plenty of skeletons (and not just those of horses) hidden it its cupboards...

We spotted a number of similar dwellings before finally reaching Tipperary Town.


'Tipperary town is much less important than it sounds. If you've already visited Clonmel, it will come as something of a shock— compared to Clonmel's yuppie prosperity, Tipperary feels somewhat down at heel,' asserted my no-nonsense 2004 *Rough Guide to Ireland*. As for older sources, there seemed to be no consensus. Whereas W.G. Blackie was rather scathing about Tipperary (as he was about most places in the world, except perhaps for London and Glasgow—he was a Glaswegian) dismissing it as, 'all dirty and ill kept; houses of stone, but with few exceptions badly built and incommodious', in 1912 Murray called it 'pleasantly built and laid out'.

Faced with those contradicting opinions, I was left to make my own judgments, and initially was in full agreement with Blackie and the *Rough Guide* (notwithstanding the century's gap between them).

The town seemingly consisted of just one long main street, from which nearby fields could be clearly seen, and looked grim and run-down. So did its inhabitants. I noticed that, for some obscure reason, most male Tipperarians were subdued, scruffy and unshaven, albeit all unexpectedly gentle, polite and friendly when approached for directions. The only two buildings of note were St Mary's Church, with its 'conspicuous tower and spire' (Murray) and the incongruous modernistic Excel Centre, right next to it. The Disney-like Centre was taller than the church, suppressing and dominating it to the extent that the latter's 'tower and spire' were now much less 'conspicuous' than in 1912.

As the eponym of Ireland's most 'demoralised' and 'disgraced' county, according to Blackie, Tipperary town, with its disproportionate number of pubs, was dotted with statues of republican fighters and one of Charles Kickham, 'Poet, Novelist but above all, Patriot'.

In accordance with some peculiar Irish tradition of monumentalism, Charles Kickham was not standing on the pedestal, but sitting in state on it. In no other country have I seen so many 'sitting monuments'. In Ennis, Co. Clare, there were several sitting statues, one monument was just a huge stone chair, onto which passers-by were encouraged to plop down. In the end, I had to conclude that—on a par with its numerous Bronze-Age standing stones—Ireland was also resplendent in 'sitting stones', i.e. statues made to sit on their pedestals, the tradition triggered not so much by compassion for the sculptures (just imagine: standing straight and still under the elements and pigeons' droppings for hundreds of years!), but by the simple fact that sitting figures required a bit less sculpting material than their upright counterparts. Or so I thought.

As for the 'above all, Patriot' bit, there was something vaguely American to it. It brought back memories of a blue plaque I once spotted in Cambridge, Massachusetts, while looking for the house of H.W. Longfellow, my favourite American poet: 'Tony George Ruggles—Patriot, lived in this house in 1764–1774' it said. I thought that 'Patriot' was obviously regarded as an occupation, a life-time achievement, or an honorary title—on a par with knighthood in Britain—in the USA. It was the same in Ireland, and I began to understand why 'patriotism' as the main focus of one's life was OK both here and in the USA, but not quite kosher in Britain (the country that—at different times and by different means—tried to stifle both Irish and American aspirations for freedom and independence).

It was getting dark, and we had to find accommodation for the night. None of the Murray-recommended hotels was any longer in place. As for the *Rough Guide*, it did not recommend staying in Tipperary at all, advising just a 'brief stop-over' to have a quick look at 'the small and intriguing museum hidden away in the foyer of the town swimming pool'.

We were already too soaked and too tired to be either tempted or intrigued by the museum-cum-swimming pool. And here my many years in Britain led me into a trap: I was misled (if not seduced) by the large sign: THE ROYAL HOTEL and forgot for a moment that I was not in the UK, where 'royal' was a synonym for 'quality' and 'grand', but in the Republic of Ireland, where it was much more likely to stand for 'poor' and 'horrible'.

'What? You want to stay here?' The unshaven and scruffy, yet perfectly civil, young receptionist looked genuinely astounded, as if we had asked him not for two rooms in his hotel, but for directions to Puerto Rico.

The hotel that could easily pass for Fawlty Towers was not just smelly and shoddy. It was clearly 'suicidal' (the adjective one Russian writer of the 1920s applied to Swiss hotels). 1960s' hit songs, played in the dark foyer, added to this sombre ambience. My room had holes in the floor and a huge bottle-shaped gap in the wall. The tiny bedside table was a real health hazard, so dirty and slimy it appeared. Everything in the room was soiled, battered, broken and/or falling apart. Except, of course, for a brand-new copy of the Bible.

Yet, whereas one could theoretically survive a night in my room, the one allocated to Jerry was not just 'suicidal' but outright murderous: the frames of both windows were smashed and could not be shut which, incidentally, did not matter, because there was no glass in either of them!

'Broken windows? They should have been fixed two weeks ago,' shrugged the receptionist when we complained. His confession made us realise that we were the first paying guests at the Royal Hotel for a fortnight, and most probably—for much longer…

'Tipperary is a very Republican, very IRA town,' Jerry told me pensively from behind his pint of Guinness as we sat in The Tony Lowry pub across the road half an hour later. Unlike our hotel, the pub was warm and cosy, its doors and windows decorated with stained glass, its walls overhung with hurling trophies and pictures of horses. Three sad-looking men and one woman were sitting at the mahogany bar, silently staring at their pints. A bald publican behind the counter was watching Sky Sports. The scene was pristine and proverbial, almost homely. 'The GAA began here,' continued Jerry. 'It was here that the first engagements of the War of Independence took place…'

I quoted to him W.G. Blackie's dismissive characterisation of Tipperary.

'Yes, it is a rebellious place,' he said. 'But also the Gaelic and Catholic heart of Ireland…'

Young and stocky local women in tracksuits were power-walking outside the windows of my hotel room next morning—just like they did on the promenade in Sandycove, Co. Dublin, where I lived.

We had breakfast in the brand-new (like the Bible in my room) downstairs restaurant of our hotel. 'They neglect rooms for the benefit of restaurants in Irish hotels,' Jerry noted hopefully as we were sitting down at our table.

As we soon discovered, that questionable Irish tradition—like almost everything else at the Royal Hotel—had been broken. I solemnly promised myself never again to come close to anything that was called 'Royal' while in Ireland.

Our progress along the town's main (and pretty much the only) street was disrupted by yet another money-delivery drama. Just like in Rathdrum, a black armoured van suddenly screeched to a halt next to the bank. A platoon of gun-wielding soldiers (some of whom looked as young as fifteen), headed by a fat red-bereted corporal, fell out of it—like peas out of a lunch box—and encircled the building, aiming their weapons at several unsuspecting pedestrians, including Jerry and myself. The only creature visibly affected by this fairly pointless (from my point of view) demonstration of military prowess was a tiny stray doggy, who kept barking at the soldiers for all it was worth during the whole of the five-minute siege. Eventually, the doggy had its way: the soldiers jumped back into the van and drove away, and the little mongrel, having struck a satisfied 'mission accomplished' look, followed Jerry and myself all the way to the Excel Centre.

The incongruity of the tall and turreted Excel building was striking. It was squeezed between a row of old Victorian cottages and a historic tower with a grassy roof. And next to Excel, the ubiquitous bulldozers were already clearing space for another 'Substantial Development Site. Proposals Invited' (as announced on the billboard).

'At least there's going to be something substantial in Tipperary,' I remarked to Jerry. 'Up to now, I have been unable to spot anything of the sort, except perhaps for the town's rebellious spirit.'

The Centre housed an exhibition gallery and a café. On one of the tables, I spotted a brochure with an intriguing title: 'The Excel Guide to Tipperary Heritage' which probably listed all the town's historic sites yet to be 'developed' (read 'destroyed'). They should have called it 'The Excel Guide to Getting Rid of Tipperary Heritage', I thought.

Outside, Jerry, having filmed enough of the remains of once historic and 'pleasantly built' town centre, was dismantling his camera's tripod.

It was time to move on.

## Chapter 4

# The View of Hy-Brasail

*'The Islands of Aran…are still believed by many of the peasantry to be the nearest land to the far-famed island of O'Brazil, or Hy-Brasail, the blessed paradise of the pagan Irish. It is supposed even to be visible from the cliffs of Aran on particular and rare occasions.'*
('A HANDBOOK FOR TRAVELLERS IN IRELAND', MURRAY, 1912)

I knew we had entered Connemara when all road signs in English suddenly disappeared, to be replaced by those in Gaelic. 'Connemara is a country you visit for its scenery rather than its history,' claimed my *Rough Guide to Ireland*. Well, the part between Galway City and Rossaveel, from where we were to take a ferry to the Aran Islands, was rather barren and had very little 'scenery', except for brown rocks and construction cranes towering above them here and there, the new milestones of the Irish landscape.

A lot of digging was going on in Rossaveel Harbour: excavators, bulldozers and heavy trucks were busily (and rather pointlessly) shifting piles of pebbles and sea rocks from one place to another. Loud blasts could be heard from the grounds of a near-by fish-processing plant. With every explosion, a cloud of shrieking seagulls would take off the rocks only to return several minutes later, to be met by yet another bang.

BLASTING ACTIVITIES! warned a serious sign on the pier.

Why couldn't they just write 'blasts'? I wondered. Or has Ireland adopted the American politically correct style of sign-posting, according to which 'food center' is preferable to 'restaurant' and 'cremation center' to good old 'crematorium'?

'What's all the shooting?' I asked the facetious pier-master.

'They must have heard you were coming—ha-ha-ha!'

In reality, as it transpired, the sounds of the blasts were broadcast at regular intervals by the fish-processing plant's loudspeakers to keep seagulls away from the fish tanks.

As we were in the Gaeltacht, Jerry was very much in his element speaking Irish to everyone, even if the replies he was getting were more often in English than in Gaelic.

On top of all the other noises, a small, yet powerful, radio was blasting away in the pier-master's shed broadcasting the news of another hostage crisis in Russia. I had noticed that the world was prone to all sorts of wars and crises while I was away from home which made me think that if I stayed permanently put, our planet would become a much quieter place.

In the café near the pier, I saw an elderly couple who had just returned from the Islands. They both had the ruddy, wind-beaten faces of travellers and explorers. Or, possibly, heavy drinkers.

'We first went to the islands forty years ago and then we learned one Irish word...' the man was saying. I was unable to find out which word they had learned as our ferry was already hooting angrily at the pier.

I have always loved islands, and over the years of my travel-writing career have visited dozens of them, including the Faroes, the Falklands, Ascension Island in the Pacific, the Hebrides (both Inner and Outer), the Channel Islands (all of them) and a number of islands and islets off the coast of Australia and Tasmania, including the obscure Three Hummock Island. The latter was then populated by hundreds of giant red kangaroos, thousands of poisonous snakes and one elderly English couple, who had their food and mail dropped from a plane once a week. Separated during Word War II, they vowed never to leave each other again and lived on the island until their deaths (within a month of each other) several years ago.

The islands' relative isolation from the rest of the world had always had a calming effect on me, and made me feel at home on almost any of them.

As the ferry approached Inishmore, according to the *Rough Guide*, 'the most tourist-oriented and least authentic of the Aran Islands', the first thing we saw was the neon sign of a Spar supermarket blinking above the harbour, like a lighthouse that had been stranded far ashore. Next to it, we saw another neon sign— SUPERMAC'S. The latter was a fraction too small to pass for a lighthouse, yet large enough to be mistaken for a beacon.

We left our bags at an empty guest house on the pier, where we were greeted by a young receptionist—an Irish-speaking dark-eyed brunette of about eighteen. In windy pitch darkness, full of the thick aromas of fish and sea, we climbed up the hill to the village. On the way, I shared with Jerry my puzzlement as to the guest house receptionist's swarthy and seemingly 'un-Irish' appearance.

'She must be a descendant of the Spaniards from the Armada who came ashore and settled here over four hundred years ago,' my knowledgeable companion explained.

Bracing myself for an evening in the company of Irish speakers, I asked him to teach me a couple of common forms of greeting in gaelic.

The Inishmore Spar supermarket was the largest of all its namesakes I had seen anywhere in Ireland. Brightly lit and modernistic in style, it looked like a UFO that had crash-landed on the island. As I found out later, it was the only shop left on Inishmore.

Inside, the supermarket was empty, not counting several sales-girls in bright red aprons behind the tills and some of the counters.

Thinking it was a good opportunity to practise my non-existent Irish, I approached a plump and visibly bored young girl in the 'Deli' section.

'*Dia is Muire dhuit!*' I greeted her amicably.

She looked at me strangely, yet with some distant recognition on her round face.

'*Vi govorite po-russki?*'[8] she asked me all of a sudden.

I would have been less surprised had she addressed me in Amharic.

Her name was Iovita, and she was a Russian-speaking Lithuanian from Vilnius.

'Most of the girls in the shop are Polish,' she told me (in Russian!) with a smile. 'Except for the one at the till who is from Estonia…'

We agreed to catch up with her the following day for possible filming (a Lithuanian living and working on the Aran Islands sounded like an interesting prospect). I had to restrain myself from practising on Iovita the second Irish phrase that Jerry had taught me: '*Slán agus beannacht!*' When we met Iovita the following evening, though, it was a disaster. Away from the Spar store, she was a shadow of her cheerful and smiling self. She complained of being lonely and kept downing one drink after another—to the point when her speech became slurred and no longer 'filmable'.

'There's n-nothing else to do here but d-drink,' she muttered, before we had to call the island's only taxi to take her home.

'It is like the plight of so many Irish workers abroad in the past,' Jerry sighed while packing up his camera. 'What an amazing turnaround!'

We trudged through the dark and deserted village in search of either of the island's two pubs. At some point we were overtaken by a lonely cyclist wearing traditional Sikh headgear. Then a couple of Aussies materialised out of the darkness and asked us where they could get some 'tucker'…authentic or not, Celtic Tiger Inishmore was ethnically mixed, or 'ethnically filthy', as my late friend Peter Ustinov used to jokingly refer to himself. In the course of a couple of hours, we had encountered many more foreigners than native islanders.

We finally installed ourselves inside the 'American Bar'— another 'inauthentic' reality of the islands, where we were surrounded by a small crowd of Irish-speaking local youngsters (the swarthy young receptionist from our guest house was among them, too). The interesting thing about their verbal exchanges was that their Irish conversation was heavily interspersed with English four-letter words. The melodious and poetic Irish tongue must not have contained swear words as colourful and expressive as the language of Shakespeare and Gordon Ramsay…

I was hastily writing down that last profound observation, when Jerry interrupted me with a warning: 'You should be careful making notes here, for the patrons may take you for a government inspector checking whether they speak enough Irish…'

'What??' I muttered in disbelief.

'The Irish speakers get special allowances for conversing in their indigenous language, but only provided they use it in everyday life…'

Despite my genuine interest in Irish and other European minority tongues, I was shocked by such a blatant case of politically correct linguistic tokenism. It suddenly became clear why, on Ryanair flights from Dublin, the attendants stumble through a couple of Irish sentences before switching into English, while making in-flight announcements. I also understood why, at the opening of a session at the Dáil, the Speaker has to go through the same meaningless rigmarole. Tokenism does little to revive a dying language (or anything else, for that matter). On the contrary, it is the surest way of killing all remaining passion for it.

Had I indeed been a government language inspector, I would have failed the youths in the pub: you cannot claim to speak your language 'enough' until you actually start swearing in it!

On the way back to our guest house, we popped into Supermac's for a take-away meal. I normally wouldn't go near a burger joint, but 'Supermac's—100% Irish' was the only catering outlet on Inishmore still open on that late-November evening.

The burger joint was staffed by one person—its manager, a short middle-aged man. Having given us our burgers, he went outside to see us off. 'I'm from Galway, but have lived on the island for twenty years,' he said.

'Do you miss Galway?' I asked him

'Not really. You see, I love the smell of rotten seaweed and miss it terribly every time I leave Inishmore.' He greedily sniffed in the cold island air which was indeed abundant with the stench of rotten seaweed.

The manager was the first Irish person, apart from the guesthouse receptionist, with whom we had spoken on the Aran Islands so far. He was also the first rotten-seaweed addict I had ever come across.

There was only one TV channel available in our guest house—TG4, the Irish station based in Connemara. All its output was in Irish, except for the commercials that were all in English, with the exception of one for TG4 itself! Another example of language tokenism? Watching one of the programmes (I think it was some sort of a literary debate in Irish) was—if nothing else—a great night cap: I was fast asleep ten minutes into it.

——

On my way to the village the following morning, I spotted a strict NO DUMPING sign on the harbour wall. Underneath the sign were two smaller-print inscriptions: one in Irish (translated with Jerry's help) threatening would-be 'dumpers' with a fine of €1,900; the other—in English—promising a...€1904.61 fine for the same offence. The price of being an English speaker on the Aran islands was therefore €4.61—not too harsh a penalty by any standards.

Next to the sign, there was a shop with a no-nonsense name 'Out of Aran' (only the missing exclamation mark stopped it from sounding rude and peremptory). It was selling locally knitted woollen sweaters, and one of its windows was adorned with another forbidding sign in five European languages (but not in Irish!) saying: 'Only five students at a time allowed into shop'. Obviously, it was not just English-speakers, but also students who were not particularly welcome on the islands.

I am of the opinion that the best starting point for exploring a city, a town—or an island, for that matter—is the local coffee shop, and we were lucky to find the Lios Aengus Coffee House right next to the Spar superstore.

Despite the café's obviously Irish name, it was owned and run by a Norwegian lady, who was serving customers from behind the counter. The coffee shop was also doubling as a 'book exchange' (due to the recent closure of the island's library, I was told), which was probably why its menu, along with the 'Soup of the Day' offered a 'Saying of the Day' which, on that particular morning, was by Arnold Bennett: 'A cause is like champagne and high heels—you must be prepared to suffer for it.' I thought it was rather tasty.

The coffee house was without doubt a focal point of the island's community. An old lady was busy dipping slices of bread in her coffee mug before consuming them slowly at one of the tables. Jerry remarked that he had not seen that peculiar way of Irish coffee-drinking since his mother had done it ages ago.

Due to the smoking ban, most smoking patrons were sitting outside. We shared a table with a twinkly-eyed local woman, whose hands were trembling as she rolled up a fag. She looked and behaved as if she were either tipsy or on drugs. Or possibly both.

Having stared at me intently for some time, she declared: 'You used to be a priest in your previous life!' She then added that there was something gaelic in me, too, and that I resembled Peter Ustinov (who, as far as I knew, with an extremely mixed background that included some Ethiopian genes, did not have a drop of gaelic blood in him). I was not sure whether to take her last remark as a criticism or a compliment. Peter Ustinov once wrote the following dedication in one of his books to me: 'To Vitali—brother, nephew, son—in spirit, in laughter, in rotundity, and in the tranquil earnestness of purpose.'

I think it was the 'rotundity' bit—more than anything else—that accounted for our slight resemblance.

The woman then went back inside the coffee house and emerged with a scratch card that, as it turned out, had won her €10. 'See: I am in direct contact with the Lord,' she commented.

The only other obvious local (if not to count two kittens playing happily on the road) in—or rather outside the coffee house—was an old man in a 'peculiar costume' (*pace* W. G. Blackie): a black woollen hat and a matching black knitted sweater. He had the same twinkly sparkle (or was it a sparkly twinkle?) in his eyes. I had noticed a similar twinkle in islanders' eyes on numerous occasions on different small islands of the world. Was in because their eyes constantly reflected the water? Or, maybe, they simply felt more grounded and secure—and therefore happier—than most mainland dwellers?

A young man at a neighbouring table was sporting a sweater with 'Ventspils' (a town in Latvia) written across his chest. 'This is Dmitri, a Russian from Latvia,' the clairvoyant woman explained. 'He does minibus tours of the island.'

Having finished our drinks, we left the cosmopolitan coffee house and went for a walk along the island's main (only) road—past the new primary school, the shed which served as a branch of the Bank of Ireland ('Open Wednesdays 1.30–3.30 p.m.') and a weather-beaten road sign which read, NEXT CAFÉ 4 MILES. From time to time, we were overtaken by horse-drawn carts, or 'traps' as they called them on Inishmore, probably heading for the 'next café'. The road soon led us to the coast, where several bulldozers and excavators were digging up the beach to clear space for more bungalows with a sea view, next to a cluster of those constructed already.

The Celtic Tiger had definitely made it across the sea to the Aran Islands. The beast could swim, after all. Yet its presence on Inishmore did not feel as oppressive and out of place as on the mainland. Maybe it was due to the fact that, despite all the mess it created, the overall view from here was still stunningly beautiful. Even if the legendary 'island of O'Brazil, or Hy-Brasail, the blessed paradise of the pagan Irish' (*pace* Murray) was nowhere to be seen.

## Chapter 5
# Looking for Claddagh

'This ancient town of Galway...has considerable
natural advantages, with which neither its
industries nor its commerce are at all
commensurate, and much of it wears an air of sad
but picturesque dilapidation.'
('A HANDBOOK FOR TRAVELLERS IN IRELAND',
MURRAY, 1912)

'When it is stated that, throughout the town of
Galway, you cannot get a cigar which costs more
than twopence, Londoners may imagine the
strangeness and remoteness of the place...Pigs are
in every street: the whole town shrieks with them.'
('AN IRISH SKETCH BOOK', W.M. THACKERAY, 1842)

'The city of Galway...has a vibrancy and
hedonism that make it unique.'
(THE 'ROUGH GUIDE TO IRELAND', 2004)

College Street in the centre of Galway was a cornucopia of
time-frozen B&Bs, with signs promising 'Colour TV in
Each Room' and such bang-up-to-date facilities as 'Hot and
Cold Water', 'Telephones' and 'Central Heating'. All of them were
totally empty, not counting Ashford Manor guesthouse, where
there was one accidental guest—*moi*.

On the day of my arrival in the self-proclaimed 'capital of
Ireland's West', the *Galway Tribune* led with the story: 'Tourism
chief rejects claims of city hotel-bed oversupply'. The article
explained that generous tax breaks introduced several years before

had allowed the cost of building a hotel to be offset against tax at 15% per annum for six years and 10% in the seventh year, making the building of hotels and B&BS (like the rest of the country's economy) hugely attractive to investors and developers. This situation led to the bizarre scenario in which many hotels in Ireland were built not so much for accommodating visitors but to take advantage of the tax breaks. The result was a huge oversupply of hotel rooms throughout the country, of which Galway's College Street, with its permanently empty B&BS and guesthouses, was a shining example.

The paper's warning signal, however, was but a cry in the Celtic-Tiger wilderness. *Tribune Life*—a tabloid supplement to the very same issue of the paper, carried an advertorial under the protracted and fairly cocky headline 'Stunning and quirky: *the g* goes where no hotel has gone before'. The 'g' was yet another new hotel opening in the city. 'Walking through the new g hotel in Galway, you can almost imagine you are in an animated movie version of *Alice in Wonderland*,' gloated the paper. 'The vivid pinks and purples, lush carpets and stunning fabrics combine to create a space that is totally different to anything Ireland, or indeed Europe, has ever seen.'

I wondered what the mysterious 'g' stood for? Goodness? Glamour? Gargoyle? The article did not provide any clues, allowing me to assume that one possible answer was *'greed'*.

Not a fan of 'vivid pinks and purples', I decided that, instead of visiting the g, I'd rather pop into the GS—another Galway hotel that came top on Murray's list of recommended places to stay in 1912. The Great Southern, formerly the Railway Hotel, was hard to overlook in the city's Eyre Square. In fact, it was much easier to overlook the rest of the square, in the throes of never-ending repairs and road works, than that graceful building originally dating from 1845 and the only structure in sight not covered in scaffolding. Opened in 1852, the hotel (together with Galway railway station) was designed by John Skipton Mulvany, architect for the Great Western Railway Company. Built of limestone, it carried Mulvany's favourite motif, stone wreaths, above its front door. The Railway Hotel accommodated Prince Louis Napoleon of France in 1857, was requisitioned by the British Army in 1918, handed over to the Irish National Army in 1922 and provided a sumptuous dinner and an overnight stay to Captain John Alcock and Lieutenant Arthur Whitten Brown after their world's first non-stop trans-Atlantic flight landed at Derrygimla bog near Clifden.

On my visit, Mulvany's wreaths still adorned the hotel's entrance—one of its very few surviving original features. Another was a cosy Victorian reading room, with a marble fireplace decorated with bronze discs carrying the Midland and Great Western Railway arms and dated '1845'. Inside the reading room and in the lobby, with bathroom-style tiled floor, the stale stench of tobacco smoke, exhaled by generations of smokers was still lingering—two years after the smoking ban!

I was shown around by the hotel's PR lady, who had the unlikely name Susannah. Whereas all PR women in Britain are called Jennifer, in Italy, Paola and in the USA, Jo, their Irish counterparts (at least, those I had come across so far) were Aoifes.

The modernised hotel boasted nothing much, except, perhaps, for its leisure centre on the roof. A modern spa bath was installed next to a capacious Victorian hot tub, from where the guests could admire the views of the town. I sincerely hoped that whatever the Victorian guests saw was more pleasant to the eye than the present-day view of Galway bus terminal and the Harbour, dotted with the eye-sores of ugly warehouses and oil tanks. My 2004 *Rough Guide* was right in describing the Galway Harbour area as 'one of the most architecturally abused spots in Ireland'. The gems of the 16th-century Spanish Arch and the medieval Lynch's Castle were all but dwarfed and suppressed by (to quote the *Rough Guide* again): 'ugly post-modern façades and bone-headed development'.

The roof of the Great Southern was an excellent time-travelling spot. Having opened my Murray's 1912, and having, in my imagination, climbed carefully (not to get burnt!) inside the steaming hot tub, I teleported myself ninety-three years back:

> 'The streets…containing several handsome buildings are narrow, inconvenient and ill kept, nevertheless, the antiquary will find very much to interest him in the remarkable architectural features of the houses, which are

foreign to a degree unknown in any other town in the kingdom…Time and modern improvements have to a certain extent obliterated many of the ancient remains, which, with some exception, are not so patent to the general tourist as might be imagined from the glowing descriptions. The old houses require looking for, and in recent years many of them have sunk into complete dilapidation, or have been destroyed in the ordinary course of street alterations or rebuildings. Some of the houses were built Spanish fashion, with a small court (patio) in the centre, and an arched gateway leading into the street; but it requires some effort of imagination to identify these ill-kept and overcrowded dwellings with the gay residences of the Spanish merchants.'

I asked Aoife/Susannah whether it was possible to go down to the hotel's basement.

Basements of old buildings are the second-best time-travelling points after the roofs, because basements (and cellars) are more resistant to change than the floors above ground. The typical basement of a big Georgian, Victorian or Edwardian hotel would accommodate the kitchen, storage rooms, laundry and other service quarters. I had a weakness for basements due to the fact that the bulk of my ever-expanding collection of old guide-books, my only real 'asset' in this world, was still stored in the former laundry-drying room in the basement of the Edwardian Metropole Hotel in Folkestone, Kent. I felt bitter about abandoning my books (even if temporarily) in the basement. My only consolation was that they were being stored in style and in their accustomed environment, too.

Susannah/Aoife (or, for brevity, 'Souife'), however, refused to take me to the basement 'for insurance reasons', as she put it, which inevitably made me wonder what dark secrets they were hiding down there—under the tacky bathroom tiles of the lobby…

Having had a good view of Galway from the roof, I had to descend back to earth and contribute to the city's traffic congestion. The reason was the allegedly faulty airbag in my car. At least, that was what the electronic dash-board kept telling me repeatedly, distracting me from driving. I was almost sure that the problem lay not with the airbag, but with the dashboard itself, yet to be absolutely certain and to avoid the airbag exploding in my face in the middle of a motorway, I had to take my Fiat to a garage on the outskirts of the city.

The drive, of a couple of miles, took me over an hour through the traffic-jammed streets. I had to negotiate numerous—and totally superfluous—roundabouts, each with its own 'personal' name. Naming roundabouts—as if they were streets or squares— had always struck me as a peculiar Irish obsession. I had ample time to ponder the historical and/or psychological reasons behind it while stuck for over twenty minutes at 'Joyce roundabout'. I wondered whether it was named after the writer James Joyce, whose wife, Nora Barnacle, had come from Galway: her family home, in Bowling Green, is now one of Ireland's smallest museums. Another 'famous' Joyce—William, aka Lord Haw-Haw (a nickname given to him for his exaggerated upper-class English accent), executed for high treason in 1946, was also a native of Galway and is buried here, too.

A fascist and a vitriolic anti-Semite, William Joyce had broadcast Nazi propaganda for Hitler during World War ii. He also contributed regular columns to the German-run newspapers of the occupied Channel Islands. During a visit to Jersey, I had a chance to read some of them in the local archive and was shell-shocked by the extent of Joyce's devotion to Nazism and his hatred of Jews.

But how did Lord Haw-Haw's remains end up in a Galway cemetery? It was due to the efforts of his daughter Heather, who approached Roy Jenkins, then Britain's Home Secretary, with a plea to take Joyce's bones to Ireland, 'the land of his forebears', in 1976—thirty years after his execution. Permission was granted, and at dead of night, the tarmac in Brixton prison, where Joyce had been buried, was dug up, and his bones were shipped to Galway.

The reburial attracted some publicity and cost Heather her marriage: her husband, who had been kept in the dark about her parentage, was worried that his wife's genealogical link to Britain's most infamous traitor could damage his hairdressing business and walked out on her. Yet Heather—still alive at the time of writing—has looked after the grave ever since.

Stuck at the Joyce roundabout, I thought that naming it after William, rather than James, Joyce would have been more logical, for if one were to pick an adjective to describe it, 'literary' or 'creative' would not make any sense, whereas 'treacherous' or 'ugly' (William Joyce had a nasty-looking scar across his face) would be much more appropriate.

I found the most likely explanation of the name's true origins in my good old Murray: 'The part of the barony of Ross between the Killaries and Lough Mask is known as Joyce Country, from the prevailing name of its inhabitants, who are descended from a Welsh family who settled here in the 13th century.'

Mystery solved. My enforced tour of Galway's permanently crammed roundabouts, strangling the city like garrottes, was not a complete waste of time, after all.

Having left the car at the garage, I walked back to the city in a mere twenty minutes!

Due to its compact size, Galway has always been a great place for walking. Chapter 16 of Thackeray's *Irish Sketch Book* starts with two sub-chapters: 'More Rain in Galway' and 'A Walk There'. In the former, the writer asserts that, because of constant rain, 'English waterproof coats are not waterproof in Ireland' and adds that 'the traveller who has but one coat must of necessity respect it, and had better stay where he is unless he prefers to go to bed while he has his clothes dried at the next stage.'

In the latter, Thackeray—an archetypal mid-19th-century English traveller, prone to comparing every foreign venue to London—describes the actual walk: 'The houses in the fashionable street where the club-house stands (a strong building, with an agreeable [*sic*—vv] Old Bailey look) have the appearances of so many little Newgates. The Catholic chapels are numerous, unfinished, and ugly. Great warehouses and mills rise up by the stream, or in the midst of unfinished streets here and there; and handsome convents with their gardens, justice-houses, barracks, and hospitals adorn the large, poor, bustling, rough-and-ready-looking town.'

He also notes that, while walking in Galway, he failed to find any 'regular bookshops', yet 'a man who sells hunting-whips, gunpowder, guns, fishing tackle and brass and iron ware, has a few books on his counter; and a lady in a by-street, who carries on the profession of a milliner, ekes out her stock in a similar way.' The writer therefore, 'when it came on to rain' (and it must have 'come on' to it fairly often!), 'had no resource but the hedge-school volumes…that present some very rude flowers of poetry and 'entertainment' of an exceedingly humble sort; but such shelter is not to be despised when no better one is to be had.'

Galway was well supplied with bookshops and even better supplied with banks, I noticed. A branch of Allied Irish Bank now occupied the former Lynch's Castle (or, in Murray's words, 'Lynch's Mansion'), 'the finest medieval town house in Ireland', according to the 2004 *Rough Guide*. Inside, some details of the original décor —the remains of old fireplaces, wood panels and vaulted ceilings —were still recognisable.

The irony of the AIB's location lay in the fact that it was from one of the Castle's windows that James Lynch Fitzstephen, then Galway's mayor, hanged his only son, a temperamental lad, who was not only guilty of murdering one of his Dad's Spanish friends in 1493, but was also a notorious spender of money.

The most striking feature inside Lynch's Castle, aka AIB, was a fine 1651 map of Galway—complete with minute graphic details of every street and lane as well as coats of arms, people, houses and even dogs and horses, lovingly drawn along its frame. A passionate collector of old maps, I was pleased to discover the following passage in my trusted Murray:

> 'From a map (of which only two copies are extant) made in 1651, by the Marquis of Clanricarde, to ascertain the extent and value of the town, it appears that Galway was then entirely surrounded by walls, defended by 14 towers, and entered by as many gates. A poetical description appended to this map informs us that—"*Bis urbis defendunt moenia turres/ Intus, et ex duro est marmore qoeque domus*".'

Since my knowledge of Latin—the result of a speedy university course thirty odd years ago—could be best summarised by a short

Latin phrase *'tabula rasa'* ('blank plate', or, in colloquial English, 'zilch'), I was unable to translate the above quote. Interestingly, Murray was not of any help either: neither he, nor his esteemed friend and rival Karl Baedeker, offered translations of the Latin and Ancient Greek expressions with which their guide-books were resplendent. Their understanding was that their readers were sophisticated enough to have those dead tongues at their fingertips. There were other Latin expressions on the fringes of the map of which only one (next to the Lynches' coat of arms) had been translated into English by some aspiring and not particularly capable modern poet:

'From one proud stock for ages known to fame
These different branches of Lynches came.'

The untranslated Latin original looked better, to be honest…

On the way from Lynch to lunch, I bumped into another 'sitting stone'—a modern sculpture of Oscar Wilde sitting on a (stone) bench, next to that of Estonian writer Edward Wilde (pronounced *'w-ee-l-de'*). A brass plate on the bench explained that, by commem-orating two writers from two different countries who had the same name, the monument was supposed to symbolise 'internationalism'.

I had a quick look at the Collegiate Church of St Nicholas, where Christopher Columbus had—allegedly—once worshipped and Mayor Lynch was definitely buried in the crypt. It was reassuring to learn that nowadays the church was shared by both Protestants and Catholics who held their respective liturgies at different times of the day. Inside the 'venerable cruciform building' (Murray, 1912), this 'largest medieval church in Ireland' (*Rough Guide*, 2004) had an unusual layout: the pews on all four sides created the impression of a large amphitheatre, with a dribbling fountain in the middle. A large sign on the wall read: Peace + Peace + Peace; that simple mathematical formula sounded right and relevant in this shared shrine to two conflicting trends of the same religion.

After the gracefulness and quiet of St Nicholas, the Harbour looked even more 'architecturally abused' than it had appeared from the roof of the Great Southern, and its dominant structure—the new-ish Jury's Inn hotel—could compete with the London Tower Bridge Thistle for the title of the world's ugliest building. Even the once-magnificent Spanish Arch, 'built to protect galleons unloading wine and rum' (*Rough Guide*)' dwarfed by a nearby 1970s' office block, looked tired and in need of repairs. Clusters of green prickly moss were bursting through its ancient stones like tufts of hair from an octogenarian's nose. It looked as if it were in need of an appointment at the nearby 'Arch Barber Gents' Hair Salon'.

One positive detail, however, was supplied by Murray: '…there is no doubt that it [Galway Harbour] possesses one advantage over other ports, viz. its proximity to America, it being 1656 m. to Halifax, 2385 m. to Boston, and 2700 m. to New York.' I squinted at the misty horizon, and, having failed to discern the outlines of New York, went off to find a place to eat.

The place announced itself as specialising in seafood. My portion of whiting was so heavily battered that I had to drill through the armour plate of fatty crust to get to the fish itself, of which there was surprisingly little. The meal brought to mind some Scottish memories: fried Mars bars and Greenock—a suburb of Glasgow and officially Britain's unhealthiest place, where I once spent a couple of days on a newspaper assignment, studying the effects of its junk food on myself.

Now, just like in Greenock, my skin started oozing fat and I had to chase the meal with an apple to beat off the horrible after-taste. Outside, I observed the city's lunch-time crowds: lots of 'alternative' ageing-hippy types and constantly snogging young couples. I rather liked the modern buzz of Galway—the city that reminded me of my whiting portion: it took an effort to vicariously drill through the crust of its tacky façades to get to the nicer bits, the best of which I was yet to discover.

I spent the evening walking off my ill-considered lunch in the dark and deserted College Street (although B&B Road would have been a more appropriate name for it), where my guesthouse was located. As before, all the small hotels were empty and could have done with having the word 'Vacancies' carved in stone above the front doors. Their forlorn owners could be seen occasionally in the bay windows—watching TV ('Colour', no doubt) in the spacious and seemingly warm ('Central Heating'!) lounge rooms, with all lights aglow.

Galway Greyhound Stadium at the end of the street was in darkness. GALWEGIANS GO BARKING! the slogan above its gates read. I smiled at the logo and went back to Ashford Manor guest house, where I had a chat with Robert, a soft-spoken Hungarian receptionist, who was happy to talk to his only guest.

In Hungary, Robert used to work as a traffic controller in the army until his country joined NATO and his job became obsolete. He had signed up as a cabin steward on QE2, then lived in Australia. When Hungary joined the EU, he had relocated to Ireland with his wife and daughter.

'I want my daughter to learn English, although I don't want her to have an Irish accent,' he said. That was why he chose to settle in Galway, where, in his words, the accent 'was not too bad: much better than in Cork'.

I asked him what he thought of Ireland in general, apart from the accent.

'It's OK,' he shrugged. 'The taxes are low…'

———

'*The Claddagh, the locality inhabited by the fishermen, should be visited by every tourist.*'
('A HANDBOOK FOR TRAVELLERS IN IRELAND',
MURRAY, 1912)

It was not often that the reserved and matter-of-fact Murray allowed himself to get emotional about a place (even the notoriously dry and precise Baedeker was more likely to get personally 'involved' with a location). So I was rather amazed when in just one paragraph of Murray's handbook I came across such words as 'interesting', 'extraordinary', 'very moral', 'very peculiar' etc., all applied to the Claddagh—a fishing village and a suburb of Galway. That village was also the birth-place of the famous Claddagh ring.

Murray's passage on Claddagh is so uncharacteristic for his usual impersonal style that I will quote it almost in full:

'Claddagh is an extraordinary assemblage of low thatched cottages, built with total disregard to system and numbered indiscriminately. Hardiman[9] writes of them as follows: "The colony from time immemorial has been ruled by one of their own body, periodically elected, who is dignified with the title of Mayor, regulates the community according to their peculiar laws and customs, and settles all their fishery disputes…" The title and office are now quite obsolete. At one time they always allowed strangers to reside within their precincts, and always intermarried with each other, but now strangers settle among them. They are a very moral and religious people. They would not go to sea or away from home, on any Sunday or holiday…The dress of the women of the Claddagh was very peculiar, and imparted a singularly foreign aspect to the Galway streets and quays. It consisted of a blue mantle, red body gown and petticoat, a handkerchief bound round the head, and legs and feet *au naturel*, but the dress is rarely seen now. The Claddagh Ring—two hands holding a heart—becomes an heirloom in a family, and is handed down from mother to daughter.'

These heartfelt words by the seemingly heartless Murray had sparked my imagination. For years I had been 'collecting' quirky bits of European culture and geography. I wrote a book, *Passport to Enclavia*, on Europe's remaining enclaves (parts of the territory of one sovereign country totally surrounded and landlocked by another sovereign state), having become the first person in the world to visit all of them, and another book on eleven European mini-states. On my travels, I had discovered a curio called Ely Place—a charming little lane in the centre of London (also a streeet in Dublin). The Claddagh, as described by Murray, sounded like a valuable addition to my 'collection'.

It didn't take me long to ascertain that the Claddagh as such no longer existed. The last mention of it as a living entity that I could find was in the 1914 *Survey Gazetteer of the British Isles*: 'Claddagh—a suburb of Galway, chiefly inhabited by a fishing population.' The 2003 *Encyclopaedia of Ireland* referred to the Claddagh as a 'now-vanished fishing village at the mouth of the River Corrib'. And, according to *Brewer's Britain and Ireland*, 2005, 'the Claddagh was demolished as part of a redevelopment in the 1930s.'

I was nevertheless determined to locate the Claddagh (or whatever was left of it) while in Galway.

Unsurprisingly, Robert, my receptionist (he also doubled as a night porter) had no idea of where (or what) it was. He looked fresh and rested after an undisturbed night's sleep.

They had no knowledge of the Claddagh in the city's tourism office either, and I had to rely on the sketchy mid-19th-century map of Galway from the 1852 *Imperial Gazetteer*, where the village was marked as a small dot on the seafront outside the town.

I got into my car (the airbag problem had been fixed) and started cruising slowly along the seafront towards Salthill. It wasn't long before I got stuck at another 'personalised' roundabout, this time bearing the name of D'Arcy, and had ample time to ponder its origins: was it named after Galway-born 17th-century politician Patrick D'Arcy or after modern Irish violinist Michael D'Arcy?

At the same time, just as in Sandycove and in Tipperary, I observed flocks of young women in track suits power-walking forcefully along the embankment. Power-walking seemed to have become Ireland's favourite sport, particularly among women. I couldn't help noticing that modern Irish women were very different from their oppressed sisters of the not-so-distant past. To begin with, they were no longer meek and taciturn and would routinely behave in a much more vociferous and aggressive way than males in restaurants and pubs. They were also playing an ever-increasing role in Ireland's politics (two female Presidents within a decade!), culture and business life.

I had to interrupt my ruminations (and observations) as the traffic at D'Arcy roundabout came into motion. Another couple of miles on, I realised that I had left the boundaries of modern

Galway, within which the Claddagh had been definitely located, and had to turn back.

I pulled over at a Salthill florist. The young man behind the counter was the first person in Galway (except for myself and my old friend Murray) who knew about the Claddagh. 'There's nothing left there,' he shrugged but agreed to direct me to the village's former location: 'Keep the sea on your right. When you see a lot of swans—you are there!'

I ended up driving nearly all the way back to the point, from where I could clearly see the mutilated Galway Harbour. It was there—half a mile away from the Harbour (and an unhurried ten-minute walk from my guest-house) that I saw dozens of swans in a small bay near an old pier, strewn with discarded snake-like mooring ropes. At the pier entrance, a battered memorial stone lay on the ground. IN MEMORY OF THE CLADDAGH MEN WHO TRAGICALLY LOST THEIR LIVES ON GALWAY BAY ON THE 4TH OF MAY 1902. Eureka! I was there!

There were eight names on the stone, and four of them were Patricks.

Three decrepit Galway hookers[10] lay on the ground like the decomposing bodies of dead dolphins washed ashore, a couple of rusty Victorian lanterns towering above them. Was this all that was left of the unique 'and 'very special' (Murray) self-governing community of the Claddagh?

Luckily, it wasn't.

Across the road from the pier, I saw a grotto. IN MEMORY OF JOSEPHINE FLAHERTY WHO TENDED THIS GROTTO WITH LOVING DEVOTION, said a faded memorial plate. The grotto was full of rubbish. While I was examining the gritty grotto, a middle-aged woman came out of a near-by office building. There was something 'special' in her look. Perhaps, it was a lively mischievous sparkle in the eyes that often characterises people living close to the sea? Or was it the openness of her face ('very moral') and her floating swan-like manner of walking? It was easy to imagine her in the Claddagh's traditional attire—'a blue mantle, red body gown and petticoat, a handkerchief bound round the head, and legs', albeit the latter were not '*au naturel*'.

I approached the woman and asked her about the Claddagh. She was in a rush, yet agreed to talk. I was right: she was born in the Claddagh, or rather on the spot where the village used to stand. Her voice was melodious, with a broad Galway accent that I thought was rather lovely. 'The village was here until about 1940, when the town council built new houses in its place. The only buildings left now are the church, the school that is now for children with learning difficulties, and the community centre on the pier where the Claddagh fishermen used to make their nets. It was a very special community, and many of the former villagers would love to come back, but it is very expensive now...'

She hurried away, and I was left alone next to St Mary's Dominican church, where morning mass was under way. The voice of the white-clad elderly priest was soft and soothing—not unlike the woman's with whom I had chatted earlier. Soon the worshippers were streaming out of the door before the prayer was even finished—like spectators in a Moscow theatre rushing out to pick up their coats from the cloakroom well before the final curtain fall.

Back at the pier, I found another reminder of the old Claddagh. ALEXANDER NIMMO (1783–1832), A SCOTSMAN, BUILT THIS PIER AS A BREAKWATER AND SHELTER FOR THE CLADDAGH FISHING FLEET, ran the weather-beaten plate attached to the rusty railings. A Gothic barn-like building of the former village hall (or, in the words of my recent interlocutor, 'community centre') now housed Galway Rovers AFC Sports & Social Club.

The swans on the quiet surface of the bay were huge, the biggest I had ever seen. Could they be the re-incarnated souls of the villagers? Or were they a reminder of the poetic and idealistic notion of Ireland that I used to nourish as a travel-hungry boy in the Soviet Ukraine?

The school bell ricocheted off the sea surface like a pebble, and kids poured out of the building to enjoy the first break of the day. I was grateful to my old Murray for helping me to conjure up my long-cherished childhood images of 'good old' Ireland—a country that did not exist any more.

## Chapter 6
# Wild and Beautiful

*'Connemara…one of the most wild and beautiful
districts that is ever the fortune of a traveller to
examine; and I could not help thinking, as we
passed through it, at how much pains and
expense honest English cockneys are to go and
look after natural beauties far inferior, in
countries which, though more distant, are not a
whit more strange than this one. No doubt, ere
long, when people know how easy the task is, the
rush of London tourism will come this way…'*
('AN IRISH SKETCH BOOK', W.M. THACKERAY, 1842)

I was having a farewell cappuccino and a cigarette outside a
Galway City coffee shop. Next to me, an elderly lady was telling
her friend, another local woman, a horror story, of which I was
able to overhear only a snippet: '…and then he fell and hit his head
on the kennel, and there was no one around (how about the dog,
I wondered). When they found him, he was dead…'

Bye, Galway.

The road to Clifden, 'Connemara's English-speaking capital'
(*Rough Guide*), was indeed no less than spectacular. The barren
landscape reminded me of that around Thurso, in the north of
Scotland: brown mountains, mirror-like lakes. I can't deny myself
the pleasure of quoting Murray's description of Connemara: 'The
tourist will observe that the country all around is of curiously
weathered limestone, strewn with ice-borne boulders, a large
proportion of which are of granite, which must have travelled a
considerable distance. Any of these are of great size, and curiously
perched in prominent positions.' I regard this short extract as a
direct challenge to Jerome K. Jerome, who once asserted that

descriptions of scenery never work in literature. Well, in guide-books, they sometimes do…

The rough and serene beauty of Connemara was so captivating that I was finding it hard to concentrate on steering my Fiat along precariously winding narrow roads, the danger of which was brought home to me by a hitchhiker, to whom I offered a lift. The elderly lady (it was my personal 'Elderly Ladies' Day'), 'a retired housewife', as she introduced herself, told me about an English female solicitor, who—being in a rush to get to Galway airport to catch her plane—drove too fast along Connemara roads and ended up falling into a lake, 'under twelve feet of water'. For just one morning, it was a horror story too many.

With relief, I let my scare-mongering passenger out on the outskirts of Clifden. Unlike W. M. Thackeray 163 years before, I was even spared the 'yelling children following the car, and crying "Lash, lash!"' to the whip-wielding driver, to whom the writer was respectfully referring as a 'carman'. (In modern Celtic-Tiger Ireland they would have been much more likely to cry: 'Cash! Cash!'). The 'car' was, of course, a horse-drawn carriage.

———

> *'After traversing the wild, heathery roads…Clifden,*
> *with its wide main street and escarped situation, is*
> *pleasant to look upon…We recommend a stay in*
> *Clifden if only to see the coast, which is worth the*
> *trouble of exploring. We have tested its air times and*
> *again, and there is none better in Ireland.'*
> ('A HANDBOOK FOR TRAVELLERS IN IRELAND',
> MURRAY, 1912)

> *'Clifden….a very small place with only three*
> *significant streets…seems to be trying hard to cultivate*
> *the cosmopolitan atmosphere of Galway.'*
> (THE 'ROUGH GUIDE TO IRELAND', 2004)

'Bad Food' was written in chalk across the blackboard above the bar of the Station House Hotel, where I was having a late lunch. Having squinted at the board, I realised that it actually said 'Bar Food', the smudged 'R' in the word 'Bar' looking very much like 'D'. It reminded me of the frightening Air Malta airline logo I spotted once, whilst sitting on the plane awaiting take-off: 'The Power of Chance' that upon closer inspection, turned out to be 'The Power of Change'. The importance of calligraphy…

A Chinese man sitting next to me and talking on his mobile spoke English with a Connemara accent, inserting 'feck' after every other word.

The Hotel was built around Clifden's old railway station that closed down in 1935. The complex included the restored station building, turned into a pub (where I was sitting), a shopping mall, an old engine shed, housing a railway museum (although the majority of its exhibits dealt not with railways but with Connemara ponies), and, it being December, a brand-new ice rink in a marquee. The lanes in this 'regenerated' (in the words of Daniel Loosely, the hotel's English-born manager)—or 'Celtic-tigerised', as I would put it—area were nostalgically named after the now-defunct railway platforms: 'Platform One', 'Platform Three' etc.

Daniel was from Somerset and came here six months before, 'to reap the benefits of Ireland's economic boom—particularly in the hospitality industry', as he himself put it while showing me around the Museum. I thought I had already witnessed the consequences of that 'boom' in Galway's ever-deserted College Street.

The Railway Museum could have been renamed the 'Pony and Marconi Museum', for apart from a large section, devoted to Connemara ponies—a miniscule horse looking very much like its Shetland sister, only without the latter's rich mane—it had exhibits relating to Guglielmo Marconi's world's first transatlantic wireless station, set up near Clifden in 1907 (the location was chosen due to the absence of landmass between the Station's aerials and the USA). There was also a small section on Alcock & Brown's first non-stop transatlantic flight that nose-dived into nearby Derrygimla Bog in 1919 (so there was a 'stop' in that flight, after all!). A pair of Captain Brown's worn-out boots, allegedly used during the flight, was on display. The boots brought back memories of different pieces of foot- and underwear that I had seen in museums around the world: from the childhood booties of an ABBA soloist in Stockholm's ABBA Museum, to Karl Marx's underpants, the star exhibit of a small gallery in Trier. To say nothing of the Museum of Socks in Canada that claimed to have a pair worn by Napoleon himself (hopefully, they had been washed at least once since leaving the feet of the restless French Emperor).

Clifden's main modern attraction was undoubtedly the ice rink that had opened a month before my arrival. Daniel told me about the difficulties they had finding 'ice marshals' to look after the rink and to stop the skaters from falling face down on the ice much too often. That was understandable, for Clifden (and Ireland in general) does not have a long skating tradition. 'In the end we hired some Russian guys from Latvia,' he said, thus confirming the *Rough Guide*'s conclusion about the town's artificially engineered cosmopolitanism.

Daniel confided in me that for the privilege of repeated stumbling and falling face down on the ice (and that was exactly what the majority of Clifden skaters were bound to do) the courageous punter had to cough up €15 per hour. It was still not too bad compared to €11,000—which is the average modern cost of a tiny Connemara pony nowadays. According to knowledgeable Daniel, one could have been 'picked for just fifty or sixty quid ten years ago.'

After lunch, I had a meeting with the head of Clifden Heritage group—a middle-aged shop-owner and Oxford-don lookalike called Brendan. I had a couple of questions which I hoped he would be able to answer:

1. What was it that made the air in Clifden so special ('there is none better in Ireland')? How exactly could Murray 'test it times and again' and was the air still the country's best?

2. What was the correct name for the mountains around the town to which Murray and Blackie referred as 'Twelve Pins', whereas both the *Rough Guide* and the local 'What's On' booklet for Clifden and Connemara called them the 'Twelve Bens'?

Brendan was unable to answer the first set of questions but instead offered to take me out for a walk so that I could judge the quality of Clifden air for myself. As for the second question, he explained that 'Bens' was actually the correct name, stemming from the Irish *beinn*—'mountain', and 'Pins' was its corrupted, or anglicised, version. No wonder Murray and Blackie—both passionate 'Britishers' chose to stick to the latter.

'Breathe in deeper!' Brendan puffed out merrily as we climbed up a steep hill. 'This is what we call Brandy and Soda Road. Can you smell it?' I could not smell any brandy. As for soda, I think I did eventually—by the time we had reached the hill top. I could also taste it in my mouth. Or could it be the smell (and the taste) of my own sweat? That was probably how Murray 'tested' the quality of Clifden air!

From the top of the hill, we had a good view of the Market Square, where the famous 'flat' Clifden oysters used to be sold. 'Loads of oysters were sent to London by train every morning until 1935, when the railway went bust, due to the fact that it was built in the wrong position—away from the coast,' Brendan was saying.

Whereas Baedeker used to grade views by awarding them stars (one view in the Lake District had three!), Murray reserved his starry marks of distinction (always limited to one) for cities, towns and villages. As for scenic views, he simply described them. Travelling in Ireland, I found Murray's descriptions of scenery precise, laconic and literary as well as artistic—a brilliant time-travelling device, for countryside—unlike city- and townscapes —normally doesn't change much in seventy to a hundred years. 'A short walk to the top of Monument Hill will give the visitor an idea of the scenery around Clifden: the view of the town backed by the Twelve Pins (*sic*—vv) has quite an Alpine look on the small scale.' I couldn't possibly miss the 'Alpine' view and hoped that the hill we had climbed *was* Monument Hill. But Brendan told me it was actually Church Hill, so we had to stumble down a rock-strewn muddy path and climb up again. It was good exercise, and the smell of soda in the air was growing by the minute.

At the end of our ascent, I came to understand why Murray, while describing Monument Hill, failed to mention the actual Monument on its top (hence the hill's name). It was a monument to the victims of the Great Famine that would have been in place by 1912. For obvious reasons, the Irish Famine of the 1840s was not a popular subject of discussion in Britain in the early 20th century.

The monument, that purported to carry the names of all Clifden victims of the tragedy, looked shabby and unkempt. It was also incomplete. Brendan said it was because the charity that had built it ran out of funds in the 1850s.

The land around the unfinished memorial was now privately owned, and the landlord was reluctant to have tourists trespassing. The Monument therefore was largely forgotten. I grumbled about it to Brendan.

'You can't stop progress and prosperity,' he shrugged.

'Yes, but progress doesn't have to be ugly! And prosperity should allow for monuments of the past to be respected.'

'You may be right. John d'Arcy, Clifden's founder and its first developer, used to fine people for not looking after their homes…'

At this point in our uphill discussion, we were approached by two Connemara ponies, which—until then—had been peacefully grazing at a distance. They probably wanted to have their say. Or, more likely, were just hoping for a treat.

I showed Brendan the following passage from Murray: 'Clifden has no antiquities to boast of, being an entirely modern creation, since the beginning of the last (19th—vv) century, of the family of D'Arcy, who were constant in labouring for the good of the locality.'

'Why can't modern Celtic Tiger D'Arcys be the same?' I asked Brendan and the ponies. None of them was willing to reply. But I was pleased that Murray had been able to put his word into the argument, on top of the hill he described so beautifully seventy-nine years before.

Bonfires of sunset were burning in the sky as we climbed down to the town centre. In Market Square, the construction of a new giant supermarket, complete with a multi-storey car park, was under way. The huge cranes looked intrusive and out-of-place, discordant notes in the otherwise harmonious symphony of old Clifden. Or like daggers stabbing the town straight through the heart.

WATCH THIS SPACE! WE THINK YOU ARE GOING TO LIKE WHAT WE'VE PLANNED! asserted the flirty message on the billboard covering the supermarket's concrete carcass. I didn't. And neither did Brendan. 'They've knocked down the town's oldest house to start building this complex,' he said. 'We protested, of course, but to no avail...Clifden doesn't need a giant supermarket. The population is dwindling and the young people are leaving, for there is no entertainment—not even a cinema. We used to have lots of tourists from England before the Troubles, but now even they stopped coming—partly out of fear of the IRA, partly because the hotels are too expensive...'

The sheer pointlessness of the new, giant shopping mall became even more evident after a quick visit to the existing (albeit much, much smaller) supermarket in the main street. It was 6 p.m. on a week day—the time when herds of happy Londoners or Dubliners routinely do their shopping on the way from work. The shop was totally empty.

I spent the evening at my hotel's leisure centre, or rather—in and out of its excellent sauna. Steam rooms had always struck me as great democratic institutions, where one's social status stopped mattering and conversations were easily struck. Two young guys, sitting next to me in on the hot wooden bench, were speaking Russian to each other. They turned out to be the very ice marshals Daniel, the hotel manager, had told me about. Ethnic Russians from Latvia, a new EU member state, they had been sent to Clifden by the Galway employment agency which they joined on arrival in Ireland. 'There was no work for us in Galway, and after a month of waiting they offered us the job of ice marshals in Clifden,' one of them explained.

'Did you have to undergo some training?' I enquired.

'Nah. We are from Latvia. We know how to skate... '

After they went for their swim, I was left in the company of a talkative, sweating local.

'Have you seen our new supermarket under construction?' he asked.

'I wish I hadn't,' I replied.

'It will create eighty new jobs for the town,' insisted he.

My hotel room was unexpectedly spacious and cosy, with every traveller's need taken into account: two 'complimentary' mini-bottles of wine, a new kettle, a good choice of teas and coffees and even a 'personal' little iron—the lone traveller's ultimate luxury. It even had brushes for shoes and clothes in the cupboard—an important detail overlooked by most five-star hotels (in one of my travel columns, I seriously suggested to grade hotels not by stars but by brushes—an idea that both Murray and Baedeker would have undoubtedly supported). I dined on the excellent room-service soup and sandwiches and went to bed with the thought that the Celtic Tiger was not always a bad beast.

Next morning, I departed Clifden from Platform 6, where my car had been parked overnight. My destination was Westport in Co. Mayo, but on the way I planned to visit Kylemore Abbey. The Abbey as such was not mentioned in my Murray, for one simple reason: it was founded in 1920. Yet, the splendid Kylemore Castle, in which it was located, had been in existence since 1871, and its description took up a couple of uncharacteristically euphoric paragraphs in Murray's guide-book:

> '...on the North side, on the shores of Castle Lake in the very best situation which could have been selected, the late Mr Mitchell Henry built Kylemore Castle. Mr Henry, an English gentleman, first attracted by the good angling in Connemara, eventually became the owner, by purchase...of large estates amounting to nearly 14,000 acres in this lovely district. By his residence among the people and large expenditure, he effected, as can be easily understood, great good...The castle is a magnificent structure in the Elizabethan style, built of granite faced with limestone, and was constructed at enormous cost. A special feature of the interior is the use of Connemara marble in the pillars and other work. Visitors are admitted in the absence of the family to the Castle and gardens, which are every extensive and beautifully laid out.'

Murray definitely loved the place, although he did not tell the full story. What he had failed to mention was that Dr Henry first visited Kylemore while on honeymoon with his Irish wife in 1849. The couple stayed at what was then Kylemore House, a workhouse during the Great Famine that had been converted into a hotel. When Henry's father—a textile magnate—died in 1862, he was left a considerable inheritance that allowed him to buy the lodge and the land around it as a gift for his wife Margaret, whom he adored. Subsequently he built a castle with a 'Romantic Victorian Sensibility'.

Yet the Henries did not enjoy it for long: in 1874 Margaret died while on holiday in Egypt. Her body was brought back to Kylemore and laid to rest in a mausoleum built by her grieving husband on the grounds, next to the Gothic church dedicated to her memory.

Kylemore proved unlucky for the Henries. In 1892, the couple's daughter Geraldine died tragically when she fell out of a horse-drawn cart into the river near the castle. No wonder Dr Henry sold it to the Duke and Duchess of Manchester in 1903 and went back to England, where he died in 1910 (*sic* 'late Mitchell Henry' —Murray, 1912).

Initially, the Duke and Duchess of Manchester were very enthusiastic about the castle and made many practical, yet extravagant, alterations to the building which they regarded as too 'romantic' for their tastes: the columns in the hall were taken down and wood panelling was put up on its walls, bedrooms were enlarged and a kitchen was built in place of the Henries' spacious ballroom. With time, however, the running costs of the castle proved too much for the Manchesters. In 1913, 'caretakers' (or bailiffs, to use a modern term) took control of the estate for seven years, until it was bought by Benedictine nuns, refugees from Ypres in Flanders, for the miserly sum of £45,000 (Mitchell Henry had sold it to the Manchesters for £63,000 seventeen years earlier!). The nuns have been in the Abbey since then. In 1923 they opened an international boarding school for girls and made provisions for visitors to be admitted to the grounds during summer.

The unwritten rules of Victorian/Edwardian guide-book writing stopped Murray from delving into the Henries' and the Manchesters' family secrets. I learned all the above and many more facts from a video introduction, presented by Sister Benedict—an elderly frail nun—in the Abbey's Visitor centre. The nuns had proved commercially astute, and the centre also housed a large souvenir shop and a café.

I was glad that the Abbey was run by Benedictine nuns as

opposed to their Franciscan sisters. Franciscan nuns, dwelling in Tyburn Covent in the centre of London (I had a chance to visit it on numerous occasions), are only allowed to speak for one hour a day—between 3 and 4 p.m. I wouldn't have been able to learn a lot from them, for it was only 11 a.m. when I started exploring Kylemore Abbey.

Luckily, the Abbey's nuns did not observe an oath of silence. Nor did the girls at the international boarding school who kept (out of boredom, I assumed) calling out to me and even blowing me kisses as I passed under the Castle's windows. I was about to return their air kisses, but from a politically correct point of view, by returning the teenage girls' innocent welcoming gestures, I would have probably committed a brazen act of paedophilia.

MOTHER ABBESS WELCOMES YOU TO THE CONVENT was written above the Abbey's entrance. IN ORDER TO PROTECT THE FLOORING, PLEASE WIPE YOUR FEET CAREFULLY! said another—somewhat less welcoming and less literate—sign inside. The moment I crossed the threshold, I was immersed in a deep deafening silence of the sort that reigns in Tyburn Convent twenty-three hours a day. The silence did not last long due to the group of vociferous Spanish tourists, who entered the building shortly after me. Their thunder-like verbal exchanges echoed intrusively, even somewhat blasphemously, into the convent's vaults.

The interior of the Abbey was plush, bordering on opulent. Somehow, it did not correspond to the video-introduction footage I had just seen, of modestly dressed, ever-toiling nuns. In one of the display cases, under a portrait of 'Lady Mary Percy, founder of the Irish Benedictine nuns order (1570–1649)', lay two mementos, brought by the nuns from their original home convent in Ypres: a foundation stone and an old tapestry. I found the display moving: all wanderers like to carry with them some small objects from home. In my case, it was my granddad's pencil holder, made of German porcelain, that used to stand on my late father's desk in Ukraine and which now adorns my writing table in London. I look at it as I am writing these lines.

The feature that added a real Celtic-Tiger touch to the place was a set of coin-operated candles near the statue of Mary and Jesus in the Community Chapel in the Abbey grounds. Until then, I had only seen coin-operated candles inside provincial parish churches in Italy—a country notorious for its pious commercialism (or commercialised piety), also manifesting itself in ubiquitous Virgin Mary icons above cash registers and supermarket tills.

I tossed a one-cent into the coin slit—the candle did not light up. I tried five cent, then ten—still nothing. The smallest coins the recalcitrant candles would accept probably of one- or two-euro denomination. I moved away from the statue before I wasted all my change and opened the bulky visitors' book on a near-by table. 'I am sorry the pomp and opulence and richness on view represents everything that is bad about the church—now and then...' read one of the entries.

A narrow path, winding past a conifer-lined lake, led to the elaborately decorated chapel, looking more like a mini-cathedral. Murray had described it with one curt adjective: 'costly'. There was no one inside. A Christmas tree lay on the floor across the aisle. A violin-and-piano recording was being played from hidden loudspeakers. From one of the pews, I picked a printed leaflet: 'All visitors to Kylemore Abbey are prayed for daily by the Benedictine Community'.

I sat down on the pew and did a brief meditation, interrupted by the noise of a car from outside. A young woman in a parka carried in a box with Christmas decorations.

'You must be the writer doing the travel book,' she said, with a clear-cut German accent. Rumours must have travelled fast in the Benedictine Community. She had probably been forewarned by the woman from the visitor centre, to whom I had shown my letter of introduction, signed by one of the Galway Aoifes and stating that I was 'a writer on an assignment with *Murray's Ireland*.' (!)

The woman was the Abbey's head gardener and indeed from Germany. 'Our duty is also to do Christmas trees,' she smiled and kindly invited me to visit the Abbey's famous walled gardens, 'now closed to the visitors'. I never asked her what her name was, but, for some reason, was almost sure she was called Ute.

The gardens, tucked away in a remote forested corner of the Abbey's grounds, next to the nuns' residential cottages, with smoke rising gently from the chimneys and the nuns' working robes put out to dry on a clothesline. They belonged entirely to me at that particular point in time. I strolled past neatly arranged flower-beds and squeaky-clean hothouses. I went across small toy-like bridges built above quiet little streams. The sweet smell of chimney smoke was drifting in the air. And although 'Ute' was not around, I could feel her presence and her touch in every single meticulously numbered tree or plant.

Despite the mercenary coin-operated candles, I had enjoyed my stop at Kylemore Abbey and even bought a nice woollen sweater in its souvenir shop. I could feel its warm soothing touch on my body as I drove into County Mayo.

STOP AND PRAY! called the banner on top of a modernistic church on my approach to Westport. It was the only one of its kind I had come across in my travels so far. Toll plazas—not churches—seemed to have become the true shrines of modern Celtic Tiger Ireland—'Stop and Pay'.

——

*'Nature has done much for this pretty town of Westport; and after nature, the traveller ought to be thankful to Lord Sligo, who has done a great deal too.'*
('AN IRISH SKETCH BOOK', W.M. THACKERAY, 1842)

*'Westport is a comfortable, relaxed town, still recognisably Georgian…'*
(THE 'ROUGH GUIDE TO IRELAND', 2004)

Having dropped my bags at The Harbour Mill Luxury Apartments, where I was accommodated for the night, I went to explore this designer town, created by the architects Richard Cassels and James Wyatt, the town that seemed to have charmed Thackeray.

It was raining, and I popped into the town's museum, which doubled as a tourist office.

'What are Westport's main attractions?' I asked the lonely woman at reception.

She blinked: 'It is the town itself, I presume…'

And she was right. Of all other Irish towns I had seen so far, Westport stood out, due to its peculiar architectural *ensemble*. Unlike Dublin, Cork, Galway or, say, Bray—which were architecturally chaotic, Westport had its own unique and readily recognisable face. This was largely due to the Browne family, long-time dwellers of stately Westport House, who were responsible for the formal planning of the town.

Westport struck me as a rather foreign-looking, 'un-Irish' place: its graceful malls, its geometrically correct central square, called the Octagon, its straight spacious streets running up and down the hill and lined with graceful Georgian terraces, made it look more French than Irish. Striking views of the sea and of the town's rooftops opened up from many a vantage point. Westport's architecture reminded me of a well-conducted symphony orchestra: no single building in itself (except perhaps for Westport House, which was closed for winter) was particularly special, yet together they formed a perfectly synchronised whole.

Why was it then that both Murray (in 1912, 'the town itself presents no object of interest') and Blackie (in 1856, 'Westport is poorly built and has a handsome fever hospital') found it uninteresting and poor? I found the answer in the Museum, to where I was driven back by the rain. 'For a hundred years, between 1850 and 1950, the town stagnated,' asserted the impressive interactive display, designed, allegedly, by two local teenagers (it allowed you to explore the town without leaving the Museum—simply by pressing buttons). The Act of Union and the Great Famine hit Westport very hard, I was informed, and led to the decline of its traditional linen and cotton industries, unable to complete with their more technically advanced British counterparts, as well as of the port. The town became extremely poor (*pace* Blackie) and largely lost its appeal (*pace* Murray). It stayed like that until the 1950s–70s, when, according to another child-prodigious interactive comment, 'poverty saved the town from insensitive development'.

I now realised why both Thackeray and the *Rough Guide* writers had a positive view of the town: the former visited it before the 'great decline', and the latter well after it. Having resolved the enigma, I walked back to Westport Quay.

'As for the warehouses, they are enormous; and might accommodate, I should think, not only the trade of Westport, but of Manchester too. There are huge streets of these houses, ten stories high, with cranes, owners' names, etc, marked Wine Stores, Flour Stores, Bonded Tobacco Warehouses, and so forth...These dismal mausoleums, as vast as pyramids, are the places where the dead trade of Westport lies buried...' wrote Thackeray in 1842.

One of those enormous 'mausoleums', aka 'pyramids', was now supposed to 'accommodate' me.

'Welcome to this uniquely reconstructed 18th-century cut-stone mill, built around an open-air courtyard,' started the glossy brochure for Harbour Mill Luxury Apartments. The 'open-air courtyard', long echoey corridors, with rows of doors facing each other, and balconies along the internal perimeter gave the Harbour Mill the look of a modernised and freshly painted prison.

My flat had a spacious lounge room, two bedrooms, two bathrooms and a kitchen—all modestly, yet tastefully, furnished and equipped. It felt almost perverse to stay there on my own. More used to small closet-like rooms (my first ever writer's 'office' was indeed inside a slightly enlarged wall closet in Moscow), I was not sure what to do with all that empty space and momentarily played with the idea of spending half of the night in one bedroom and then relocating to another...

It took me ages to sort out where all the electric switches were located, whereas in a 'normal' hotel room I would usually find them instinctively). I felt like an intruder into someone else's empty home.

The little detail that upset me most, however, was the electric doorbell on the front door. Nothing emphasises loneliness as much as a useless doorbell on the door of a flat, in which a traveller spends his one and only night in an unknown town, where there's absolutely nobody who could pay him a visit.

I didn't feel like watching TV in a large and empty lounge-room. Instead, I installed myself in one of the wood-panelled bedrooms and opened a copy of the *Western People*—County Mayo's daily broadsheet. My writer's curiosity was sparked by the very first paragraph of the lead story: 'Gardaí in Mayo are liaising with police in Northern Ireland after it emerged that Knock Airport has been identified as a potential target for an Al-Qaeda suicide bomber.'

Intrigued and ashamed of my own ignorance (it was the first time I had heard about the existence of Knock airport), I kept reading: 'Claims that the West's airport was a target for Osama bin Laden disciples…is (sic—vv) of considerable concern to gardaí, the *Western People* has learned.'

Of course, it all made perfect sense: while police forces all over the globe were focusing their attention on Heathrow, JFK and LA airports, the cunning bin Laden was about to strike where he was least expected—by knocking out Knock!

The next several paragraphs of the story, headlined 'Knock Airport was on Al Qaeda hit-list', however, were a cold shower: 'A garda spokesperson told the *Western People* that the gardaí *had no definite information* (italics are mine—vv) regarding…plans for Mayo's airport…Knock Airport bosses have dismissed the reports, saying they are *not aware of any evidence* to support the claims. "We are also not aware of any high-risk alerts," Head of Operations, Robert Grealish, told the *Western People…*'

I silently praised my journalist colleagues for this brilliant example of making a lead non-story out of absolutely nothing…

To my surprise they told me at reception the next morning that the Harbour Mill didn't have a room for breakfast, and so I'd have to go to The Helm pub next door.

The pub was located in another converted warehouse. Its walls were pasted with clippings from 1916 local newspapers—a gift for a time-traveller.

One article was called 'Execution of MacBride'. The name was familiar from the monument that I had spotted in town the day before. 'IRA Major John MacBride. Died for Ireland in 1916,' had been carved in stone under the statue. According to the article, the execution was ordered by 'the British commander'.

Next to it, there was a copy of another order of the same 'British commander', allowing all shops selling 'intoxicating alcohol' to be open only from 2 p.m. to 5 p.m.—almost like in Gorbachev's

Soviet Union! Soviet associations did not end there, for the next paragraph of the Order said: 'These restrictions do not apply to officers in military uniforms.' In special 'closed' shops, for the Soviet Communist-Party apparatchiks, no restrictions used to apply either. The British must have been busy in Westport, I thought, ordering executions and restricting sales of alcohol for those not executed yet.

My appetite negatively affected by the gruesome displays, I looked around. There were two more patrons breakfasting in the pub: an elderly French couple, with the baffled look of accidental tourists (or *touristes accidentales, si vous voulez*) on their faces. I overheard snippets of their dialogue with the waitress:

'Cereal?'

'What?'

'Cornflakes?'

*'Non.'*

'Tea or coffee?'

'What?'

And so on.

'What' was obviously the only English word they knew.


'Thanks for mentioning us in your little article!' the receptionist at the apartments said as I was checking out. They were clearly misinformed, but I didn't feel like arguing: at least they hadn't mistaken me for either Murray or Baedeker. What a pity!

Chapter 7
# A Village Called Ireland

'*Roscommon is a neat-looking county with little beauty of situation to recommend it.*'
('A HANDBOOK FOR TRAVELLERS IN IRELAND', MURRAY, 1912)

'*Roscommon has the...reputation of being the most boring county in Ireland.*'
(THE 'ROUGH GUIDE TO IRELAND', 2004)

Pints of Guinness were popping up on the bar in front of me like the blades of flick-knives concealed under the counter. This was my first ever night in a 'typical' country pub (The Corner House), in what had been described as a 'typical' Irish village—Ballinagare, Co. Roscommon. I was speedily approaching my personal absolute record in Guinness consumption and thinking of entering it into my own imaginary *Guinness Book of Records*.

Since my very first days in Ireland, I had wanted to visit a small and seemingly unremarkable Irish village, for—from what I knew—it was there, and not amidst the chaotic urban piles of Dublin, Limerick and Cork, or the carefully laid out Westport from which I had travelled, that the elusive 'Irish soul' was dwelling.

Celtic Ireland was entirely rural: towns were a fairly recent Irish creation. In my imagination, it was like one huge sprawling village, populated by warriors, druids (or dreamers) and poets.

My first evening in Ballinagare, to where I had been invited for a weekend, did little to confirm that romantic vision.

The Corner House's ambience was rather reminiscent of a scene from *McCarthy's Bar*, by the late Pete McCarthy: men drinking at the counter, women reclining on sofas along the wall—a timeless setting. The only reminder of the 21st century was a poster, advertising salsa-dancing classes in the village hall.

I felt as if I had known all the patrons for donkey's years. After the fifth (or was it the sixth?) pint, Dublin, London, elections in Ukraine and the war in Iraq—all receded, faded away, blended into distant insignificance—overshadowed by the really important issues: the previous week's closure of the old village post office and a new housing-development project, approved by the County Council…

'These thirteen new council houses will ruin the village,' a retired teacher, sitting next to me, was saying.

'That's right! Besides, what are the newcomers going to do here? There are no jobs, no childcare, no public transport and no infrastructure for them,' echoed one of the women from the sofa.

The residents of Ballinagare had been fighting a losing battle against the housing project for several years, their rationale being that one simply could not increase the village population of seventy-two almost threefold without drastically changing its way of life and its historic architectural pattern. Yet, despite numerous petitions and protests, the construction of new houses was under way: three of them were already in place—a Dublin-style 'in-fill development' in miniature…

In-between the pints that seemed to grow from the bar in front of me, I would pop out for a smoke. The tiny village outside was immersed in peaceful slumber. To a hardened city dweller like myself, it resembled a neat little old lady, who had dozed off quietly on a park bench. I thought I could even hear her snore ever so gently…

Next morning, I was woken up by the deafening silence outside my window. A pot of steaming coffee looked (and tasted) like a pint of hot Guinness. With Pat, one of my hospitable hosts, we went for a drive around the area. We could have walked of course, but modern Irish villagers love their cars…

One of the two settlements of the parish of Kilcorkey,

Ballinagare stands on a large Bog—'little beauty' (Murray) indeed. For centuries, this area was the domain of the O'Conors, the famous Gaelic chieftains and landowners. The most prominent of them—historian, poet and manuscripts collector Charles O'Conor—lived in Ballinagare in the mid-18th century and later retired to a secluded farmhouse called the Hermitage. After his death, the house became a writers' retreat and then a training centre for the Irish Free-State Army.

A listed building, it was in a deplorable state: roof and chimneys overgrown with grass, the windows' gaping eye-sockets covered with sheets of plastic. Right next to the house stood a modern cottage, occupied by the Collins' family—descendants of Charles O'Conor's herd. The woman who opened the door told us that they had been trying to maintain the Hermitage on their own money. 'It cost us a fortune. For twenty years we have been waiting for some assistance from the County Council, but it claims to have no funds for the house's upkeep...'

We moved on to Ballinagare's semi-ruined old church which, it seemed, had been turned into a tip, its grounds strewn with rubbish, broken bikes and rusty washing machines. A similar fate befell the historic Old Market House in the neighbouring village of Frenchpark, the only difference being that, unlike the church, it was enclosed by a shabby fence. Once an impressive structure that, among other period features, had indoor toilets—a highly unusual detail for a 17th-century Irish interior, it had more recently been used for food storage. For me, this brought back memories of Communist Russia, where many old churches were turned into vegetable depots. 'The Temple of St George on Potatoes'—as Muscovites used to joke uneasily in the mid-1980s.

The USSR, of course, was very poor and, at the time, spent almost half of its budget on 'defence' (read arms race), but how come the powerful and seemingly peaceful 'Celtic Tiger' cannot find the means to preserve the country's heritage?

We drove on to the village of Tulsk (a deceptively Russian-sounding name), overlooked by Murray, that lay in the midst of what the local tourist brochure called 'a unique sacred landscape'. The area was dotted with Bronze-Age mounds and ancient burial grounds. Indeed, there was a modern state-of-the-art visitor centre in Tulsk. But what did we see next to it? Bulldozers and excavators digging up that very 'sacred landscape' for all they were worth to create a modern housing estate! The same brochure obviously got it wrong when it called the people of Tulsk 'proud custodians of this unique ritual landscape'. One could see with a naked eye how greed and big business were hastily transforming Ireland from the Emerald Isle into the 'Concrete Isle'.

Perhaps Russian associations were not that far-fetched in Tulsk.

To be fair, we did eventually find one old church that had been properly, even lovingly, restored by Roscommon County Council, Portahard, on the edge of Frenchpark. The reason for that was simple: the grave of Dr Douglas Hyde, the first President of Ireland, was in the churchyard, next to the Douglas Hyde 'Interpretive Centre', of course. To me, this was a classic case of Soviet-style window-dressing that simply underlined the neglected state of other, no-less-important historic buildings that could not boast of having the tomb of a prominent Irish statesman on their grounds.

The old graveyard of Ballinagare did not have any 'prominent' graves either—just those of 'ordinary' Irish village folk—all victims of the Great Famine, the Black and Tans, 'Crown Forces' and the plain hardship of everyday life. That was probably why its present-day state was not just deplorable—it was disastrous.

To get to the cemetery, Pat and I had to negotiate rivers of mud and hillocks of cows' droppings. We had to dive under spires of torn barbed wire—erected by the County Council instead of the promised restoration. 'Dancing' gravestones in different stages of collapse—fallen, semi-fallen and still almost upright—were hardly visible behind thick vegetation, mostly weeds. The ground under our feet was disturbingly bumpy, and every bump signified an abandoned grave. Or rather—a forgotten life. It was like trudging through the necropolis of the Irish countryside itself.

It was getting dark. The short winter day was coming to an end.

———

Despite this gruesome excursion, I did find a number of signs to support my romantic image of an Irish village in Ballinagare. It was a place where locals still left their cars and houses unlocked; where wild pheasants could be seen unhurriedly crossing the 'main road'; where Tommy Connor, the oldest resident, in his mid-90s, and a devoted former Gaelic football player, vividly remembered 'how farmers walked their pigs a hundred miles to the nearest terminal, from where they would take them to England'; where people still believed that a child whose father died before he was born could cure thrush by blowing on the sores.

I was delighted to learn that the village—just like the whole of Ireland—had always had a disproportionate number of able, if somewhat surrealist and tongue-in-cheek amateur poets. 'Oh, Ballinagare of fame renowned,/A church without a steeple,/At every door there stands a whore/ To laugh at decent people…' This à-la-Jonathan-Swift rhyme was written by Frank Browne, a Ballinagare native, who died in 1998.

And this is how he described his experience of the Hill pub in Tulsk: 'Between "Hill" and Hell there is but one letter/ And if "Hill" was in Hell,/Tulsk would be a lot better.'

A similar sparkling poetic wit could be found in the works of two other deceased locals—Bob Loftus and Seamus Dockery ('As I walked into the park one day,/ I could not believe my luck./ I spied upon the river bank/ a fine big mallard duck./ I had to scheme a brilliant plan, it was all down to me,/ How could I catch that lovely duck to have it for my tea…')

Luckily, not all poets-cum-eccentrics in the area were dead. Sean Browne from neighbouring Castlerea ('an uninteresting town, rather prettily situated on the Suck', according to Murray—and here I have to restrain myself from coming up with a modern pun to the effect that 'the town Sucks') may never have written a single verse, but I was inclined to regard him as a true poet for what he had managed to achieve. A train buff from childhood, he bought a disused Irish Railways A55 locomotive in 1996 and installed it inside his pub, Hell's Kitchen. On my visit to the pub, I admired this diesel-electric 'monster', surrounded by signals, points, badges, conductors' caps and other railway paraphernalia from all over the world, and, as a fellow trainspotter, could not help admiring Sean's ingenuity and stamina (he had to overcome lots of bureaucratic hurdles to purchase the locomotive) in having his dream realised.

'I did it purely out of love,' he said to me proudly.

'Pub owner goes loco!' ran the headline in a 1996 Irish tabloid that also quoted one of Sean's customers as saying that his pub gave a whole new meaning to 'suppin' diesel'. As for me, I was thrilled to see in Sean's collection the badge of the Kharkov Institute of Railway Engineers, from my native city in the Ukraine.

Poets and dreamers (read eccentrics) were precisely the types I had been hoping to find in my imaginary Irish village. So, in this particular respect, my short visit to Ballinagare—a microcosm of the whole of rural Ireland—was a success.

And although, having been born elsewhere, I couldn't follow John Noone, another home-bred Ballinagare poet, who emigrated to America in 1904—'Ah, Ballinagare I think you are/ The sweetest place on earth./My thoughts do fondly cling to you,/ I've loved you from my birth…'—my own thoughts will 'fondly cling' to this 'unremarkable' hamlet in Roscommon—a once lovely historic area, chewed up by the omnivorous Celtic Tiger and regurgitated as 'Ireland's most boring county'.

'We all live in the present moment of the past'—I had noticed these words by T.S. Eliot on a poster inside Tulsk Visitor Centre. Leaving Roscommon, I was hoping that one day they would be noticed and taken on board in this old and once-beautiful village called Ireland.

Chapter 8

# The Eagle Eye

'West Cork is bigger than Ireland.'
('IRELAND OF THE WELCOMES', IRISH TOURIST
BOARD, 2005)

'The motorist who visits Ireland, intending to tour
through it in his own car, without previously
having a suitable route drawn up for him, is likely
to have a very varied experience...'
('A HANDBOOK FOR TRAVELLERS IN IRELAND',
MURRAY, 1912)

I was in for a long drive across the western side of Ireland to
Beara Peninsula. Having ignored Murray's advice (see above),
I didn't have 'a suitable route drawn'—just followed the signs,
stopping to ask for directions from time to time. It soon became
evident that, even ninety-odd years after Murray's warning, such a
light-minded attitude to 'touring through' Ireland was fraught
with danger.

I left early in the morning, hoping to arrive at Bantry, where a
hotel room had been booked for me, seven or eight hours later.

The road signs were few and far between, and most of them, as
Wicklow had earlier with Bahrain, proclaimed that this or that
town had been 'Home' to Singapore, Estonia, Kyrghizstan and
other countries. The fact that Newcastle West, say, hosted disabled
athletes from Martinique several years before was certainly
educational, yet it did little to steer my Fiat in the right direction.

Most roads were also overhung with bright, attention-grabbing
banners wishing good luck to local footballers, in one case—

rather self-critically it seemed to me—to 'minor' footballers.

As for the few 'proper' road signs, they were often either misleading or made no sense whatsoever, like the one saying 'Galway' and pointing right, straight into the wall of a house in the middle of a street, with no trace of a right- (or left-) hand turn for at least a mile in both directions.

Asking pedestrians for directions was even worse, because there were so few of them. The Celtic Tiger Irish, whose attitude to money was like a teenager's attitude to sex—having just discovered it they couldn't have enough of it—simply did not walk, but preferred to drive everywhere. As a result, I would normally end up asking a Pole who had only just arrived in Ireland, had no clue as to where he was himself (to say nothing of how to get from Tuam to Gort) and did not speak any English anyway.

Those rare pedestrians who actually *were* Irish wanted to know first where I was from ('I can't place your accent…')—a question that took some time to answer. Having satisfied their curiosity, they would be willing to tell me all about the sights of their own little town, providing me with lots of valuable information on when the local church was built and how many 'people from Dublin' had already snapped up the town's best residential properties. The directions they eventually supplied were sketchy and often misleading.

My car dragged its wheels along tree-lined narrow country roads—squeezing into them like a dagger into a sheath. It drove through the main streets of countless little towns, each displaying a traditional set of Spar and Centra stores, bakeries, hairdressers, bookmakers, charity shops (for some mysterious reason, almost all of them had books by Virginia Andrews on display), pubs and funeral parlours. The best old building in almost every town was the Victorian Court House. The British occupation was obviously *trying* for the Irish. But at least they were tried in style.

In the disproportionate numbers of hairdressers' and funeral parlours, many Irish small towns reminded me of the Russian 'regional centre of N.' from my favourite satirical novel of all time, *The Twelve Chairs* by that brilliant tandem of pre-wwii Soviet satirists Ilya Ilf and Evegeny Petrov:

'There were so many hairdressing establishments and funeral homes in the regional centre of N. that the inhabitants seemed to be born merely in order to have a shave, get their hair cut, freshen up their heads with toilet water and then die. In actual fact, people came into the world, shaved, and died rather rarely in the regional centre of N. Life in N. was extremely quiet. The spring evenings were delightful, the mud glistened like coal in the light of the moon, and all the young men of the town were so much in love with the secretary of the communal-service workers' local committee that she found difficulty in collecting their subscriptions.'[11]

I was very pleased to add Ilf and Petrov to the list of my time-travelling companions...

In one town, where I stopped for a snack, there was actually a funeral parlour doubling as a pub (or was it the other way around?). I popped in and asked for a sandwich. A little old man in a dark suit materialised from a dark recess behind the bar (the whole room was very gloomy and sombre). 'We don't do sandwiches any longer,' he said with a professional undertaker's grin.

'What do you do then—coffins?' I asked.

'Yes,' he muttered and receded back into darkness.

I had a snack at a 'Supermac's Gaelic Restaurant' (!) next door where they tried to force chips on me—as a 'side dish', with the fattiest burger I had ever had. No wonder the town's undertakers were busy.

To compensate for a lack of proper road signs and to while away the time, I kept ticking off curious names of shops and pubs, some of which were brilliant: 'The Off' off-licence shop, 'The Why Not?' pub, 'Mr Mister Menswear Shop' (my favourite) and so on. Eventually, I reached Co. Kerry, where I had lunch in a small town. While using a public toilet in the town square, I noticed a red-faced man lingering near the sink—as if preparing to wash his hands—and looking around himself nervously. To me, he resembled a perverse priest in search of a victim, and I immediately castigated myself for such a brazen generalisation, brought about by local Irish newspapers' obsessive coverage of their clergymen's sins. The lead story of that day's issue of *The Kerryman* was—unsurprisingly—'Priest resigning after man's claim'. To my own embarrassment, I couldn't help thinking that it was him—the resigned priest—I had spotted in the toilet... Bombarded with such stories on a daily basis, seventy per cent of the Irish (according to a survey in the same newspaper) thought the Catholic Church should no longer be allowed to run schools.

The real trouble started at a petrol station near Killarney, when I thought I was no more than a couple of hours away from my destination. The man at the counter was very helpful and volunteered to give me directions to Bantry, even though I hadn't asked for them: for once, I had had a proper look at the map and thought I knew perfectly well how to get there. Having enquired whether or not I was German, the man dissuaded me from driving through the town centre as I had intended (correctly, as it turned out), and insisted I take the N72 to Cork instead.

It was like that old Irish joke recounted to me once by Peter Ustinov:

'Do you know the way to Dublin?'

'No, sorr, I don't. But let me ask my friend over there...'

'Don't worry. I'll ask someone else on the way...'

'Don't, sorr. I've just spoken to my friend.'

'And what did he say?'

'He doesn't know either...'

Irish jokes were to remain my only consolation for the following four hours as I got increasingly and irretrievably (as it seemed) lost.

When I discovered that my inquisitive advisor from the petrol station was wrong, it was too late to turn back. In any case, I wouldn't have been able to find the way back for a million pounds (let alone euro).

It was dark, misty and pouring with rain. Having already spent over nine hours behind the wheel, I started panicking. 'Calm down, Vitali!' I said to myself, pulled over and took out the map. Squinting at it in the treacherous light of a pocket torch, I decided

to drive towards Macroom and then take the R584 to Bantry. I
should have known better: if the system of road designation in
Ireland was in any way similar to that of Britain, where the lowest
grade of a road was 'B', 'R' roads were bound to be the same
category as Alpine goat paths, strewn with rocks and opening up
to a precipice. R584 was probably even worse. The truth is that I
never found it. Macroom was unreachable: the road that was
supposed to lead to it had been closed for repairs, and I had to take
an alternative route via country lanes.

The fog was so thick that I could hardly see my windscreen
wipers, and it took me a considerable effort to keep from veering
into the large trucks (also on the 'alternative route'!), splashing
fountains of mud from under their wheels. Soon I realised that I
had actually been moving in the opposite direction to my
destination. I turned back—and got lost completely. So much for
my old, semi-ironic, dictum that the ability to get lost is the most
important quality of a travel writer.

'Your tongue will lead you as far as Kiev,' goes an old Russian
proverb, the English equivalent of which would probably be,
'When everything else fails, ask the locals.' The problem was, there
were not many locals around, if not to count some stray sheep, into
which I narrowly avoided bumping from time to time. The good
thing was they (the sheep) were white and hence discernable.

I thanked my lucky stars when the murky silhouette of a
drenched postman on a bike, snatched out of pitch darkness by the
headlights, materialised in front of me. What was he doing
paddling up a country road late in the evening, a bulky mail bag
on his back? Then I remembered that my mail delivery in Dublin
used to arrive well after lunch time, if at all, so this man could
easily have been on his way to deliver the morning post.

Having patiently listened to the postman's detailed description
of local sights and attractions (from which I deduced I was still
nowhere near Bantry); I finally managed to extract one piece of
advice from him: 'Drive through the centre of the next village, then
turn right.'

I was not able to follow that useful tip, for I failed to find the
bloody village! Instead, I ended up on a dirt track, where my car
started skidding. In despair, I steered towards a detached house,

semi-hidden by the trees. Its windows were dark, but I decided to knock on the door anyway. The moment I got out of the car, I was pounced upon by two large dogs. I couldn't see what breed they were, but from the sheer aggression of the creatures, I decided they were Pit Bull terriers and dashed back inside the Fiat.

After that encounter, I all but gave up and just kept on driving 'to where my eyes looked', as they say in Russia. Bracing myself for the night on the road, I suddenly saw a faded sign with the word 'Bantry' on it. A colleague of mine once said that the best words in the English language were 'cheque enclosed'. He was wrong: the nicest-sounding word in the language of Shakespeare and Joyce was 'Bantry'!

I got lost several times more before, having spent almost twelve hours driving, I finally reached my destination. West Cork was indeed 'larger than Ireland'. Or so it seemed...

————

> *'With the exception of the Main Street and the quay, with their whitewashed and slated houses, Bantry is a town of cabins. The wretchedness of some of them is quite curious...I declare I believe a Hottentot kraal has more comforts in it; even to write of the place makes one unhappy, and the words move slow.'*
> ('AN IRISH SKETCH BOOK', W.M. THACKERAY, 1842)

> *'Bantry...consists of two parallel streets, irregularly and indifferently paved; some good houses, but the greater portion are squalid huts, imparting to the town altogether a very mean appearance.'*
> (THE 'IMPERIAL GAZETTEER', W.G. BLACKIE, ED., 1855)

It was late, yet in the amazing anti-climax of my journey, the few streets of Bantry (from what I could see, there were now more than two—*pace* W.G. Blackie) were solidly clogged with traffic. Having negotiated hundreds of miles of deserted country roads, I got stuck in the biggest traffic jam I had ever seen. Bantry, one of my favourite towns in Ireland (I had visited it before), was choking on its own new-found prosperity, and the congestion was largely due to road works and construction sites, with which the place was literally dotted. But for once, I didn't begrudge the queue that seemed to welcome me back to civilisation.

'I am not Irish,' said the dark-skinned girl at Reception in the tired-looking 1970s' West Lodge Hotel.

'Neither am I,' I reassured her.

I guessed that she had probably wanted to say, 'I don't speak English' but was unable to do so, because she didn't speak English.

Our conversation sounded approximately like this:

I: 'What time is breakfast?'

She: 'Town centre two minute car…'

I: 'What TV channels do you have?'

She: 'Yes, you can make phone call from your room.'

It was like asking a pedestrian how to get to a post office and hearing in response: 'It is half-past eight in the morning.'

As it turned out later, she was French. Whenever I was about to ask her a question, she would strike that peculiar half-defensive half-aggressive pose, like Manuel in *Fawlty Towers*, as if expecting a provocation…

A rectangular mark on the carpet in the middle of my miserly furnished room testified to the fact that a second bed had once stood there. It must have been removed to make sure I didn't invite a lodger. There was no shampoo—just a tiny, almost transparent, piece of soap in the bathroom. In need of a proper wash after my twelve-hour drive, I went down to the hotel's 'leisure centre'.

A father and son were sitting on a bench inside the steam room. The moment I entered, I realised that the heater was not on. The room was freezing.

'There's no steam here,' I said to them.

They nodded, stood up and went out.

A bald fat man was luxuriating in a Jacuzzi, with its pump off. I pressed the button on the wall, and the water started bubbling. The man said: 'Thanks!' and turned over onto his stomach.

What a strange nation, the Irish…

_____

*'Skibbereen…is principally associated with distress,*
*this locality having suffered to a fearful extent in the*
*famine year.'*
('A HANDBOOK FOR TRAVELLERS IN IRELAND',
MURRAY, 1912)

*'Cheerful Skibbereen smartly painted and set on the*
*River Illen…'*
('THE ROUGH GUIDE TO IRELAND', 2004)

The long-suffering, yet now supposedly 'cheerful', town of Skibbereen was my main West-Cork destination after Bantry. Chiefly, due to *The Southern Star*, the local newspaper incorporating the legendary *Skibbereen Eagle* that had bravely announced to the world in its famous 26 August 1898 editorial that 'it will keep its eye on the Emperor of Russia and all such despotic enemies—whether at home or abroad—of human progression and man's natural rights, which undoubtedly include a nation's claim to self-government.'

The *Eagle* eye watching Russia from a tiny famine-ravaged Irish town remains one of the biggest scoops in the history of Irish journalism. Easily dismissed as either a silly joke or a classic manifestation of the provincial inferiority complex, the 'eye on Russia' editorial was in fact neither. It was a masterful publicity gimmick, masterminded by the paper's then editor and proprietor, Frederick Potter. The sensation it created saved the paper, then on the verge of financial ruin, from going bust for another thirty-one years (the paper finally wrapped up in 1929). Since that artificially engineered outcry, the paper's weekly chronicle page was printed under the heading 'The Outlook from Eagle Watch Tower'.

It has to be said that, until its very last days, *The Eagle* eagerly wore its self-made mask as Russia's vigilant watchdog and published an inordinate (for a provincial Irish rag) number of mostly critical articles on Russian and Soviet affairs—a game picked up by *The Southern Star* that came to replace it. In 1946, the latter printed a political cartoon depicting De Valera and Stalin enjoying a pint. 'Between ourselves, Dev, Russia has never quite forgotten that article in *The Skibbereen Eagle*,' said the caption.

In Joyce's *Ulysses*, J.J. Molloy mentions 'our watchful friend *The Skibbereen Eagle*'. Thus, a small provincial newspaper became part of classical literature.

And although I had never heard of *The Eagle* while in Russia and only learned about the whole saga when living in Dublin, I found the story fascinating.

At a first glance Skibbereen did look rather 'cheerful', and definitely not distressing—not any more. Its brightly painted façades reminded me of Torshavn, the smallish capital of the Faroes, where locals paint their houses in bright colours to make up for the lack of sunlight and the overall drabness of their tree-less windswept islands.

My contact in town was Michael Manning, the local tourism officer—an engaging and extremely knowledgeable man. I felt immediate affection for him from the moment I learned that he did not own a mobile phone. Neither did I. Prior to meeting Michael, I had even thought I was the world's only remaining person over sixteen not to own a mobile. As it turned out, there were actually two of us…I immediately suggested we should start up club of conscientious objectors to mobile phones. The suggestion was accepted unanimously.

My conscientious non-ownership of a mobile was triggered by the extremely pushy pictures editor of a big newspaper where I worked several years before. From the moment I set off on an assignment (at times, even before I hit the road!), he would start pestering me with calls demanding to know what photos I wanted with my column. Eventually, I returned my mobile phone to the paper saying that from then on I would be contacting the picture editor myself—from a public phone!—when I was ready, and have lived happily ever since.

It was Michael who organised my meeting with Liam O'Reagan, the *Southern Star*'s incumbent editor. The appointment was set up on the spot by a single short phone call (from a landline in the tourist office, of course!).

I popped into a newsagent's to ask for directions to *The Star*'s offices. A very old and untidy woman was dozing in a chair behind a counter, littered with newspapers and other items.

'Where is *The Star*?' I asked her. She woke up with a jerk and replied angrily pointing at a pile of newspapers: 'Here it is!'

It was entirely my fault: I should have formulated the question differently. I bought a copy of *The Star* to look at later.

I met Liam, a gentle soft-spoken man, in his tiny office, brimming with old newspapers and folders (one—worryingly—said 'Bantry Hospital') and with a tattered map of Ireland on the wall. *The Star* had been in the hands of the O'Reagan family since 1946, with Liam representing its third generation. He had been Editor for over twenty years.

Liam told me that *The Star/Eagle* had two main claims to fame: the 'eye on Russia' editorial of 1898 and an apology made by *The Irish Times* of 1882. Having referred to *The Eagle* in somewhat disdainful fashion, *The Irish Times* later apologised, regretting its 'hasty and inadvertent blunder'. The paper then praised *The Eagle* as a 'well-conducted journal, still flourishing and useful.'

*The Eagle*, in its turn, reacted to the apology in its habitual self-assured fashion, in an editorial: '*The Irish Times*' allusion was unworthy of an important and influential journal' and (wait for this) was 'so discreditable and unwarranted that we treated it with silent contempt.'

That small, yet proud, newspaper definitely possessed a huge amount of self-confidence and cheek, also known as chutzpah...

'We have been maintaining the Russian theme through the ages,' Liam was saying now. He told me that *The Star* now employed a staff of twenty-eight, only three of them full time. That was not counting five freelance writers and twenty (!) sports reporters—a typical scenario for a provincial Irish newspaper, he assured me. According to him, *The Star* was presently selling 16,000 copies 'all over the West' (of Ireland, no doubt).

Fascinating as it all was, I was more interested in the paper's past than in its present-day achievements and asked Liam whether it was possible to see some of the 1912 issues of *The Eagle*.

Liam led me to a small room upstairs where I was faced with an antediluvian microfilm reader, the like of which I hadn't seen since the mid-1970s, when I had to use them quite a lot as a graduate translator in Ukraine. Strange, for, according to a local tourist brochure given to me by Michael Manning, *The Star* was 'one of the most technically up-to-date newspapers in the country'.

'We have old issues on microfilm only,' explained Liam. 'The picture is upside down at times.'

'No worries,' said I. 'I'll simply stand on my head then...'

It turned out that it was not possible to print the images either ('It has to be special paper, and it is very expensive...'), so I had to copy the articles by hand. *The Star* was obviously going through difficult times.

Having excused himself, Liam went out for lunch. The rest of the staff (his deputy and a secretary) were out of the office, too. I was left alone with a film roll of issues published in 1912—the year when my *Travellers Guide to Ireland* had come out. Reading them on the blinking screen of the faulty projector was like peering through the veil of time.

I decided to look first at the 14 December 1912 issue that was precisely—almost to the day (*The Eagle* was a weekly) ninety-three years old.[12]

> BANDON. CHRISTMAS IN THE SHOPS.
> 'In accordance with our usual custom, we are again called upon to give a description of "Christmas in the Shops" in Bandon. Owing to the way in which our space is taxed, the reference to each establishment must be brief, but we shall endeavour to mention them all. The article must be extended into two issues of the paper.'

I was pleasantly surprised by the tightness and fluency of the style —a stark contrast to the ear-grating clumsiness of many modern newspapers—Irish and British.

'Last year the Christmas trade was seriously handicapped by continuous rain during the preceding fortnight. We hope the traders will be more fortunate this year in the matter of weather and that the people of the town and district will support local shopkeepers, and also encourage Irish industry by purchasing Irish goods whenever possible.'

The last sentence sounded rather modern. I wondered whether Bandon traders of 1912 used to display 'Proudly Irish' signs above their shops.

The natural thing to do now was to see what Murray wrote on Bandon (which I hadn't visited) in 1912. I opened my trusted old guide-book:

'Bandon* (pop. 2830), an important agricultural centre. It is pleasantly situated on the rt.bank of the Bandon River, in a broad open valley, bounded on the N. by the Clara Hills. Spencer calls it—'The Pleasant Bandon crowned with many a wood.' With the exception of the handsome modern Church and a modern R.C. Church (obviously, in Murray's terms, the only proper 'Church' was a Protestant one), the town itself contains very little that is interesting to the tourist, except for the Earl of Bandon's Park of Castle Bernard, that stretches along the banks of the river to the W. and which is open to the public. Golf Links, a nine-hole course, have been laid out here...'

I was mystified by the fact that Murray had given his coveted asterisk (star) to such a seemingly uninteresting place.

Looking for a more 'piquant' human-interest story, I came across the following in *The Eagle*, in the section 'Bantry Notes':

BANTRY LADDIE

'On Monday last at the Petty Sessions Court a case of much local interest was heard. A gentleman named Mark Sullivan sought for an order to have a dog named "Laddie", the property of Miss Crowley, destroyed, as he alleged the animal bit him. The complainant went to show that the dog was of Scotch descent, as the name implied, but the defendant's solicitor contended that "Laddie" had as much right to live in Bantry as any Irish dog, be he "Paddy", "Jim", or otherwise. A number of witnesses were called, including a dispenser of medicine, locally called "The Doctor", and the mark on Mark (a rather awful pun!—vv) was graphically described. But the majority of the magistrates refused the order for execution, and transported "Laddie" to Clonakilty (God help us!)[13] to a friend of his former owner. The case was the most amusing one, but the owner of "Laddie" had the satisfaction of knowing her pet will not be destroyed.'

I was coming to realise why *The Eagle* had enjoyed such a good name in the late-19th and early-20th centuries. Its popularity was further highlighted by the following editorial 'Note' on the Letters page: 'Owing to extreme pressure on our space, we are compelled to hold over to our next issue several letters & items of news.'

Underneath the Note was a sentence that would have probably been called 'Quote of the Day' in a modern newspaper: 'Money making is one of the industries in which Quantity is considered before Quality.' A wisdom generated possibly by the paper's legendary editor, Frederick Potter, himself.

I turned over the page to look at the ads section. Wherever I travel, I always find ads in a local newspaper extremely evocative. I wondered what the 93-year-old 'classifieds' would be able to tell me:

WANTED.
—Girl, about 17 years of age, to assist in housework. Good home. Apply—"Girl", Eagle Office.

For better or worse, political correctness did not exist in 1912.

A general servant, able to wash, plain cook, for small family in suburbs of Cork. Comfortable home to suitable person. Small farmer's daughter preferred (it was unclear whether they wanted a small daughter or the daughter of a small farmer—vv). Apply by letter to 'Domestic', Eagle Office, Cork.

A boy able to care horses and do general farm work. Good wages to suitable person. Apply to Joseph Walsh, Clonakilty' (this time without, 'God help us!'—vv).

Here I couldn't help recalling my precious *Baedeker's Manual of Conversation in Four Languages*, published in 1886—a precursor of modern phrase books. In the chapter on 'Engaging a Servant', Victorian travellers were offered a 'model' of a question-answer verbal exchange. It is quite possible that the 'boy to care horses', sought after by Clonakilty's John Walsh was 'interviewed' in the following Baedeker-recommended manner:

'How long have you been in the habit of acting as servant?'
'It is now fifteen years, Sir.' (From what we know the 'boy' could have been in his forties or fifties—vv)
'Can you take care of a horse?'
'Yes, Sir, and even two or three if necessary.'
'Are you given to drinking?'
'I like a glass of wine very well, Sir, but I never get drunk.' (Don't we all say that?—vv)
'What wages do you ask?'
'Five francs a day.'
'But you have not always had so much as that.'
'Oh! Sir, sometimes I have not had more than thirty sous.'
'You must always be clean and well dressed. I must tell you before hand, that if I take you into my service, you must be exact in the execution of my orders; and if you happen to get drunk, I shall discharge you at once.'
'My masters have always been satisfied with my services, and I hope you will be so too, Sir.'

'You may return here tomorrow, as I must make some inquiries before I engage you.'

And so on.

Reading this, one could be forgiven for thinking that political correctness was not such a bad thing, after all.

The next ad in *The Eagle* was hard to overlook:

'PIGS! PIGS! PIGS!'

It sounded like the angst-driven outburst of a depressed misanthrope. But it wasn't:

'I will receive pigs fortnightly at Ballineen Station— Thursdays 12 noon to 3 p.m.—all risks taken. Highest prices obtainable.'

And underneath it: 'Frank Daunt—agent for J. Matterson & Sons Ltd, Limerick—Bacon Curers of Worldwide Reputation.'

This last ad was printed three times on the same page of the paper, a fact that made me wonder whether the above-mentioned 'pressures of space' did not apply to pigs and bacon curers.

On the following page, next to a story with a headline that would have gone down well with any modern tabloid—'45 Pounds in an Old Mattress'—there was an extraordinary report:

WIFE WANTED FOR CHRISTMAS
'The applicant wrote to the Castlerea Guardians on Saturday: "I am a man of 50, healthy, industrious, and a good earner, and has (*sic*—vv) a nice house and garden, together with a couple of pigs (pigs seemed to play a significant role in the life of post-Victorian Skibbereen—vv). Still I am never happy, because I am all alone and never married…I hope you will consider my case and make me happy for Christmas. An inmate (*sic*—vv) aged 40 or 45 would suit. I am not very hard to please…"
The Master was commissioned with the delicate task of

finding if there was anyone in the House willing to comfort the lonely applicant.'

I thought I had come to enjoy *The Eagle's* tongue-in-cheek style of reporting.

The paper carried a section called 'Questions in Parliament' (which then meant Westminster, of course); a catalogue of Christmas presents; an article 'The Irish Unionist Party and Ireland' by Stephen Gwynn, MP, 'Special to *The Eagle*'; a debate on the state of Irish self-government on the Letters page (one quote: 'Legislation of the past few years treated Ireland as if she were non-existent'); and another set of reports under tabloid-style headlines of the type 'Dublin Tragedy: Publican Cuts His Wife's Throat' and, 'Lady's Death While Singing a Christmas Carol' ('During the afternoon, while the company was singing a Christmas carol, Mrs Marlow suddenly fell back in the chair and died immediately...').

I looked out of the dusty office window. It was raining, and in the grey satin light of a winter afternoon, horse-drawn carriages were rattling along the wet cobbles. The rare passers-by were all dressed in Edwardian costumes. I thought I could even hear pigs squealing in the distance (probably on the way to the 'bacon curer'), and the muffled barking of poor 'Scotch' Laddie, chased by some pure-breed Irish mongrels along the street.

I switched off the microfilm reader, left the empty office of *The Eagle/Star* and went out into the streets of 1912 Skibbereen.

In their entries on Skibbereen, both Murray and W.G. Blackie noted that it was among the places hardest hit by the Great Famine in Ireland. Why Skibbereen? To find out, I visited the permanent Great Famine Commemoration Exhibition in the town's heritage centre. I had been reluctant to do so, fearing I might discover another tacky 'interactive' display and nearly ran out of the centre, having spotted 'The Famine Walk' inside—footsteps painted on the floor—and *The Irish Potato Cookbook* tactlessly on sale in the gift shop. Yet, the factual side of the display was both educational and to-the-point.

I learned that by the time the potato disease *phytophtora*

*intestanis* came from America (in 1844), Ireland was one of Europe's poorest countries, with West Cork being the most destitute area of Ireland, and Skibbereen the most deprived and abject town in West Cork. The area was heavily dependant on potatoes, of which an average family would consume thirty pounds a day.

The exhibition reproduced a number of drawings from *London News Illustrated*, which commissioned its artist to visit Skibbereen, 'a seat of extreme suffering', in February 1847: he drew emaciated bodies, soup kitchens, scenes from Skibbereen Workhouse that accommodated 500 dying people (each person had just two square feet of space, except for the patients of the 'Infirmary for Idiots, Epileptics and Lunatics', privileged enough to share one cell between two or three).

'The people are dying fast,' wrote a *Cork Examiner* reporter, who had accompanied a government inspector, O'Donovan, on his visit to Skibbereen. The journalist described 'a local family of nine—all sick and dying, awaiting death eagerly, with not a single item of nourishing in the house.'

Over a million people died in the Great Famine, and almost ten thousand of them were buried in mass graves near Skibbereen.

Whereas all previous Irish exhibitions, films and books on the Great Famine that I had seen or read carried a strong anti-British message (to the point that the whole tragedy was engineered by the British establishment to suppress Ireland's drive for independence), the one in Skibbereen was different. It even displayed an impressive list of British donations to the victims that included 2,500 pounds (now worth a quarter of a million) from Queen Victoria, 175 shillings—from 'convicts of Woolwich prison', and fifty pounds (now four-and-half thousand)—from 'journalists of Punch'.

'What part did the British government play in the tragedy?' I asked the exhibition's curator.

'It did have a role, but its efforts simply didn't work. Unlike other similar displays,' she went on to explain, here we do not look for culprits. We just tell the facts. Most Famine exhibitions in Ireland are very anti-British, yet, as you could see, the British people donated money—even prisoners did. Our aim is to inform about the Famine and let visitors make their own judgment.'

After the macabre experience of the heritage centre, I wandered aimlessly around Skibbereen trying to cheer up. In Bridge Street, next to The Tsar Restaurant (to commemorate the famous *Eagle* editorial, no doubt), I saw a sign: 'Bridge House B&B. Victorian Accommodation. Winner of the Most Unusual B&B in Ireland' and popped in (who wouldn't?).

The house was brimming with Victorian knick-knacks: dolls, clocks, old photos, antediluvian gramophones and bathroom utensils. A dishevelled elderly woman in a long dress that looked like a night-gown came down the stairs to meet me. Her name was Mona Best, and she eagerly introduced herself as a 'Victoriana-maniac'—my sort of a person.

'It is a very decadent house, and I am trying to maintain in it an original Victorian clutter,' she said with a cackle. I was not so sure about the decadence, yet she had certainly succeeded in having 'cluttered' the place with Victorian junk, to bursting point.

'Can you feel the Victorian smell? Can you?' she kept asking.

I certainly could. It was stale.

One thing about Mona pleased me much more than all her 'decadence' and 'clutter': like Michael Manning and me, she did not have a mobile and could therefore qualify as member number three of our newly formed club of mobile refuseniks!

It felt strange, yet vaguely significant, that two thirds of the club's membership were based in the small West Cork town of Skibbereen.

——

'*Glengariff\*, the Rough Glen, the brightest and most beautiful spot in Co. Cork...Many medical authorities assert its claims as one of the finest climates in Europe for invalids.*'
('A HANDBOOK FOR TRAVELLERS IN IRELAND', MURRAY, 1912)

'*...within five miles round the pretty inn of Glengariff there is a country of the magnificence of which no pen can give an idea. I would like to be a great prince, and bring a train of painters over to make, if they could, and according to their several capabilities, a set of pictures of the place.'*

('AN IRISH SKETCH BOOK,' W.M. THACKERAY, 1842)

SITE WITH PLANNING PERMISSION. SOLD. I saw this sign in Glengariff, on the spot where, according to my calculations, the famous Roche's Hotel used to stand. And what a beautiful sight the 'site' apparently was! 'The grounds of Roche's Hotel...are delightful and thickly planted down to the very water's edge; through them a pretty stream makes its way over a rocky bed,' wrote Murray in 1912.

Everything was still there: the wavy edge of the blue-ish sea, and —stemming right from the surf's edge—a patch of thick evergreen growth looking fresh and radiant even on that drab and rainy December morning; and the bubbly creek. Only one thing was missing: the hotel itself. It had been pulled down in 1939 to accommodate 'holiday homes'. Celtic Tiger tendencies were obviously in fashion in Ireland long before the arrival of the beast itself.

Unlike Baedeker, who used to include his recommended hotels in the description of a place, Murray, with very few exceptions, listed them in the Index section of his 'handbooks'. Murray's entry on Glengariff, therefore, was highly unusual, because in it he actually described two local hotels—Roche's and the Eccles. One could expect any hotel included in the text to be nothing but spectacular.

Luckily, the second of the two—the Glengarriff Eccles Hotel— was still there. Opened by Thomas Eccles, who leased the 1745 building and twenty-five acres of land from the Earl of Bantry, it was one of Ireland's oldest. In the 1850s, the Eccles became a popular wedding venue, and, according to the hotel's brochure, 'Charlotte Brontë spent one night of her honeymoon' there (with her groom, I would assume). In the early 1900s, it briefly functioned as a rest and recuperation home for British War veterans.

With its gabled turrets, pagoda-like porticos, Georgian terraced balconies and bay windows, overlooking the Bay (for once, an architectural term made complete sense!), it still looked magnificent.

The hotel's interior was full of Victorian grandeur: a blue-walled dining room with a conservatory, guests' lounge room-cum-library, Biedermeyer sofas, fireplaces, carpets, mirrors, ornate chandeliers, spiral staircases. The Eccles' original moulding had been tactfully preserved under modern wallpaper.

A kindly, bored receptionist took me upstairs to the 'Yeats Suite', where the poet, allegedly, used to stay, and left me alone there. The view of Bantry Bay from the room's enormous bay window was, according to Murray, 'in itself an inducement that very few places can offer.' Only now—in full accordance with the rules of Celtic-Tiger hedonism—the same 'inducement' could also be enjoyed from a large jacuzzi in the Suite's state-of-the-art bathroom. I wondered whether Yeats would have been able to generate his poetic images in the relaxing warmth of a modern bubble bath. Charlotte Brontë, on the other hand, would have loved it—I was sure!

In his description of the Eccles', Murray mentioned 'the pictures in the dining room' from 'the collection of the former proprietor'. To my sheer delight, the collection of these 1830s' pictures was still on the walls, only not in the dining room, but in the lounge. It consisted of several dozen engravings on Shakespearean themes by some obscure 19th-century artists: 'Midsummer Night's Dream, act 4, Scene 1'—and so on. The 'pictures' were mediocre, yet for a time-traveller their value was unquestionable. Like scenic views, they were part of history's 'frozen carcass', for I could look at them through the eyes of the long-deceased Murray, and be momentarily transferred (teleported?) at least ninety-three years back in time.

The other distinguishing feature of Murray's Glengariff entry was that in it he uncharacteristically quoted another writer's opinion of the place. That writer was none other than one of my time-travelling companions, W.M. Thackeray: ' Were such a bay [Bantry Bay—vv], said Thackeray, 'lying upon English shores, it would be a world's wonder. Perhaps if it were on the Mediterranean or the Baltic, English travellers would flock to it by hundreds. Why not come to see it in Ireland?'

It was a significant moment, confirming that Murray did carry a copy of Thackeray's *Irish Sketch Book* on his travels—as I had previously surmised in my travels in Galway City. Glengariff was therefore an important point of my journey—the place where my two trusted sources/travel companions merged together—like the Meeting of the Waters.

'Rainy Days in Glengariff' is the title of Chapter ix of Thackeray's book. It looks as if rain accompanied the writer through most of his Irish journey (again, see Galway City in this book) which prompted him to remark: '…there is more rain in this country than in any other.'

It was a rainy Sunday morning and the whole of Glengariff was empty. No one was willing to be 'induced' by its magnificent views and curious subtropical flora. The famous Bamboo Park was closed for the season, and ferries to Garnish Island were not running. A lonely-looking man in a raincoat was walking his no-less-lonely-looking dog on the beach. Victorian street lanterns were burning all through the day. And the December day itself was brief and bleak—like the final flash of a dying electric light bulb.

Umbrella above my head, I walked past the harbour, where several months before, on another visit, I had caught my first and only 'Irish' fish, during a short angling expedition with my son (he caught nothing—so our damage to the Irish natural environment was minimal) and headed for the village's only open pub.

A tattooed rough-looking couple, with a baby in a pram parked next to their table, were having a 'full Irish breakfast'. At midday! Their verbal exchange consisted almost entirely of one brief English (or rather—*Irnlish*) word and its derivatives. They duly paid tribute to 'feckin' weather', 'feckin' food' and to some mysterious (to me, at least), yet no-less-'feckin' Liam. I could easily imagine their baby joining them in that lively family chat with his (her?) own profound comments on 'feckin' milk' and 'feckin' nappies'. All three of them were clearly enjoying their 'feckin' weekend treat…

Driving back to Bantry, I spotted a black rock jutting out of the sea a hundred yards away from the shore. My map said it was called Priest's Head, and indeed it looked a bit like the head of a hooded monk. Had I been a modern guide-book writer, I could have easily invented a folk legend explaining the origins of its name: a desperate, yet shy paedophile priest fell in love with a beautiful choir boy and, being unable (due to his shyness alone) to consummate his passion, threw himself into the sea from that rock. Not very original perhaps, but certainly topical!

Back in Bantry, I spent one of my life's loneliest Sunday afternoons.

Everything in the town was shut—including the French Armada Centre in Bantry House. I whiled the evening away browsing the Web at an Internet café which was open only because it was run by Poles. At some point, even my PC fell asleep: froze and wanted to shut down.

A pimpled elderly man next to me was engrossed in chatting up some virtual ladies on an Internet dating site. Probably not such a hard thing to do: one striking fact about modern Ireland is the huge—and totally disproportionate in terms of the overall population—number of dating sites. If you type in 'Dating in Ireland' in the Google.com search engine—2,420,000 pages pop up: a page for every two Irish residents!

Significantly, the number of female members of these sites is normally four to five times higher than that of males.

A closer study of international dating websites (which I undertook on that lonely afternoon in Bantry—purely for the purposes of research!) showed another enormous disproportion. For example, www.adultfriend.com (a website for those in search of sex and casual relationships) had 52,000 female members in the USA and 27,000 in Ireland (with over 5,000 male Irish members!). What a blow to the globally accepted stereotype of Ireland as a straight-laced society where religious values were still of paramount importance.

Was this a backlash, I wondered, a revenge, particularly by Irish women, on generations of enforced puritanism and male-domination? Or perhaps a subconscious return to the matriarchal order of some ancient Gaelic tribes?

Had Irish women gone wild perhaps? They drink more than men; they shout louder in pubs, they show more aggression, in business, politics and in family life: 'Celtic Tigresses' indeed!

I didn't have a chance to complete my 'research': the Poles probably (and rightly!) got fed up with two middle-aged Internet-browsing men as their only clients and announced they were closing, too. We stood up and went to the exit. My fellow patron's ruddy face was beaming: he must have secured himself a date!

Before going to sleep, I opened my copy of *The Southern Star* which I had accidentally acquired from the sleepy old lady in Skibbereen. The paper (12 December 2005) had certainly deteriorated in the last ninety-three years—both in style and in content. The ads that it ran these days would have certainly puzzled its 1912 readers:

> 'Part-time Graphic Artist required to work in the artwork (a classic case of tautology—vv) department at Rowa Pharmaceuticals, Newtown, Bantry, Co. Cork. The suitable applicant should be proficient in the operation of the Apple Mac computer and associated software such as Quark Xpress, Adobe Illustrator, Photoshop etc….'

The only two words a post-Victorian reader would understand in that ad were probably 'artist' and 'required'. Our civilisation had certainly progressed since then, yet I would still very much prefer the good old 'boy able to care horses and do general farm work'. To me, it sounded a bit more…er…human, if you wish.

Another ad on the same page did not contain any computer terminology, yet it would have probably been even less comprehensible to Murray and his like:

> 'Proposals for Afforestation in Environmentally Sensitive Areas. Public Consultation Note.'

'Afforestation'? As a member of the public, I did exercise my right to 'consultation' and consulted all available Web dictionaries. To my relief, the unpronounceable lexical monster was nowhere to be found! I bet that the editor of the old *Eagle* would have crossed this word out and replaced it with something in English, like 'planting trees', say…

Just like its predecessor in 1912, the modern three-section *Southern Star* covered several court cases:

> 'It was the case of brother against brother at Schull District Court, when one sued the other for the injuries sustained during an assault outside a pub in Ballydehob. The court heard the evidence by Michael William Lynch—better known as "Billy", against his brother, Steven Lynch—better known as "Stevie"…The sixty-nine-year-old plaintiff said his younger brother "drew a belt" into his chest outside Vincent Coughlan's pub…The plaintiff…who was seeking compensation for the loss of a blood-stained shirt and tie (!-vv), also alleged that the two remaining teeth in his upper jaw were knocked out when Stevie hit him in the face. Whilst on the ground, he said his brother kicked him in the back and Mary Lynch—Stevie's wife—sat on him…'

Reading that, I couldn't help thinking that all the Apple Macs and Quark Xpresses had done little for the development of the human spirit.

I found further proof of that on the same page: 'A 48-year-old former Baptist pastor from Bandon who held up staff at gunpoint and made off with over 3,000 euro from the local bank where he was a customer has been given a two-year suspended jail sentence…'

Call me a retrograde, but browsing through the modern paper, I felt a pang of nostalgia for the bygone early 1910s. As well as for the vanished high standards of newspaper reporting—precise, stylistically impeccable and charmingly tongue-in-cheek.

Chapter 9

# Brave Naivety

*'Baltimore\* (pop. 597)…is finely situated on the*
*E. coast of the Bay of the same name, which is*
*sheltered on the W. by the island of Sherkin.'*
('A HANDBOOK FOR TRAVELLERS IN IRELAND',
MURRAY, 1912)

*'The population of Baltimore, together with its*
*prosperity, is rapidly declining.'*
(THE 'IMPERIAL GAZETTEER', W.G. BLACKIE, ED.,
1855)

On the way to the island of Sherkin, I stopped in Baltimore, where I intended to visit an English family, friends of a Dublin friend of mine; according to the latter, 'refugees from Thatcher's Britain'. Myself a refugee, I was curious to find out why they had left the UK and what they thought of Celtic-Tiger Ireland.

Ireland's own Baltimore looked very pretty—much more appealing than its (much, much larger) American namesake. The house I was looking for stood on the edge of the village. Inside, I found the whole family: Jill, William and their daughter Ruth. I happily joined them for a 'nice cup of tea'.

One look at Jill and William was enough to establish that they were a happily married couple. The way they looked at each other and listened to each other's remarks testified to a strong and loving relationship. They were also in total agreement with each other on all the issues we discussed and each would only use the pronoun 'we' when recounting their experiences. At times, it seemed they were speaking with one and the same voice, as if it was not Jill and

William, but one unisex 'Jilliam' I was talking to. It was unnerving, yet reassuring, for a multi-divorcee, like myself, who hadn't quite lost hope of finding his own soulmate one day.

My conversation with 'Jilliam' therefore felt more like a dialogue. That was how I wrote it down in my notebook.

*vv*: 'Why Ireland?'

*Jilliam*: 'We always dreamed of having our own farm. In the late 1980s, we came here on holidays and liked the place. On returning to England, we sold our house and bought this 1820s' farmstead. Baltimore was very poor then, and the property was cheap.'

*vv*: What did you do for living?'

*Jilliam*: 'One of us is an artist, the other, a gardener. Our food comes out of the garden onto our plates. We built an open-air amphitheatre in our backyard and started staging performances of folk music. Next to it, we built a gallery and a little theatre that had Shakespeare's plays in its repertoire. We performed ourselves and also invited professional actors and musicians. Initially, the attendance was poor, but with time the locals started coming in droves and did not want to leave. Shakespeare must have punctured their Celtic Tiger existence...'

*vv*: 'You've just mentioned the Celtic Tiger. What do you think of the beast?'

*Jilliam*: 'We are very disappointed with certain aspects of modern Ireland. The people here seem to be overwhelmed with new wealth. They don't know how to cope with it and often go crazy. The obnoxious consumerism, however, seems to have reached its peak, so there is hope that one day they will come back to their senses...Baltimore is dying culturally. The only things that are being built here are holiday homes on tax breaks. Yet the fact that some people from Dublin sell their houses and come here to live inspires some hope. Everything we do is pro-culture and anti-consumerism. We've become a sort of an artistic engine for Baltimore, although the locals haven't quite accepted us yet...'

*vv*: 'You mean there's some anti-British feeling?'

*Jilliam*: 'Yes, the prejudice is still going strong. We had never experienced discrimination before, but here we did feel it. Perhaps

our accent was a give-away, because it was OK until we opened our
mouths. At times we felt as if we were the only black people in a
totally white environment. Our kids felt it at school, too...'

At this point, Jilliam's daughter Ruth joined in the conversation.
*Ruth:* 'I felt particularly uneasy at history lessons. We had an Irish
history book on the Great Famine saying it was all Britain's fault
—I wanted to hide inside my desk...On the other hand, the
awareness of being different eventually made me more defined as
a person.'

After our conversation, we walked around the couple's spacious
garden and William showed me the impressive amphitheatre he
had built in a former cow-shed, and his detached little studio—a
plywood hut with a view of the bay. He had built it himself on the
premise that 'an artist should be able to go to work like all other
people'. He said he didn't do landscapes, for 'there were too many
of them around', and he couldn't compete with nature.

William was also a keen fisherman and boasted of catching a
200-pound skate in the bay. 'It took me two hours to get it into the
boat...' He then invited me to go fishing with him the following
day and I was tempted to agree before remembering the long
journey that lay ahead...

'Baltimore was a big shipping port in the 1920s and 30s,' William
told me. 'Freshly caught fish was sent by train to Billingsgate
Market in London where it was on sale the following morning.
There were so many fishing boats in the harbour that one couldn't
see Sherkin Island across the bay...'

Thus a logical connection to my next destination was made. I
apologised for not being able to accept his kind invitation and,
having said goodbye to the eccentric English family and their no-
less-eccentric pets (goats, dogs, geese etc.), who were all called
Kupin (!!) I climbed into my car.

As I was driving to the pier, past the elegant Victorian terraces
and crescents of the village centre, I wondered how William was
able to describe the Baltimore harbour of eighty years before—
something that he had obviously never seen—so graphically?
Perhaps like so many people endowed with an inquisitive mind
and powerful imagination, he was a time-traveller too?

*'Sherkin Island is 3m. long and 1,5m. wide, the E.
coast of which is bold and rocky, but has a safe
landing-place; it has a pop. of about 400...Fuel is
scarce and has to be imported from the mainland. The
inhabitants are brave and expert fishermen and pilots.'*
('A HANDBOOK FOR TRAVELLERS IN IRELAND',
MURRAY, 1912)

*'Tiny Sherkin Island is a delightfully pretty place...'*
(THE 'ROUGH GUIDE TO IRELAND', 2004)

I was about to visit Sherkin—another island in my peripatetic life.
Having not been to a *proper* isle since the Aran Islands (to forget for
a moment that Ireland itself is one too), I was craving an island and
couldn't wait to get there. But my island-craving had to be kept in
check, for the next ferry was not due for another hour or so.

The gregarious owner of the Harbour Newsagents was duly
puzzled by my accent.

'We have all sorts of people in Baltimore: Poles, Russians...In
fact, two Russian girls from Turkmenistan work in a local
restaurant...'

'Calling Turkmenistan Russia is like calling Ireland England,' I
remarked dryly while browsing through the shelves. Among the
items displayed were several Sherkin Island colouring books for
kids and the magazine-format *Sherkin Island Community
Newsletter*.

'This Newsletter is published by an English dentist who lives
next door,' explained the loquacious shop owner. 'It sells like hot
cakes. I've already disposed of twenty-five copies today...'

I coughed up two euro, opened the Newsletter and was
pleasantly surprised by the relatively high quality of its contents
and design—not bad for a 'community' that had shrunk five-fold
since 1912. There were now fewer than eighty people permanently
on the Island.

In the 'Sincere sympathy' column of the 'Announcements'
section, I spotted a distinctive Russian name—'Alenka Dunaeva'

(the sympathy was expressed to her family and friends). The name puzzled me somewhat: firstly, one wouldn't expect to find a Russian on Sherkin Island (well, at least, *I* wouldn't); secondly, the diminutive suffix 'nk' in Russian personal names is normally reserved for little girls (the lady's name in that case would have been 'Alena'). There was little doubt that some sort of a tragedy had occurred.

The punters of the only harbour pub were drinking their pints outside, their backs towards the strikingly beautiful bay, to which Murray referred as 'fine'. It was obvious they were all locals.

The ferry finally docked at the pier. She was called *The Black Point*. When I was already on deck, a man ran out of the harbour pub and jumped on board. He was the skipper.

The ten-minute crossing cost €7 one way—which put *The Black Point* on a par with the Heathrow Express, the world's most expensive train.

A boy of about twelve, probably the pub-loving skipper's son, was selling tickets on board. The boat carried just a handful of passengers, among whom was a man with a camera tripod going to Sherkin to take some scenic shots.

It was a bright sunny day, and the island itself was clearly visible all through the journey. Sitting on top of a rock was a phallic white lighthouse. Here I cannot deny myself the pleasure of quoting Murray's description of the structure:

> 'The new Lighthouse (1889–1904) is one of the most important off the W. coast of Europe. It consists of a granite tower, 147 ft. high, with the focal plane of light 160 ft. above high-water mark. It rises from foundations which stand at 11 ft. above low-water mark. The tower is a magnificent specimen of masonry; it was erected in sections in the contractor's yards in Cornwall to test the fittings before shipment. The dioptric apparatus is supplied with an incandescent petroleum burner, and the brass is a five-second flashlight, with a 750,000 candle-power. It was designed by the late Wm. Douglas, Engineer to the Board of Irish Lights, and erected at a cost of 90,000 pounds. The coast peasantry have a superstition that the rock sails a mile to the westward at daybreak, on the 1st of May every year.'

Incorporating history and technical details and providing a nice human touch in the end, it was one the finest descriptions in the whole of the book. It made me feel sorry for the global demise of lighthouses, these magnificent poetic structures that had helped our ancestors to find the right direction in their lives...

Although it was not 1 May, the rock, with the lighthouse on its top, had indeed been moving closer and closer. In reality, of course, it was actually *The Black Point* that was approaching it. I could already see the pier, to which we were about to moor, and next to it a pile of picturesque ruins. These were most likely the remains of the 15th-century 'Friary for Franciscans' (Murray), founded by the O'Driscolls. Destroyed in 1537 'in an attack by Waterford citizens',[14] they were 'in a fair state of preservation' in 1912, according to Murray. By 2005, as I could clearly see from the boat, their 'state of preservation' had deteriorated, and several island cows were grazing peacefully amongst a cluster of moss-covered 'standing stones', made of crumbling red bricks.

Dozens of cars were parked near the island's pier. Remembering that Sherkin was just 3.5 square miles, this was surprising and could serve as further proof of my observation that the Celtic Tiger Irish could not (or rather didn't want to) walk and would soon mutate into Americans (about whom Ilya Ilf noted as far back as 1935: 'Americans' legs will atrophy soon and will be replaced with special gadgets for pressing pedals.') Among the parked cars, there was even one Sherkin taxi!

On the similar-sized Isle of Sark, all forms of transport, except for bikes and a handful of tractors, had been banned, and they seemed to be coping without cars beautifully—as I could see for myself during my visit there several years before.

I resisted the urge to book that island taxi for the hundred-metre ride up the hill...

Following the island's only paved road, I soon reached an isolated hut with a sign: O'NEILL'S SHOP. The shop was shut. Rolls of toilet paper were prominently displayed in its dusty windows. Such a display would have been a huge hit in pre-Perestroika USSR, with its chronic shortages of that essential product.

The shop also doubled as a post office which, in its turn, doubled as a library. All three important island establishments seemed to be closed forever. Not a single living soul was in sight, and the silence was so intense it made my teeth ache.

A dishevelled cat came out of the shop and rubbed against my leg. I was glad to have some company on this island that felt as if it had been unpopulated since the bellicose 'citizens of Waterford' ravaged it in 1537.

On the shop's locked doors there were several notices. One was for 'Cinderella Wants a Fella'—a play at the island's community hall. Next to it, there was a rather mystifying sign: TOILETS AVAILABLE AT THE ISLANDER'S REST. From the map I had picked up on the boat, I knew that Sherkin had two pubs: The Islander's Rest and The Jolly Roger. Having in mind the island's minuscule size, the establishments must have been in fierce competition. The kind invitation to the toilets was probably a clever marketing gimmick in that rivalry, and I wondered whether it meant that The Jolly Roger did not have toilets at all?

At least, there was something to investigate. There was also the urgent need to check the state of the publicised facilities, and not just for the purposes of research.

The publican was smoking outside The Islander's Rest in the company of a patron (until my arrival—the pub's only one). They were the first two living creatures I had come across on Sherkin, if not to count the friendly cat, of course. I could overhear snippets of their conversation: 'It was like a feckin' Siberia in feckin' Russia,' the landlord was saying. He was probably referring to the previous day's weather which had been truly awful indeed. At least, geographically he was more advanced than the Baltimore Harbour newsagent.

Inside, the pub was empty. The only seafood dish on the blackboard menu above the bar was tuna steak—a sure sign that the island's glorious fishing traditions were no more.

I picked up the pub's leaflet from the bar stand: 'The newly renovated bar is one of the island's informal meeting places. Here you can enjoy panoramic views in comfortable surrounds (*sic*— vv). The feeling is "Just sit back, take it easy and enjoy yourself".' Well, it was all true (including the 'surrounds'), apart perhaps from the 'enjoy yourself' bit…

The toilets, however, were in place and functioned properly.

The Jolly Roger, Sherkin's second 'informal meeting place' was about a hundred yards away. My footsteps were echoing in the air as I walked towards it. Halfway between the competing pubs, I stumbled upon a roadside map, with arrows pointing to local landmarks:

Abbey
Castle
Lighthouse
Church
Post Office
Beach
School
Community Hall
Wildlife Nature Reserve
Library
Accommodation
Telephone

It was like a graphic imprint of the island's life.

The map made me realise that, having walked no more than 300 yards around the island, I had 'covered' most of Sherkin's 'sites', with the exception of the 'Wild Nature Reserve' and the 'Telephone'. The latter was ten yards away, and it worked! I ticked off yet another island attraction in my notebook.

The Jolly Roger was twice as busy as The Islander's Rest: not one patron, but two—a young local couple. Yet it was still anything but 'Jolly'.

I sat outside and had a snack and a cigarette (Ireland's smoking ban was in force on Sherkin, too!). A friendly little robin landed on my table, and I shared the sandwich with it.

Having looked around, I realised why The Jolly Roger did not advertise its toilets: they were outside and not particularly fragrant. On closer inspection, they were also very basic: just a hole in the ground. I hadn't seen 'facilities' like those since my visit to Romania in 1996. In the Australian Outback, they would call such a toilet a 'dunny' ('as lonely as a brick dunny in the desert' was my favourite Australian simile).

'It was so quiet in the pub that one could hear a fly fart,' my good friend Bill Bryson wrote famously in one of his books.

I was reminded of his profound, if grossly down-to-earth, observation, when the young couple at the bar took turns to use the outside 'dunny'. It was so quiet that I could hear...

Before leaving The Roger, I asked the landlady about 'Alenka Dunaeva', whom I had read about in the paper.

'She was the toddler daughter of the Russian doctor who came to the island with his family three years ago,' she told me. 'Once she was playing near the school's swimming pool, fell into it and drowned. The whole island was in shock for weeks. The doctor and his wife were normally very careful and watched their two children like eagles. It was only once they overlooked her...Since then, no one has seen much of them, although sometimes they do come to the church choir rehearsals. There's one tonight and you can meet them, if you wish...'

It was the second offer (the first being to join William on a fishing trip) I had to refuse on that day. Only for entirely different reasons.

Like every other populated bit of our planet, the tiny island of Sherkin did have a life, with its own joys and dramas.

It was time to retrace my (few) steps to the pier to catch the day's last ferry to the mainland. On the way to the harbour, I passed by another locked and abandoned plywood hut, with the sign JOSEPHINE JEFFRIES ART GALLERY on the door. One of the works, displayed in the window, was called 'Brave Naivety'. I rather liked the title: it nicely summed up the very act of opening an 'Art Gallery' on a tiny windswept island. I felt affection for Josephine Jeffries and for her dry and self-deprecating sense of humour.

The cold winter sun was setting behind the ruins of the Abbey as I stood alone on the pier waiting for the boat. The last rays of the ungenerous winter sun were being dissolved in the sea, like drops of milk in a tea cup. With every soft splash of the surf, the sky above my head grew a little bit darker, and the sea—a tiny bit lighter. Soon the sun vanished on the horizon, and the water began emanating fading translucent 'sunrays' of its own, as if slowly releasing the light it had accumulated during the day. A curious seal poked his rodent-like head out of the water, had a quick look at the sunset (and at me) and disappeared.

I was alone on the pier, surrounded by the islanders' rusty jalopies that seemed to have been parked there for ages. Most of them had no road tax stickers on the windscreens, and some didn't even carry number plates. 'Brave naivety', indeed!

The ferry was nowhere to be seen, and I was suddenly hit by a mild fit of panic. What if the last boat of the day had been cancelled for lack of passengers and I would have to spend the night here, on the pretty, yet comatose, Sherkin? For all my love of islands, the thought did not feel very appealing. It made me realise with sudden clarity that islands were only perfect for brief get-aways. Having spent the first three years of my life inside the impenetrable compound of a Soviet 'secret town', itself embedded in the much larger cage of the former USSR, I had experienced a certain 'dark' nostalgia for enclosed spaces. Yet it was massively outweighed by the innate desire to break out of them.

'No man is an island, entire of itself; every man is a piece of the Continent, a part of the main,' wrote John Donne.

I was grateful to Sherkin for making that revelation clear to me.

As my worries about the ferry grew, a woman and a boy—both wearing parkas—stepped onto the pier. Seeing them meant I was no longer on my own, no longer 'an island' on the island.

Across the bay, I could discern the tiny black dot of *The Black Point* leaving Baltimore Harbour and heading towards us.

Having thrown a last glance at Sherkin from the ferry's deck, I had the impression that the rock, crowned with Murray's favourite 'Lighthouse', which had become just a smudge of white on the darkening canvas of dusk, had moved again. Only this time, it had sailed not 'to the westward', but away from me—to the east.

———

'Did you enjoy your trip?' The Harbour newsagent was waiting for me on the pier in Baltimore. His shop had been closed for the day, but he had been lingering on the pier to greet me back to the mainland.

He probably felt a bit guilty for referring to Turkmenistan as part of Russia.

But I had already forgiven him.

Chapter 10

# Dublin as a State of Mind

*'Few cities in the world have such magnificent surroundings as Dublin.'*
('A HANDBOOK FOR TRAVELLERS IN IRELAND', MURRAY, 1912)

*'The oldest part of Dublin…is composed of narrow, filthy streets, lined by mean houses, and inhabited by a miserable squalid population… Even in the better parts, when turning off the main thoroughfares, similar dwellings, similarly tenanted, meet the eye…Its principal streets are broad and present a fine appearance, but the domestic architecture, as a whole, is plain, and wanting in character.'*
(THE 'IMPERIAL GAZETTEER', W.G. BLACKIE, ED., 1855)

The old chimney, with me inside, was trembling, as if swinging ever so slightly to the accompaniment of the wind's hooliganic whistles.

With some exalted American tourists, I stood on what our guide called 'the best viewing platform in Dublin'—at the very top of the chimney of the former Jameson Distillery, now turned into a 'viewing tower'.

There was a sad symmetry in the fact that the unsightly Dublin cityscape, dominated by concrete boxes, smoking chimneys and occasional church spires, could best be viewed from inside yet another chimney, even if disused. From my very first day in the Irish capital, I could clearly see that Dublin in its entirety was not a beautiful place. Even so, having looked down at the capital from the top of the chimney, I found myself thoroughly unprepared for the sight.

Writer and journalist James Cameron's description of Dundee —a place 'of unparalleled charmlessness, an absence of grace so total that it was almost the thing of wonder', could equally apply to Dublin, as could the destruction of a once thriving and pretty Scottish city that had been meticulously (and successfully) mutilated by 'city fathers' and 'developers' for over 130 years. I use it here because I had considered modern Dundee the most architecturally messed-up metropolis in the Western world. Until I saw Dublin.

If architecture is indeed a 'frozen music' (the metaphor, attributed by different sources to Goethe, Schelling and Le Corbusier), the panoramic view from the top of the chimney could be compared to an ear-grating cacophony, played by a madman. Dublin's chaotic cityscape was reminiscent of a huge sack of potatoes that had burst at the seams and had been carelessly dropped onto the ground. Or of a pebble-strewn beach after a storm.

Like pieces of amber among pebbles, however, there were gems to please the eye here and there: the graceful dome of the Custom House; the brown-green smidgen of the Phoenix Park ('one of the finest in Europe, and which no visitor should leave Dublin without seeing', according to Murray), skewered by the disproportionately massive and phallic Wellington Monument; the pillars of the magnificent Blue Coat School in Blackhall Place straight underneath me. The latter is the only surviving 18th-century structure in a formerly fine-looking area, disfigured by Corporation housing and so-called 'in-fill developments', i.e. cramming every vacant space with as many hideous, yet profit-making, concrete apartment blocks as possible. As I could see from the top of the chimney, the frantic 'filling-in' construction was still going on.

'First we shape buildings, and then buildings shape us,' Winston Churchill once famously remarked. One could argue that the architectural turmoil of Dublin eventually 'shaped' it into a depressing and largely dysfunctional metropolis, with a high crime rate, all-permeating corruption, an unworkable transport system and one of Europe's worst-dressed populations—in short, into a city that is much less attractive than its painstakingly created PR image.

When did it all start and who is to blame for the ugly pockmarked face of one of Europe's former spiritual and artistic capitals?

Unlike in Dundee, the money-grabbing Celtic-Tiger developers of the not-so-distant past are not solely responsible, for even as far back as 1727 Jonathan Swift, himself a Dubliner, called the city 'the most disagreeable place in Europe'. And in 1937, Oliver St John Gogarty, a Dublin writer and a model for Joyce's Buck Milligan in *Ulysses*, remarked sardonically that 'Dublin has one advantage: it is easy to get out of it.'

A number of Irish historians and architectural experts throughout the years have referred to 'the planning nightmare of Dublin' and the city's 'decayed physical fabric'. From Frank McDonald's book, *The Destruction of Dublin*, I learned that at the time of writing, Ireland was in breach of EU law relating to the protection of architectural heritage. Yet none of the pundits provided a coherent answer to one simple question: why?

In search of an explanation, I had to descend from the chimney of speculation to meet Simon Walker, an architect, a tutor in UCD and a native Dubliner—for a short and strictly down-to-earth 'guided tour' of the capital.

Walking to my meeting place with Simon, I stopped (purely out of habit) at some pedestrian lights, ignored by most other passers-by. And by drivers, too. A New York friend of mine once told me that the freedom-loving residents of the Big Apple ignored traffic lights, because they found them 'too suggestive'. 'No one is telling me when to cross the road!' he snapped. In Dublin, the reason was more practical: it was generally as safe to cross the roads at red pedestrian lights as green ones. Like some demented old gits, the traffic lights were winking chaotically without any connection to the lunchtime traffic so dense and slow that it gave the impression of crawling backwards.

Looking up at the façades of buildings and trying to find synonyms for 'ugly', resulted in my brain's in-built thesaurus seriously overheating. Most of the houses were indeed 'plain' (in the best of scenarios), 'unattractive' and 'unprepossessing'. They were also 'disagreeable' and 'distasteful', whereas many were truly 'frightful', 'hideous', 'horrid', 'monstrous', 'repugnant', 'repulsive', 'shocking' and 'vile'.

Passing through two of the city's five remaining Georgian squares was like getting two sudden deep breaths of fresh air. I made sure I had a good eyeful of both before plunging back into ugliness ('unattractiveness', 'unsightliness', 'repulsiveness', 'hideousness').

In his attitude to traffic lights, Simon was a typical Dubliner, resolutely pushing his bike in between the rows of stationary traffic with a total disregard to designated road crossings and angry honks. I could hardly keep up with him.

'Irish people never had a sound relationship with spaces of public appearance, and the real culture was always relocated to rear parts of houses,' he was saying as we raced along Grafton Street. With some fiendish satisfaction, I remembered that the Dublin street, where I myself then resided was designated as 'Rear'. The 'Front' bit ran parallel to it. In no other city of the globe had I come across a similar division.

'This is why,' continued Simon, 'architecture was always approached very pragmatically. If the spirit was something immaterial and not ostentatious, then appearance didn't really matter...'

He pointed at a flock of some particularly scruffy passers-by. 'The best planner Dublin ever had was James Butler, the 17th-century First Duke of Ormond. As for the beautiful Georgian and Victorian buildings, they were always perceived as something belonging to the enemy power—England—and therefore not worth preserving. There was even an attempt to make Dublin into a Celtic city in 1924–25...'

'But as far as I know, Celtic Ireland was a hundred percent rural and had no towns at all,' I interrupted. 'How could they re-create something that never existed?'

'Well, they couldn't. The Irish always enjoyed a direct relationship with the land and felt alienation in towns. In any case, the people of Dublin have never been interested in preserving whatever architecture they had.'

We turned into Westmoreland Street. 'Here's a brilliant example of the typically Dublin phenomenon known as "façadism",' Simon pointed at the eclectic-looking Westin Hotel across the road. 'A row of fine houses that stood in its place were disembowelled, with only the façades kept intact, and their interior taken by just one hotel. The ESB Building Society next door underwent a similar mutilation: a Georgian mansion was destroyed, but the middle of its façade was kept and stuck to the modern building with its ridiculous mirror-like windows...'

The distorted reflections (including those of Simon and myself) in the façade of the building made the street feel even more congested and claustrophobic than it was already. I thought that 'façadism' could be connected to the infamous 'Potemkin Villages' —painted images of plenty, made of cardboard, and displayed by the inventive 18th-century Russian Prince Potemkin on the banks of the Dnieper. Their purpose was to mislead Catherine the Great when she sailed down the river to inspect her domains, and to cover up the indescribable poverty of the villages behind them.

We proceeded to the Quays of the Liffey, dominated by the new Liberty Hall that could be best described with one capacious Italian word '*casuccio*'—'a huge and ugly house'. The shabby concrete box of the Department of Health, looking as if it was in need of plastic surgery, peeped out cheekily from behind Corn Exchange—like an untidy primary-school upstart stretching both unwashed hands into the face of a myopic history teacher.

'Cheap and nasty...Just money and no art...No architecture here at all...' such were my learned guide's comments as we moved past various concrete blocks—all in different stages of ugliness— lining what could have otherwise been a truly beautiful embankment. The Old Custom House, the exquisite late-18th-century creation of James Gandon, stood out like a visitor from outer space in this parade of modern architectural atrocities.

I didn't notice that we'd crossed from the First World into the Third (somehow bypassing the Second) and ended up in once-fashionable Gardiner Street on the north side of the river. And it *was* quite a different world: rough, run-down, shabby and unclean. Badly dressed people with sullen faces stared at us with hostility. English and Russian swear words flew in the air like sparrows. A couple of burly policemen were pushing a screaming woman into a garda van.

The architecture—or rather total lack of it—corresponded to the atmosphere (or was it the other way around?). Original Georgian houses in the lower part of the street had all been 'obliterated' and replaced with five ironically named concrete blocks of private apartments, ('Custom Hall'), 'façadised' with fake 'Georgian' features and imitation red brick.

'This is what private capital would do, if allowed,' Simon said bitterly. 'The apartments are all dark and tiny: not big enough to swing a cat in. There are no gardens, trees or even courtyards…'

Black rubbish bags were displayed on miniature balconies: there was probably no space for them inside the flats.

'No light, no space, no air,' summed up Simon. 'And the reasons are obvious: greed of speculator builders and the incompetence of the conniving city authorities.'

Before rushing off to teach his students, Simon took me to Summerhill, the site of the now-defunct Luke Gardiner estate in the centre of Dublin.

'This area used to have four-to-five-storey Georgian tenements, all destroyed in the 1970s and '80s. Instead, rows of standard two-storey suburban cottages were built here—in the heart of the city, whose very fabric was ruined as a result. This is a good example of how the whole of Dublin was emasculated and made into something that looks truly horrendous.'

'What is the solution, if any?' I asked.

'To begin with, there has to be a comprehensive development plan. The City has to purchase land in the centre and take it from there…'

Simon jumped on his bike and pedalled away. I watched his receding figure for a while—until he turned the corner and disappeared behind a dilapidated Victorian chapel, now functioning as a garage.

————

*'You'll come across people vomiting in the streets after
a night out, so just watch where you're walking
(especially ladies in sandals)…If you're out in Dublin
at 2 a.m. on a Saturday night, you won't believe the
amount of public dumping (from top and bottom)
that goes on…'*
('VIRTUAL TOURIST GUIDE TO DUBLIN', 2005)

*'Saint Patrick was a gentleman,
Who through strategy and stealth,
Drove all the snakes from Ireland,
Here's a toasting to his health.
But not too many toastings
Lest you lose yourself and then
Forget the good Saint Patrick
And see all those snakes again.'*
(AN OLD IRISH TOAST)

As revealed by the *Guardian* newspaper in 2005, the Irish spend €6 billion on booze each year, consuming more alcohol per capita than any other European country, except for…the Duchy of Luxembourg—the world's officially wealthiest nation! Do wealth and booze always go hand-in-hand?

In any case, drink-related deaths, road accidents, crime and lost working hours, allegedly cost the Irish state €2.65 billion. And yet the state still makes a substantial profit from drinking, all whilst introducing a raft of anti-boozing measures, which would seem to be a contradiction.

If we are to believe the *Guardian*, binge-drinking has become the norm among young Irish men, who do so on 60% of their nights out and consequently are three times more prone to getting into drunken brawls than their European counterparts.

How about the women? The paper stayed mum about them, and I had to address the question to a Latvian acquaintance of mine working as a waitress in a Dublin pub.

'I haven't seen anything like this anywhere else—in Latvia, in Sweden, even in Russia,' she said. 'Irish girls and women drink to complete oblivion, and their behaviour in the pub is usually rowdier than men's...'

My contact has never been to Luxembourg, but I have and can tell you straight away that multi-lingual Luxembourg females are no competition for their Irish sisters-in-drink. It was no coincidence that President Mary McAleese mentioned 'binge-drinking' among the five biggest woes of modern Ireland—the other four being suicide, racism, street crime and corruption—in her inauguration address.

I have written a lot about drinks and drinking and even travelled once (for eleven months!) through the booziest parts of Europe to research *Borders Up!*—one of my books. So, I decided to check out the *Guardian* statistics for myself, and to look at Dublin's booming drinking scene.

I set off on a nippy Friday evening in November. I decided to stay away from Temple Bar which, according to a different article in the same paper, has become 'one of Europe's top drinking destinations', a touristy 'Ibiza in overcoats', snubbed by Dubliners and the Irish in general. Having once spent nine hours in a 'traditional Irish pub' inside Dubai airport waiting for a connecting flight to Australia, I thought I knew precisely what the paper meant.

Below is an account of my solitary Dublin pub-crawl:

*8.30 p.m.* The Pavilion Bar in the grounds of Trinity College was full of young people, most of whom were probably students. Their discarded backpacks were scattered along the floor like body bags after an earthquake. The bar is famous for its Bavaria beer—admittedly, the cheapest in Dublin.

Innumerable Bavaria cans—full, empty and half-empty (or half-full, if you prefer) grew from tables, windowsills and from the floor, like clusters of stalagmites in a dark cave. I counted nearly fifty of them on just one table, occupied by two slim, smartly dressed girls. Even at mere €2.20 per can, this collection must have cost a small fortune. Several days before, I attended a second-hand book sale inside Trinity College and was able to buy a dozen of great old folios for just five euro! So they could have bought themselves a whole library instead, I thought and immediately told myself off for sounding like an old fogey.

Outside, empty 'tinnies' were rolling on the steps like shell cartridges on a battlefield. As I was making notes, while having a fag, a somewhat unstable youngster, who got suspicious of my memo pad, approached me.

'What are you doing here, sir?' he enquired.

I explained myself.

'So, you want to uncover the truth!' he concluded solemnly. 'It is too early for that, sir. In Dublin, the truth can be heard only after midnight…'

Carefully holding his precious can of Bavaria in front of his chest—like a torch or a relay baton, he staggered back inside the Pavilion.

*9.30 p.m.* The streets of central Dublin were gradually being filled with cheerful Friday-night revellers. Despite the evening chill, most young girls in the crowd were scantily dressed, and some looked as if they had left their skirts at home.

The interior of The Stag's Head (off Dame Street) was decorated with a number of stuffed heads from some unfortunate (former) stags. Withdrawn and glassy-eyed, they were staring at the similarly glassy-eyed patrons with reproach. A drunken beggar was trudging along Dame Court asking for change. 'Sorry, mate, I need it for my drinks,' some passers-by would mutter, and he would promptly leave them alone, for that was obviously a good enough excuse.

*10.30 p.m.* The throng of revellers was somewhat unsure of where it was heading. Pedestrians were bumping into bollards, or possibly it was the bollards that were becoming aggressive and were getting in people's way.

A young man, wearing pyjamas on top of a suit, was gleefully spanking the rear of a van that had stopped at traffic lights. A fuming red-faced driver jumped out, but quickly appraising the size of the stag party to which the spanker belonged, got back into the van and drove away.

The crowd inside SoSuMe (now Dragon) in Great George's Street was falling over itself (almost literally), to correspond to the description in the *Time Out Dublin 2004* guide-book: 'Look in through the large plate glass window and you may well witness ugly scenes of boisterous civil servants loosening their collars and trying to cop off with travelling hen parties.' I moved on.

*11.30 p.m.* To me, Café en Seine on Dawson street had a clearly American, rather than Parisian, feel in its sheer size and its brazenly eclectic interior. It was filled with patrons to such an extent that if one more person somehow managed to squeeze in, the whole place would be in danger of imploding. Upstairs, a man was trying (unsuccessfully) to juggle three empty beer glasses, and some girls with rabbit's ears on top of their heads were posing for photos by lifting their tops in unison.

In search of a contrast, I wandered into the Dawson Lounge, allegedly the smallest bar in Dublin, and ordered a 'Baby Guinness'. It was the first pub on my route where one could actually have a conversation.

I was soon joined at my table by an Australian youngster, who used to work as a barman in a Temple Bar nightclub until he was sacked for accidentally spotting the pub owner sniffing cocaine with his 'mates'.

'In Temple Bar pubs and clubs, they have their own laws and own wage scale,' he said sipping his drink. 'Most of the staff have no work permits and are paid under seven euro per hour—less than the price of one drink. You never get payslips—just cash in hand. Despite the 3 a.m. restriction on selling alcohol, most nightclubs serve it until 5 a.m. They always get an advance tip-off about an impending raid or inspection, leaving them enough time to create the impression that they abide by the rules...'

He also told me how some greedy pub owners routinely ordered staff to mix together the remains of unfinished drinks and to resell them. My so-far excellent 'Baby Guinness' suddenly acquired a bitter aftertaste...

*12.30 a.m.* My interlocutor from The Pavilion bar had been right: it was only after midnight that the true picture became visible. All hell broke loose. I could hardly believe my eyes, in front of which the Saturnalia was unveiling…By now, every single person in my sight was either very drunk or totally plastered. In every other gateway, people were relieving themselves—in teams of two and three. Dark streams of urine were running across the pavements…

I was extremely puzzled by the Dublin drunks' strange propensity for removing their clothes in public—something I haven't seen anywhere else in the world, not even in the extremely boozy Moscow of the late 1970s (at any rate, not in winter). A bearded man in a stylish jacket stood on a street corner with his pants down around his ankles. A young woman across the road was stripping methodically to the applause of the gapers. She demanded payment for taking off her knickers. Someone from the crowd handed her a crumpled five-euro note, and the knickers duly went down. Two gardaí, filing past, looked the other way, pretending they were preoccupied with emptying onto the ground the contents of beer bottles they had confiscated from some street guzzlers.

I tried to hide in Bruxelles bar off Grafton Street, but had to flee ten seconds later—pushed out by the deafening rock music tearing at my eardrums.

*1.30 a.m.* My way home lay through Temple Bar, where I stopped for a quick chat with a young rickshaw-driver, patiently waiting for clients in the middle of a littered square. A musician by occupation, he needed the job to supplement his income.

'You haven't seen anything yet,' he said with an uneasy smile. 'It's at 5 a.m. when things become really mad—guys beating up girls, girls beating up girls, guys beating up guys…People start having sex in the streets…Yeah, it's then that the real madness begins. You must stay on and see for yourself… '

Having observed enough madness and dipsomania for one night, I did not follow the rickshaw-driver's advice…

It was a good thing I hadn't taken Murray with me on that memorable pub crawl. An ardent proponent of temperance, he would have found it truly deplorable.

——

*'When I came back to Dublin I was court-marshalled in my
absence and sentenced to death in my absence, so I said they
could shoot me in my absence.'*
(BRENDAN BEHAN)

Another way of understanding a city is by visiting its courts.
During my time in the city, I spent a couple of days at Dublin's
District Court, where I recorded some of the following sketches in
my notebook:

'All Rise!'
We spring up from hard wooden benches.

From behind the door, marked PRIVATE. NO ADMITTANCE, a black-
robed female judge appears. I can hardly see her face in the
uncertain blaze of electric lamps hanging from the ceiling, their
bleak and superfluous glow mixing with the grey, satin daylight
behind the windows to create a permanent semi-darkness.

The pencil box of a courtroom smells of dust, disinfectant and
human sweat—a peculiar scent of despair characteristic of
prisons, courts and social security offices all over the world. There
is nothing in it to please the eye, except perhaps for an 'Exit' sign
—its one and only reassuring feature.

It is the second day of my 'familiarisation' with the workings of
Dublin's Metropolitan District Courts, and by now I cannot help
the feeling that the whole of humankind consists exclusively of
judges, claimants, witnesses and defendants, whose roles are both
transitory and interchangeable; that we are all actors in this never-
ending and somewhat antiquated real-life drama of crime and
punishment.

Approaching the Four Courts, a fine architectural creation of
James Gandon, is like entering a different dimension—a peculiar
alienation zone, out of which all joy and happiness has been
sapped by a squad of JK Rowling's storybook 'dementors'.

People heading for the courts, seem to have left their smiles at
home, and the first passers-by I bump into are two hand-cuffed
young men, chained to a couple of burly gardaí, who drag them

towards the Criminal-Court wing of the building. They are followed by a lonely paparazzo, a huge telescopic lens dangling from his hip like a gun.

The oblong courtyard of the district court is semi-enclosed by a concrete fence, topped with barbed wire. From one side, it is blocked by the wall of the adjoining garda station building, its doors, facing the courtyard, adorned with forbidding notices, one of which says NO ENTRY and another GO AWAY.

It is morning, and the courtyard is filled with waiting crowds, the very people targeted by the no-nonsense GO AWAY sign. Subdued and sullen-faced, they chain-smoke forgetfully, their verbal exchanges reduced to an absolute minimum. Even so, I overhear some muffled snippets of conversation—in English and in Russian, the latter with a distinct Ukrainian accent.

What amazes me most, however, is the way the crowd is dressed. Almost everyone—men, women and children—are sporting track-suits, all well-known brands, clearly fake, the most popular being counterfeit Adidas. A sallow youngster on crutches is clad in a tracksuit, too. Do tracksuits constitute the standard 'uniform' for court attendance in Ireland?

Whatever it is, the courtyard looks like a mysterious open-air gym for grossly unfit people. Or, more aptly, like the exercise yard of a unisex low-security jail.

The eyes of many a tracksuit wearer are vacant, as if extinguished. They blend with equally pale, as if discoloured, faces.

It is 10 a.m., and the crowd, having dumped cigarette ends onto the ground, pours inside the building, where several courts are about to start sitting. A polite receptionist tells me that in the morning the courts mostly consider 'procedural matters', with 'real cases' starting at 2 p.m.

I consult a long list of defendants' names on a notice board. About one third of the names originate from different republics of the former USSR—Russia, Ukraine, Byelorussia, Lithuania, Latvia, Georgia and Armenia. Reading through the list is like embarking on a vicarious mini-excursion through post-Soviet geography.

I spend several hours wandering from one courtroom to another. What happens in each of them can be best described as a conveyor belt of justice: people entering and leaving at random, secretaries calling out defendants' names (for no reason, I am a bit worried that one will call out mine), judges sitting in state on their podiums—stamping away at papers and mumbling something past the microphones on their desks in defiance of the multiple strict signs urging them to USE THE MICROPHONES PROVIDED. I wonder whether all of them are secret members of the US-based International Organisation of Professional Bureaucrats, one of the three main mottos of which is, 'When in Doubt—Mumble'? Or, maybe they do it deliberately to further intimidate the already intimidated people (many of them with very poor English) in the courtrooms?

Despite the judges' semi-coherent whispers, I manage to decipher some of their pronouncements:

'It is a waste of further resources: the defendant is on legal aid.'

'Hands out of your pockets! You are in court!'

'I find your explanation unrealistic. You were simply there looking for trouble.'

'I am not concerned with that! Back here in two weeks' time.'

One angry judge, setting the date for a new hearing, whispers emphatically, as if inserting an exclamation mark after each word: 'Eighteenth! July! Court! Fifty!'

Another struggles with the foreign name of a defendant: 'Do you understand the charges, Mr Na...sim...sam... ba...ba?'

Each courtroom swarms with very young uniformed gardaí, some of whom look almost like teenagers—in stark contrast to the defendants, who, despite (or possibly because of) their track-suits, all appear prematurely aged and malnourished.

I wander off to Richmond Hospital (a ten-minute walk from the Four Courts), where another set of district courts is located.

The largest room there is crowded to bursting point. This court seems to be dealing exclusively with the offence of not paying one's TV licence. The judge is working particularly hard and is processing, on average, one defendant per minute. From the sheer number of defendants, however, I deduce that not paying a TV licence fee must be the most popular 'crime' in modern Ireland.

To me, the very fact that one does require a TV licence in Ireland comes as a shock, for I had assumed that since both RTÉ channels broadcast lengthy and much-too-frequent advertisements, they were run on a commercial basis and did not need to be supported by the public. I was wrong.

This court is dealing with those who failed to produce a valid TV licence in…October 2003. It is now March 2005 and the overload of cases must be so huge that only now—seventeen months later—can a slot for them to be heard be found.

Each of the offenders is 'processed' to the same quick pattern. One of the two impassive licensing inspectors present in court reads his report, stating the date and time of his visit to the defendant's house.

Judge (to defendant): 'Do you have any reasons for not paying your TV licence?'

Defendant (in most cases, a young woman) shrugs her shoulders which can mean both 'yes' and 'no'.

Judge: 'Are you working?'

Defendant: 'No.'

Judge: 'Do you have children?'

Defendant: 'Yes, six', (variants: two, three, seven…One African lady claims she has ten).

Judge: 'A hundred-and-fifty-euro fine and two months to pay. Next.'

Naturally, occasional deviations from this model do occur. In one case, the defendant, a young Polish man with practically no English, insists that he didn't understand what the licensing inspector wanted of him. In a couple of others, people assert that the licence was to be supplied by their ex-spouses and/or landlords, or that they had moved from the house before the licence fee was actually due.

None of them, however, manages to avoid the fine. Not even the man who apologises, saying it was an 'oversight' on his part, and asks not to be issued with a conviction, for it can impair his chances of getting a job in the USA, to where he is about to move. 'The conviction will have to be issued!' concludes the judge.

Several defendants fail to appear. Their cases are heard in absentia, with resulting fines being twice the 'normal' amount.

In just thirty minutes the judge earns a small fortune for the Irish government—literally out of thin air. Or—even more literally—out of a thin TV aerial.

Before lunch break, I witness a lucky escape. One of the testifying inspectors, drowning under the pile of his typed 'summaries' and reports, fails to produce the relevant piece of paper while the defendant—a young Asian man—is waiting in the box. As the inspector keeps rummaging through his files, the judge loses patience: 'In the absence of evidence, the summons is dismissed!' he declares.

The fortunate young man disappears from the courtroom like greased lightning.

The following day I listen to several other cases dealing with drugs, domestic violence, drink-driving and so on. The judges handle most of them expertly and without much arrogance. At times it even feels as if they no longer mumble incoherently past their microphones.

Or maybe, it is just me getting used to the tricky acoustics of Irish court rooms?

With my own experience of courts largely limited to closed, 'telephone-rule' trials in the former Soviet Union (as an investigative journalist, I was often summoned to give evidence), the openness of Irish court proceedings is reassuring. Only once does a garda ask me: 'In what capacity are you making notes in the court room, sir?'

'In a writing capacity,' I reply in unintended legal-speak.

'Welcome!' says he and smiles.

It is the first smile I see in Dublin's District Court.

It is good to know that in Ireland people can still smile (even if not too often) while in court.

'You are heading in the right direction, Mr Joyce!'—a judge reassures a bedraggled unshaven man in the defendant's box.

I spot this unkempt man again as I leave the court building several minutes later. He stands in the courtyard smoking, as if hesitant as to where to go.

Having finished his fag, he turns and resolutely walks away from the court.

Hopefully, in the 'right direction'.

------

When does one start feeling at home in a new environment?

Having lived in dozens of places in as many countries for the last fifteen years, I often ask myself that question.

On arrival in a strange town or city, I routinely visit three places on my very first day there: a café, a bookshop and a railway station (to make sure there's an escape route—just in case). As someone who was forcibly locked up for over thirty-five years in the world's largest cage, the former USSR, I simply could not stop travelling and was finding it hard, if not impossible, to settle down anywhere in the world.

In a way, I was like a strongly depressed (in more than one sense) spring that had suddenly been released and hadn't been able to stop bouncing frantically since.

Unsurprisingly for someone who had spent most of his life as a reluctant 'armchair buccaneer', I might have contracted 'dromomania'—a psychiatric condition, characterised by 'an irrepressible passion for purposeless travelling'.

In the beginning, I didn't like Dublin. As you can see from the above. The city looked drab, ugly and alien. The only consolation was that the cottage that I rented with my son was called 'St Jude's', and someone told me that he (St Jude) was a patron saint of lost souls. 'A lost soul'—that was precisely how I felt.

Another redeeming feature of my new Dublin abode was that it stood next to a railway line, and the rattling of train wheels outside my bedroom window was a constant reminder of an 'escape route' that was still open.

Several months later, however, I no longer felt like escaping. Even a released metaphorical 'spring' is destined to come to a stop sooner or later, or so I thought.

By then, I had my own favourite 'enclaves' in Dublin. One of them was the enclosed compound of Trinity College, 'the Silent Sister', once brilliantly described by Walter Starkie as 'a paradise in the oriental sense of the word, that is to say, a place surrounded by a high wall.'

Another newly discovered haven of mine was a little street off Merrion Row.

When living in London, I would wander off to Ely Place—a quiet little cul-de-sac off Holborn Circus. Passing through the ornate iron gates, separating this street from the hustle-and-bustle of the city, was like entering a mysterious 'fourth dimension', the name of which was 'dislocation'. Very few people know that this straight tree-less lane, the former residence of the Bishops of Ely, is not geographically a part of London. It is a little corner of Cambridgeshire, still enjoying freedom from entry by the London Police, except by the invitation of the Commissioners of Ely Place—its own elected governing body. When I was there last time, the results of the latest elections, duly dated and certified by 'J. Franks, Esq., Clerk to the Commissioners', were duly displayed on the notice-board of the magnificent St Etheldreda Chapel—the oldest Roman Catholic church in Britain—half-way up the street.

In the local pub, whose licensing hours were until fairly recently set by the justices of the Isle of Ely, one could view a stack of recent letters addressed to Ye Olde Mitre Tavern, Ely Place, Holborn Circus, London, Cambridgeshire.

Why did this place agree with me so well? Why did it evoke in me the peculiar feeling of being elsewhere—the sensation both calming and disturbing? Was it due to the fact that as a Ukrainian-born Russian, with Australian and British passports, now living in Ireland—I was a thoroughly 'dislocated' person myself?

Since settling in Dublin, I had been missing my Ely Place, and would often look up with nostalgia at an old print of it on my bedroom wall. I desperately needed a similar spiritual shelter, where I could quietly contemplate my future and my past. But there was only one Ely Place in the world. At least, that was what I had thought until one day a flier for a Dublin Thai restaurant, called 'Papaya', was dropped through my door.

I was about to put the leaflet to the recycle bin, when I spotted the restaurant's address, printed in the corner: '8 Ely Place'.

So there was an Ely Place in Dublin, too!

It was interesting, although I was sure that it would have little, if anything, in common with 'my' Ely Place: many old Dublin streets had been named by the British, but had no resemblance to their London namesakes.

This assumption was strengthened after a visit to Dublin City

Library. From books on local history I learned that, unlike its London sister street founded in the 13th century, Dublin's Ely Place was laid out in 1770 and bought in 1773 by an eccentric Irish nobleman, Henry Loftus, the Second Earl of Ely. The very name 'Ely', in the latter case, came from the Gaelic territory of Elye O'Carroll in King's County (now Co. Offaly), was pronounced 'ee-lai' (with the emphasis on the last syllable) and, allegedly, had nothing to do with the Cambridgeshire Isle of Ely (pronounced 'ee-li', with the first syllable stressed) that gave its name to London's Ely Place.

For someone trying to find a twin of his favourite 'dislocated' spot, it was disconcerting.

My last faint hope of connecting the two streets lay in the fact that, according to some sources, the Loftus family were rather anglicised, knew London well and might have been influenced by its architecture...

In short, I needed to see Dublin's Ely Place with my own eyes.

It was only a ten-minute walk from the street where I lived, if I was to believe the city maps.

Having criss-crossed the globe many times, I had come to the conclusion that it didn't really matter where you travel. The important thing is what you discover. To make a discovery, one doesn't need to go to the end of the earth. It is like poetry, for which, according to Boris Pasternak, you don't have to look high up in the mountains, since there's plenty of it scattered in the grass under your feet. You only have to bend down and pick it up. Travelling in just one town, or even one street, can be no less exciting than exploring the North (or the South) Pole. Provided, of course, you are armed with a pair of keen, wide-open eyes.

One early sunny morning, I set out on my journey to Dublin's Ely Place. Travelling by association is my favourite way of exploring a new place. Particularly early in the morning, when everything is still closed and there's no one around to talk to, except for houses.

On the way, I had an unhurried espresso in a café. Knowing that the chances of rediscovering my London island of dislocation in Dublin were small, I was subconsciously trying to delay the inevitable moment of disappointment.

Yet, as soon as I reached Merrion Row and had my first glimpse of Ely Place, I saw that it was, if not a twin, then definitely a close relative of my sought-after London lane.

Like the latter, it was a cul-de-sac, blocked from one side. Only in London, it was the wall of the famous Bleeding Heart Tavern, here it was the back entrance of some secretive office block, with a beam and a sentry box (was it the HQ of the Irish Intelligence Service, I wondered, before learning that it was a different, if no less enigmatic, organisation—The Office of Public Works).

The sentry box looked almost exactly like the booth of a beadle at the end of London's Ely Place.

The two streets were of almost the same length and width and were architecturally similar. But the biggest likeness—the one that I was only able to sense after walking the length of Ely Place several times—was the feeling of being elsewhere,—'neither here nor there', so to speak—the feeling that, for me, meant 'home'.

A memorial plate at No 4 Ely Place assured me that the poet George Moore lived there in the early 1900s. To me, he was mostly memorable for calling Ireland 'a little Russia', which I quote at the beginning of this book.

Despite the early hour, I could already sniff the faint aroma of curry from the basement of No 8, the famous Ely House, the former residence of the Earl of Ely, now covered with scaffolding.

The smell originated from Papaya restaurant, thanks to which I had learned about the street in the first place. Its location was somewhat incongruous and reminded me of the Bonn house where Beethoven was born, that accommodated a huge Chinese restaurant (and nothing else) in the early 1990s. I thought then that, had Beethoven been alive, he would have probably composed a Yum Cha Sonata…

On the corner of Ely Place and Hume Street, famous for the 1970s' stand-off between conservationists and developers, a sign FAILTE! ('Welcome!') adorned the façade of the old skin and cancer Hospital. Here I couldn't avoid parallels with the 'Do Us the Honour' Funeral Home in the 'regional centre of N.' from our friends Ilf and Petrov.

I instinctively moved away from the welcoming cancer hospital…

In the meantime, numerous Ely Place offices were already open for business. By the end of the working day, I had visited most of them.

I stared at the 'Unpainted Mountain' installation (it was supposed to be enveloped in smoke, but, unfortunately, THE SMOKING MACHINE IS OUT OF ORDER, said the sign put up by a receptionist) at an exhibition of conceptual art in the Royal Hibernian Academy at No 15.

I was invited to join the Labour Party at their national headquarters at No 17.

I spoke with Michael Kirk, the knowledgeable Warden of the Ely University Centre—a students' hall of residence, run by Opus Dei—an organisation that I wasn't asked to join.

I had a light organic lunch at the multi-award-winning Ely Wine Bar, where I perused the spectacular wine list, but stopped short of ordering a bottle of Alvaro Palacios L'Hermita 1998, priced at €380, or any other of the 419 wines it featured.

The interiors of all the offices, except for that of the Labour Party, were beautifully preserved and—as Baedeker or Murray would have said—'truly magnificent'.

Yet none of them could come close to that of Ely House itself, now housing the headquarters of the Knights of St Columbanus—another hitherto-unknown-to-me Catholic Order, one of whose aims was 'to counteract the proliferation of non-Catholic ideas in every sphere of life', to quote the brochure I picked up inside.

Mr William Roe, Supreme Secretary of the Knights (his official title) kindly took me around the building that the Knights themselves were now painstakingly restoring. The features included rich stuccowork by Michael Stapleton, Venetian windows, fireplaces, medallions on walls, even an in-house 'Attic Theatre'.

The highlight of the splendid interior was the staircase of three flights of Portland stone, with a life-size figure of Hercules at the bottom.

I shared with Mr Roe my humble observations about the seeming similarities between the Ely Places in London and in Dublin and asked whether Henry Loftus could have consciously recreated the atmosphere of the former.

'Well, he did copy the staircase from a house in Brussels, so I don't see why he could not have reproduced his favourite London street in Dublin,' he replied—to my obvious satisfaction.

For the purposes of symmetry (no wonder—after spending so many hours in the well-proportioned Georgian interiors), I consummated my day with dinner in the vaulted basement of Ely House, now occupied by Papaya—the best Thai meal I had had since visiting Thailand in 2001.

I was reluctant to leave Ely Place, that looked even more mystifying and quirky at night time than in the light of the day. A microcosm of Dublin life, it now basked in eerie silence. Unlike London's Ely Place, whose iron gates were closed at 10 p.m., thus blocking the lane from both sides to allow the night watchman to start calling out the hours, the Dublin cul-de-sac remained invitingly open.

———

It did feel like the end of an era—a cross between a funeral and a banquet.

On the last morning before closing for business, Bewley's Café in Grafton Street was packed with grieving customers. They turned up in their hundreds to vote with their feet (and stomachs) against the closure of this famous 164-year-old Dublin institution. The staff, in their familiar black skullcaps, were serving two types of Irish breakfast—'large' and 'small'—while trying to suppress tears: sausages, bacon and scrambled eggs were bound to taste saltier than usual. A little old lady, who had worked at Bewley's for fifty-five years, was sobbing openly at an impromptu guest-book stand, to which the sullen-faced patrons were queuing patiently to record their last tributes.

The café's interior looked grand, if somewhat tired. It reminded me of the famous Café New York in Budapest. Only the latter was not in danger of closing down—either because Budapest rents were still a fraction of Dublin's, or due to the fact that Hungary had not introduced a total smoking ban as yet.

But, most likely, Café New York—unlike Bewley's—was thriving due to the persistently Central European ways of the Hungarians, who do not agonise over spending an hour or three sipping one cup of coffee before ordering a succulent goulash (as opposed to the unwholesome 'Irish breakfast'), followed by a generous slice of Napoleon cake (as opposed to a stale scone or a sticky bun).

'Irish eating habits are changing,' a representative of the Campbell Bewley Group Ltd told me in Bewley's on that morning of mourning. 'They don't seem to want this sort of food any more...'

It was then—during my first (and last) breakfast at Bewley's—that I ate my first (and, most probably, my last) white Irish pudding. Two of them actually. On the way back home, I popped into a souvenir shop in Nassau Street. On one of the shelves, a glossy volume of 'traditional Irish recipes' was displayed next to a book on the history of the Great Famine...

Dublin eventually became the base from where I undertook my time-travelling expeditions around Ireland—North and South, and I enjoyed returning to my temporary home city—a fact that automatically turned me from a vagabond, who had no place to come back to, into a traveller.

With time, I found nice places to eat out and to have a coffee in Dublin. I had a handful of favourite bookshops and 'vantage points', from where I could observe Dubliners while remaining unnoticed myself. I had walking itineraries to be followed without thinking.

I had also accumulated a collection of Dublin characters: a long-haired chap in a worn-out Soviet Army cap, in The Ginger Man on Fenian Street of an evening, bragging of his amorous adventures; a bearded drunk feeding swans on the canal bank in Baggot Street (next to the place where a statue of the bespectacled Patrick Kavanagh sits on his eternal park bench staring myopically at the opaque water); a dishevelled street poet selling his books across the road from Trinity College. Every great city or town has a bunch of its own 'resident eccentrics', and Dublin is no exception.

I was slowly but surely coming to grips with the peculiar 'state of mind' called Dublin. Becoming a 'local' (person—not pub) does not necessarily imply having a passionate love affair with the place where you live. It is rather a love-hate relationship—a mature marriage, in which you can see your 'partner', warts and all, and eventually learn to accept, possibly even to like, the very qualities you have hated. It is a difficult liaison—at times romantic and at times oppressive.

Yet the main reason for no longer regarding Dublin as my personal 'centre of paralysis' (in the words of James Joyce) was that I had found new friends there.

One was a young Irish woman, whom I called 'Pevitsa', which in Russian means 'singer'. She played the guitar and often performed her own heart-rending songs in the pubs of Temple Bar. We had met a couple of years before, when I was visiting Dublin from the UK, and she introduced me to Irish folk music and to her father—an artist and also a musician. I was extremely moved when he played a pleasant Irish tune on his tin-whistle and dedicated it to me. He then quickly drew a sketch of an Irish landscape—with a ball pen on a beer mat (we were sitting in a pub)—and gave it to me as a gift (this sketch of his is now hanging on my bedroom wall).

The morning after my first visit, I flew back to London, where I soon received a parcel from Pevitsa. It contained a book of poems by Pat Ingoldsby, the very same 'dishevelled street poet' above, with the following dedication: 'It is probably rude to rededicate a book, but I am sure that Pat wouldn't mind…I hope this book provides snippets from a Dublin life that cannot be viewed simply…It is also through the eyes of a Native and I hope you have some joy from it.'

The most touching thing was that—throughout the book—all Pat's poems (and separate lines) that were in Irish had been painstakingly translated by Pevitsa into English and written on the margins in longhand:

'Quiet and the music
Quiet and the wind

Quiet and the quiet
Between you and me.
Quiet and the trees
Quiet and the day
Quiet and the dreams
Between you and me.'

When, a year later, I was agonising over which few books from my ever-growing collection I could fit into my jalopy and take to Dublin, this volume was one of the first on my list. How could one leave behind a beautifully poetic token of human friendship?

Pevitsa and her father visited our cottage of 'lost souls' and—together—spent half of the evening drawing on the wall above the mantelpiece. The formerly white patch was now covered with two impromptu 'paintings'.

I called my other new friend 'The Angel of Dublin', although he himself preferred to be referred to as 'Ardán' which in Irish means 'platform', for, in his own words, that's what he had strived to be—a supporting and welcoming 'podium' for other people. It was he who urged me to watch the moon on a solitary and 'officially depressing' January evening.

Ardán was a familiar figure in Dublin. Walking the city's streets with him was next to impossible, for he bumped into people he knew every ten seconds. We first met at some noisy party, where he—dressed in a set of old pyjamas (!)—was distributing sweets and toothpaste to all the guests. He then struck me as an engaging white-faced-clown sort of character, with a good deal of thoughtfulness and sadness behind the mask.

Ardán's main purpose in life was bringing people together. A lecturer at a Dublin college, he helped 'depressed loners' and newcomers to Dublin by finding them jobs, making them feel welcome and inviting them to pub crawls, cliff walks and the parties that he himself tirelessly organised almost on a nightly basis. One of those was 'the international soup party', to where guests from different countries were asked to bring their own 'national' soups that were shared by everyone.

One evening, when I was stuck at home writing, he rang to invite me for a meal out. I told him I was up against a deadline and would have to skip dinner or supper. Half an hour later, there was a knock at my door. To my consternation, no one was outside, but a hot takeaway meal had been left on the doorstep, with 'Happy writing!' scribbled on top of the wrapping paper.

An Irish-Canadian by birth, Ardán loved Dublin—the city where he finally threw an anchor after a tough childhood (his parents split up when he was six) in Edmonton and many years of wandering the globe. A compulsive traveller like myself, he measured his early possessions in 'backpacks'. 'I came to Dublin with one backpack, but now I have accumulated about twenty-five backpacks of stuff,' he told me once as we walked in Iveagh Gardens—another hidden Dublin 'enclave' that he had helped me discover.

Ardán had no plans to leave Dublin and not just because of his twenty-five backpacks of accumulated baggage. 'I felt lost while living in London and in New York, but Dublin is compact, and I always feel in the centre of things.'

I hoped he would never leave, for if he did, the city would lose its 'Angel', and 'the spirit of Dublin' would suffer as a result.

# Part II

# Neither Here nor There, or, a Visit to the Neuro Zone

*'Newry is a place of great antiquity. It is a clean and well-built town and much changed since the days when Swift wrote of it—'High church, low steeple,/Dirty streets, and proud people.'*
('A HANDBOOK FOR TRAVELLERS IN IRELAND', MURRAY, 1912)

*'Newry has little to sustain more than a short visit, and you are unlikely to be tempted to stay.'*
(THE 'ROUGH GUIDE TO IRELAND', 2004)

As I was preparing for my first time-travelling foray across the border to Northern Ireland, the advice of my omniscient Dublin friends was categorical: 'Don't poke your nose into politics, and you'll be OK!'

Well, to be honest, my poor nose was not in a condition to be poked anywhere: a respiratory infection contracted the week before had made it swell to the size of a large Irish spud. Was it because in Dublin I was constantly forced to pay through it (my nose) for food, toiletries and other basics?

Whatever it was, I was only hoping that 'The Gap of the North', another name for Newry, would be wide enough to accommodate it.

I was keen to visit Newry, and not Belfast, in the first place because having written a lot on borders and frontiers of all kinds, I was instinctively curious about the first town (sorry, city: the status was conferred on Newry in 2002) on the northern side of the border, separating the euro-zone from the pound-zone and Ireland from...er...Ireland.

My intention was to focus exclusively on mundane cross-border matters: currency, roads, healthcare, communications, prices and —remembering my friends' advice—to stay as far away from politics as possible.

To be able to look into all those properly, I made a short 'laundry list' of the things I needed to take:

1. Some euros. 2. Some pounds sterling (I could only get hold of a £20 note, issued by the Bank of Scotland). 3. Some letters to be posted to Britain and to Southern Ireland. 4. My swollen, yet running nose. 5. My British passport (I was going abroad, after all!) 6. My faithful ninety-three-year-old guide-book. 7. My British NHS card.

My rationale for the inclusion of the last item was simple: why should I cough up €50 to see a GP in Dublin, when I could see one for free on British territory, i.e. in Newry?

A writer's life itself often becomes research...

The bus journey towards the border was smooth. But after Dundalk, the road became much bumpier. I was looking out of the window, blowing my nose and munching a stale sausage roll, acquired in Dublin for staggering €3.50 the day before—a sum that could have bought me one week's accommodation including breakfast in The Imperial Hotel in 1912, Newry's best (if we are to believe Murray).

The border itself was ghostly and easy to overlook for someone who wasn't watching. But I was.

First I spotted an oblong shed with a mysterious sign: CUSTOMS FACILITATION OFFICE (as far as I knew, there were no customs barriers between Ireland and...Ireland, i.e. they had already been 'facilitated' to the extreme). Then came a row of dodgy-looking money-changing outlets. BRITISH SPY POST. DEMILITARIZE NOW! ran a colourful billboard, topped with skull and crossbones. Having guessed it had something to do with 'politics', I pretended not to have noticed it.

The road signs suddenly became dark green, strictly monolingual and showed distances in miles, but it was only when I ticked off 'Give Way' instead of 'Yield' that I yielded (sorry, gave way) to the fact that we were in the UK.

Having dropped my bag at the Canal Court Hotel (the 'Imperial' was no longer there, and nor was the Empire itself, for that matter), I briefly contemplated the idea of having a pint in one of the inviting little pubs in Co. Down, across the bridge (the hotel was in Co. Armagh, on the opposite bank of the Newry Canal), but rejected it and decided to visit a pharmacy instead.

That could well have been a life-saving decision, but I didn't know it then...

'How do you live there, in the rip-off South?' asked the friendly pharmacist at Felix McNally's drug-store when I pretended (for the purposes of research, why else?) that I only had euros in my wallet. She agreed to accept them, at a 'special Newry exchange rate', whereby €10 was equal to £6.50. Even so, I paid half of what the pills would cost me in Dublin.

Having popped into a take-away shop next door and not feeling particularly hungry, I could not resist the temptation to buy another sausage roll, this one priced at an incredible 80 pence! Even with the shop's own 'special Newry exchange rate' of just £6 for €10, it was an unbelievable bargain compared to Dublin.

'Can it be that a third, phantom, currency—"*newro*"—is circulating in this town/city'? I wondered, puzzled by the evasive exchange rates fluctuating from shop to shop.

It was 7.30 p.m. As I was putting my untouched €1.20 sausage roll into a bin, a gunman,wearing a cheap Halloween mask, stumbled into the crowded McSwiggan's pub in Newry's Water Street (a couple of hundred yards from where I stood) and shot a man and a woman sitting at the bar in the legs three times before escaping. I only learned about the incident from the following day's papers.

The rest of the evening was spent in my hotel room, trying to work out the intricacies of cross-border phoning. It was encouraging to be able to call London and Edinburgh (both hundreds of miles away from Newry) at discount national British rates. It was mildly intimidating to have to dial the international code (and hence to pay international rates) to get through to Dundalk, just ten miles across the border. Luckily, I didn't know anyone in Dundalk and was therefore spared the expense of calling it.

Contrary to Filson Young's assertion, made in *Ireland at the Crossroads*, about Ireland being a land of comfortless hotels— Newry's Canal Court was one of the best I had ever stayed at. The worst being in the Turkmenistan town of Mari on the Afghan border. I ended up there accidentally in the hot summer of 1983. A bearded Turkmen woman solemnly gave me the key to the hotel's only 'luxury suite'. The room was full of flies and smelt like a mortuary. It was forty-two degrees outside, but the air-conditioner did not work. Nor did the shower. The biggest surprise, however, was that I was supposed to share my room, and the only medium-sized bed, with a male Soviet Communist Party official from Ashkhabad. He snored and fretted on his side of the bed all night, and I when I finally managed to nod off, I dreamt of an earthquake. Also, I got severely poisoned at the hotel's restaurant (it only had eggs and cucumbers on offer, but this was enough) and nearly died...

I was able to appreciate the comfort and warmth of The Canal Court in full due the fact that I had arrived there with my cold. Having stumbled into my room, however, I immediately felt a touch better—so bright, spacious and inviting was it. And the bed...My God...It was the size of the square in a mediaeval town —so vast and spacious that sleeping there on one's own could easily constitute a minor offence.

Feeling too sick to go down to the hotel's restaurant for dinner, I ordered a two-course room-service meal.

When the procession of waiters entered my room fifteen minutes later—pushing food trolleys and carrying silver-topped trays—I thought they must have made a mistake: I had only ordered some sea-food pasta for a starter and sautéed chicken for the main course—not a banquet for twenty-five people.

But there was no mistake involved: with all the side-dishes, vegetables, spices etc my modest dinner was too big to be set on the dining table, and half of the plates had to be accommodated on the bed—a fact that somewhat mitigated my unintended offence of lone-sleeping.

The size of both courses, including the starter, was truly gargantuan and the quality and presentation superb. It was by far the best seafood pasta I had had since leaving Australia twelve years before. The price of the whole feast was…you won't believe it…just under £20! I ate it in the company of my surrogate TV family—the *Sopranos.*

By the rule of contraries, alongside the borstal-like doss-house in Turkmenistan that nearly killed me, I will always remember the Canal Court in Newry, Northern Ireland. No doubt, Murray would have recommended it to his readers, had it been in existence in 1912. Maybe, he would have even stopped short of generalising about all Ireland's hotels as 'inferior to those of England, Scotland and the Continent'.

Nonetheless, the next morning I felt lousy. My distended nose was blocked. An uninterrupted buzzing noise from the headphones I wasn't wearing resounded in my clogged ears. A faulty didgeridoo (or was it a broken Irish bagpipe?) was playing inside my brick-heavy head. I needed to see a doctor. Luckily, Newry Medical Village, comprising a number of surgeries, pharmacies and a hospital, was just outside my hotel.

I chose Meadowlands Surgery at random. It was full of people, mostly little old ladies, patiently waiting for their call.

'I need to see a GP,' I said to the receptionist, brandishing my NHS card.

It transpired that the card was unnecessary, for residents of Southern Ireland are entitled to free treatment in the UK. I looked at the old ladies, 'God's dandelions', to use a nice Russian expression, and wondered whether they were all visitors from the South, too.

'What if you fell ill while in Dublin?' I tactlessly asked Dr J.J. Torney, a facetious bespectacled man, as he was measuring my blood pressure.

'I would have to pay to see a GP, but could claim the money back on return. It's interesting how many people from the South suddenly feel unwell when they come here on shopping expeditions…I don't mean you of course,' he chuckled.

The antibiotic prescribed by Dr Torney soon took effect, and in no time I was sitting inside a café perusing the morning newspapers and sipping an espresso. The espresso was awful, but, on the positive side, I was able to puff away for all I was worth—the smoking ban having not yet come into effect in Northern Ireland. An almost-forgotten delight.

Everyone was smoking in Newry—as if the town (sorry, the city) itself was suffering from some collective tobacco-related *newrosis*. Smoking seemed compulsory in most pubs, cafes and restaurants.

Remembering my Dublin friends' advice, I rather enjoyed leafing through the totally apolitical *Armagh–Down Observer* that seemed to contain just two types of 'coverage': reports of unruly local drivers and sets of family and school photos. 'Motorist Accused of Stopping Suddenly' was one of the paper's headlines that reminded me of a heading I once saw in the *Shetland Times*: 'Driver Swerves to Avoid Sheep'.

The stories, carried by the Belfast-based *Irish News*, however, were different: 'Sectarian attack on youth group', '22 children victims of shootings and attacks', 'Man is shot in lower leg', and next to it—'Two hurt in pub shooting'. That was how I learned about the previous night's incident in Newry.

Peace Process or no, staying away from politics is not that easy in modern Ulster.


'The attack had nothing to do with the paramilitaries—it was just a copy-cat attempt to resolve a family feud,' Rory Murphy, a young barman at McSwiggan's assured me from behind the bar.

I was the only customer in the pub that early afternoon. I simply couldn't leave Newry without finding out what had happened in the pub.

A strong smell of disinfectant was hanging in the air, and fruit machines were winking sinisterly in the semi-darkness.

Rory, who witnessed the attack, readily 're-enacted' it for me *en situ*. He then pointed to a fresh bullet scratch on the wooden bar stand, about twenty inches above the floor. I thought I could discern two dark spots under a stool next to it.

'It is so out of character with the town now,' sighed the barman.

His view was shared by Henry Reilly, the popular mayor of Newry—the first Unionist mayor in the whole history of this predominantly Catholic town—whom I met an hour later.

'We have generous and genuine people here,' he said. 'They have gone through a lot of suffering, and it will take several generations to change the violence-oriented sectarian mentality completely. It is changing already. Look at me: I served in the British Army—and still I am accepted...'

He was right about the mentality, of course. Old habits die hard, and euthanasia doesn't quite work here...Time is indeed Newry's best and only *newropathologist.*

Newry is pretty—'clean and well-built' indeed. Enclosed by the Mourne Mountains, it combined the hustle-and-bustle of a mini-city ('one of the most progressive and up-to-date towns in Ulster', according to *The Ulster Guide* of 1949) with the friendly cosiness of a small town to create a truly welcoming spirit, unspoiled by the disproportionate number of windswept—both outside and inside—shopping malls, targeting bargain-hunters from the South.

The historic Newry town hall, to which Murray awarded his coveted asterisks, was built in 1893 on a bridge astride the river, dividing two counties—allegedly, to settle the rivalry between the people of Armagh and Down. It stood there now as a classical red-brick memento of the all-but-forgotten, yet much-needed by modern Ulster, art of compromise.

It is hard to imagine a town more peaceful than modern Newry, where two currencies, two counties and two countries seemed to co-exist rather happily. Not so long ago, however, it was one of the world's most dangerous places. In the local museum, I was shown an official report, according to which '13% of all the Troubles-related fatalities in Northern Ireland took place in the Newry region...that accounted for only 5.3% of the Northern Ireland population'. It was 'the fifth most violent urban area' in Ulster.

The last thing I did before leaving Newry was post two letters—one to a friend in London (it cost me 26p) and another to Dublin

(40p), just to check which one would arrive first. The one, sent to London, was delivered to the addressee the following day.

In Dublin, my friend is still waiting for my letter from Newry.

# Part III

# A 'Skeleton' Tour of the North

If America and Britain, according to that émigré Irish wit Bernard Shaw, are two countries divided by the same language, then Northern and Southern Ireland can be called one country divided by the same religion—Christianity.

Since the primary subject of this book is time-travelling in the new Celtic-Tiger Ireland, my journey north was bound to be shorter than the 'Tour through the South'. Indeed, as part of Great Britain, Northern Ireland has until recently remained all but unaffected by the Southern economic boom. On the other hand, in order to honour my travels back in time to 19th- and early-20th-century Ireland, I had to visit Ulster, then as much part of a united non-sovereign Ireland as Wicklow or Cork.

Obviously, there were no mentions of the North as a separate geopolitical entity in either of my main literary 'time machines': the 1855 Blackie's *Imperial Gazetteer* or in Murray's *Handbook for Travellers in Ireland*, 1912. That was why I had to recruit another full-time time-travelling companion, namely the *Ulster for your Holiday* Guide, 'an official publication of the Ulster Tourist Development Association', published in Belfast in 1949. The fact that by then Ulster was no longer politically a part of the island of Ireland is cautiously mentioned in the foreword to the Guide, contributed by 'The Right Honourable Sir Basil S. Brooke, Bart., C.B.E.,M.C.,D.L.,M.P., Prime Minister of Northern Ireland' from his residence at Stormont Castle. 'As Northern Ireland is part of the United Kingdom, tourists from Great Britain are not troubled by customs formalities.' With the North/South political divide being still fresh, the confused 'tourists from Great Britain' had to be reminded that it was safe to leave their passports at home.

The absence of 'customs formalities' is the one and only touch of politics in that innocuous and euphoric (if not to say 'orgiastic') holiday guide, where the most frequently used adjectives are 'happy', 'friendly', 'beautiful', 'wonderful' and (occasionally) 'irresistible'. As much as Baedeker and Murray were economical with epithets, the *Ulster Guide* was overflowing with them: 'Ulster folk are renowned for their hospitality. They welcome visitors with unaffected sincerity and do everything to make them feel at home. This happy contact with friendly hosts is one of the many abiding pleasures of an Ulster holiday,' wrote the Right Honourable Basil S. Brooke, Bart., etc. etc. (for reasons of space, I'll have to avoid all his other 'designations', which make his official title look like the number plate on a German car).

Reading that, I could not help remembering the joke about the Northern Ireland Tourism Board attributed to Brendan Behan: the Board conducted a quiz for its clients where the second prize was a two-week free tour of Ulster, and the first prize—a one-week free tour.[15]

It also brought back to memory the disastrous 'Brighten up Ulster' campaign of 1974–75—this at a time when the devolved Ulster government was collapsing, the IRA was bombing Birmingham pubs and only two years after 470 people had been killed in the province. The aim of the campaign was both to cheer up the beleaguered Ulster residents and to attract tourists from the rest of Britain to what was then effectively a war zone. Among other morale-boosting measures, the British government considered organising a big Morecambe and Wise performance at Stormont, an inter-town knockout rugby competition, a 'Miss Good Cheer' beauty pageant, a 'Sociable Week', with the message: 'Don't Let's Be Downhearted' and a series of 'Good Cheer Conferences' along with special 'Good Cheer' supplements with 'positive' news stories in local newspapers.

To me, the officially engineered campaign echoes the infamous Soviet motto: 'Life is improving and is getting more cheerful' of 1937—at the peak of the Stalinist terror and purges. Another reminder of the simple truth that one can not make people smile by decree.

I decided that occasional references to the 'cheerful' 1949 *Holiday Guide* could bring an interesting time perspective on Ulster, but have to urge the reader to take them with a good pinch of salt.

My own experience of the North had, before now, been insignificant: a visit to Belfast in 1994, as a roving reporter/ columnist for the now-defunct *European* newspaper. I flew into Belfast on a gloomy February morning and drove to the city past a couple of checkpoints and was overtaken by several grey APCs. Piles of dirty snow on the streets reminded me of Moscow. But most of all I was struck by the painfully familiar 'Soviet' expression on many of the locals' faces, what I came to call 'the seal of oppression'—that haunted I-am-waiting-to-be-hurt look, moulded by years of fear and humiliation, by the daily struggle for survival and repressed emotions, the look that made my former compatriots so easily recognisable from the distance, no matter what sort of chic Western clothes they were sporting. As if they were constantly expecting a blow from behind.

'We live under constant stress here,' one of my Belfast hosts told me.

To me, Belfast of 1994 did not feel part of the free world, for the real danger of being blown up or shot at any moment destroyed all existing liberties of Western civilisation. The dead have no use for free expression.

With the Peace Process in full swing, I hoped that travelling there with one eye on the past would allow me to bypass the Troubles (which proved impossible), to visualise Ulster as it used to be before partition and to compare it with what I was seeing today.

'A Tour of the North' was how Murray entitled one of the 'skeleton routes' in the introduction to his 1912 Handbook. By 'skeleton' he probably implied 'essential, reduced to a minimum'[16] —a semi-forgotten and outdated meaning of the familiar word.

Murray's recommended 'Skeleton Tour' was meant to last for a month. For various reasons, I had to complete mine in just twelve days in November–December 2005, trying to follow my old guide-book's directions wherever possible. Even though my routes were more skeletal in places than Murray's, the reality in front of me was often disjointed, inconsistent and discombobulated. It also concealed a number of 'skeletons in the cupboard', thus adding to the 'skeleton' nature of my trip.

## Day One
# Enniskillen

*'It would be impossible to imagine a more charming or romantic district for the holiday maker than can be found in...Enniskillen.'*
('ULSTER HOLIDAY GUIDE', 1949)

*'Enniskillen\* is one of the prettiest places in Ireland, a circumstance to which, together with its stirring Protestant associations, it owes its principal attractions, for it is destitute of any archaeological objects of interest.'*
('A HANDBOOK FOR TRAVELLERS IN IRELAND', MURRAY, 1912)

The lobby of the Murray-recommended Old Railway Hotel in Enniskillen is smoked through to such an extent that it appears smouldering: patrons in the lounge-room bar, made to look like the interior of a Pullman carriage, are puffing away with abandon—as if there's no tomorrow. One can almost smoke kippers or burn DVDs on top of the reception desk without any additional equipment. For the first time, I feel in favour of the smoking ban in the South.

The 1949 Ulster Holiday Guide ad for my hotel runs:

'Cosiest Country Hotel in the Six Counties. Recently Enlarged. Hot and Cold water in All Bedrooms. FULLY LICENSED. OPEN ALL YEAR ROUND. Kitchen has "Esse" Cooker and Frigidaire. Garaging for 40 Cars adjoining Hotel. Phone, Enniskillen 2084. Proprietress, MRS. R. BYRNE.'

The thing that interests me most in that ad is the mysterious 'Esse' cooker in the kitchen. Is it still there?

The room allocated to me initially has no light and feels depressing. I ask to be transferred to another one that turns out to be peculiar. It comprises a huge and totally superfluous entrance hall, furnished with a single chair standing it in forlornly—like a monument to itself. I add my soaked umbrella to the hall's furnishings which does little to make it less dangerous for an agoraphobic: a couple of hundred umbrellas can be safely left there to dry and even then only a fraction of the space would be taken up.

In comparison to the hall, the room itself is tiny—like a small hut on the edge of a prairie. In the middle is a podium with three steps leading to a square stage-like platform which makes me wonder whether it used to be a local drama-society rehearsal venue. Am I expected to perform on it? If so, where is the audience?

In the end, I decide to use the podium as my desk (for there is no other place for writing in the room), on which I can scribble while kneeling on the steps.

The room's idiosyncrasies do not end there. It also has a fire door leading straight to the balcony. The problem is, the moment it springs shut, you can't get back! The rationale behind it probably is that one can shout for help from the balcony in case of fire. As the fire instructions for guests of the Alma Ati hotel in Kazakhstan, where I once stayed, went: IN CASE OF FIRE, OPEN THE WINDOW AND SCREAM FOR HELP.

In the bathroom, there's a capacious spa bath, yet no shampoo —just a couple of used (!) mini-bars of soap.

To cap it all, the window overlooks the hotel's old kitchen, and the loud buzzing of the kitchen fan can be clearly heard throughout the day. The receptionist assures me the fan goes off at 9 p.m. It's only 5 p.m. now, so to beat the noise that is driving me bonkers, I have to get out.

Outside, it is dark and pouring with rain. The wind is whistling like a bully and breaking in two any rare umbrella. Through the veil of mist I spot the concrete bulk of a Dunnes Stores, with a Bank of Ireland ATM and forget for a moment that I am in the UK, not in the Republic of Ireland. The cash machine dispenses the

Northern Ireland breed of suspicious-looking British pounds (twenty-five million of which were recently stolen from a Belfast bank—hence the suspicion), yet shows the balance in euro. And there is no 'Gaeilge' option for the customers.

I wonder whether AIB stands for 'Alternative Irish Bank'.

The town is empty, sullen and silent, except for the time-muffled echoes of the Troubles...

Back in my room, I switch on the telly (to drown out the noise of the kitchen fan) and watch *Ulster News*. The seemingly routine news items of the day are as follows:

1. The arrest of a group of terrorists
2. A bomb explosion in a house3.The discovery of another bomb that failed to explode
4. A Northern Ireland policemen claiming compensation for having suffered PTSD (post-traumatic stress disorder) during the Troubles
5. Several bomb scares and bomb warnings in Belfast
6. Suspects of the Belfast bank robbery arrested
7. A sectarian murder
8. A petrol-bomb attack, targeting a politician
9. An arson attack
10. Promises of another miserable day and gale-force winds for tomorrow (the weather forecast).

What is supposed to be a laconic chronicle of yet another day of Northern Ireland's burgeoning Peace Process sounds like a series of reports from a war-zone.

When travelling in the USA, I remember being surprised by the sheer number of school shootings reported daily by American local TV stations. Most of them, as it turned out, never found their way onto British (or other) news bulletins. The same is true, it appears, with the ongoing conflict in Northern Ireland: only a fraction of the shootings and explosions are picked up by the mainstream British media.

At around 7.30 p.m., I get an official excuse to leave my quirky noise- and news-ridden room to meet John Byrne, former owner of the Old Railway Hotel. I want to talk to him for one simple reason: there are not many Murray-recommended hotels remaining in Ireland, North or South, and this is one of them

From my background research, I know that Mr Byrne became the owner in 1966, when he took over from his dad, and ran the hotel for over thirty years, until 1999, when it was acquired by another proprietor.

I descend to the hotel's lobby where Mr Byrne is already waiting, nursing a pint of Guinness. He is a shy and quiet man, with a warm smile.

'I've been here for a while enjoying my pint. My wife is now away in the UK looking after the grandchildren,' he says.

I am tempted to remind him that we are in the UK as well, but decide not to.

'My family bought the hotel in 1852,' he is saying in between small sips. 'Enniskillen was then a stop for Dublin coaches, so the establishment started as a coach house. Then the railway came. The station was across the road, where the Lidl supermarket is now. The railway disappeared in 1956, and the hotel became a convenient stopping place for CTs; commercial travellers, or, as they say now, "reps". They constituted the bulk of the clientele when I took over in 1966. It was the year when ladies were first allowed to stay at hotels unaccompanied and to drink at the bar on their own. I had to go through a two-week trial period—like all the rest—and had to do everything: cleaning, carrying CTs' luggage, polishing their shoes. The guests' shoes were left outside the doors, and the full B&B cost seven shillings and six pence…The hotel was always viable commercially, even during the Troubles…'

He seems reluctant to talk about 'the bombs'.

'Enniskillen had just one big bomb and that, unfortunately, put it on the map. The hotel itself was never affected—neither bombs nor bomb threats nor warnings…'

I ask him whether any famous people have stayed at the Railway, expecting to hear De Valera's name.

'We were always an unpretentious and down-to-earth establishment,' he shrugs (I don't tell him that I have noticed that already). 'De Valera stayed here once...'

The former President of Ireland must have had an extremely peripatetic life.

'Do you come here often these days?' I ask Mr Byrne.

'Not really. Too many memories, you know...'

Having asked for permission, I pop into the hotel's kitchen and make sure that the much advertised 'Esse cooker' is still there. The handmade cast iron oven is very much in use, and I wonder whether Murray saw it in 1912. Quite possible, for 'Esse' was invented in 1854. He definitely did not see the 'frigidaire' that first appeared only in 1913. The latter, although broken, is in the kitchen, too, but is now being used as a storage cupboard.

'Ovens have souls,' the restaurant's chef mutters, stroking the cooker's charred door almost lovingly.

Soothed by this unexpected historical perspective, I sit down to dinner in the hotel's restaurant, which seems to be specialising exclusively in the railway variety of food (down-to-earth and starchy) and puzzle the staff by ordering a fruit salad. By their response, you might suppose that the last fruit salad was ordered here somewhere around 1912...

Later on, in my room, I watch a fascinating UTV documentary. During World War II, De Valera was worried that, if fifty German paratroopers landed in Counties Fermanagh and Tyrone and proclaimed themselves liberators, that would become his Sudetenland, or the fifth column: the people in those counties were ardently opposed to partition and wanted to be in the South.

At about midnight, the kitchen fan finally goes off and allows me to have some sleep.

Day Two

# Enniskillen

*'Enniskillen...is well-built, cleanly and thriving; has lately been lighted with gas, and in other respects greatly improved...The town has two tanneries, a brewery, a manufactory of leather, a small cutlery establishment and the females make straw plait, and sew muslin.'*
(THE 'IMPERIAL GAZETTEER', W.G. BLACKIE, ED., 1855)

*'A pleasant, conservative little town.'*
(THE 'ROUGH GUIDE TO IRELAND', 2004)

The following day, I discover, round the corner from my hotel, the modernist cubist block of the Clinton Centre, built on the site of the Remembrance Day Bombing of 8 November 1987—the 'very big bomb' that, according to John Byrne, put the town on the map. The bomb killed eleven people (and injured 61). Twelve, to be more exact: Ronnie Hill, a local school headmaster, went into a coma after the explosion and died fourteen years later—in 2001. Ironically, the World War 1 memorial, with the inscription 'Our Glorious Dead' was the only structure that stayed intact on the bomb-ravaged site. It is here today, still commemorating the victims of that War, and twelve more 'glorious dead' of Enniskillen, in whose memory bronze doves have been added to the cenotaph.

The Clinton Centre, comprising a hostel, a gallery and an Internet café, was built on the spot of the blast in 2002 (and opened by Bill Clinton himself) as part of the 'Higher Bridges' project to bring the town's Catholic and Protestant communities closer together.

There is no one inside the Centre. The building is imposing, yet lacking in substance (dare I say it, 'Clintonesque').

Having checked my e-mails in the Centre's Internet café (as I do so, the café's proprietor—a Romanian immigrant—tries to sell me one of the computers), I wander off to the Buttermarket to meet my guide for the day. I walk along the main street, past two churches, a Catholic and a Protestant—both disproportionately large and intimidating—across the road from each other and without any visible 'bridges' between them.

The Buttermarket, once a thriving Victorian institution, where the area's agricultural produce was sold, has been taken over by local craftsmen and has become 'a creative space where artists and craftspeople are designing and making.' I quote from one of the Buttermarket's multiple 'interpretation' signs—all written in stilted and stylistically illiterate, yet *ad nauseam* politically correct, English: 'The area was formerly called "Boston"; or "Boston Quay". It was used by the people who were very poor to cross the River Erne by ferry to the workhouse.'; "Boston Quay" is the name of our craft shop and *thereby* will preserve the old reference to Boston.'; another example: 'Rebecca Dick was the first person to sell freshly baked bread in Enniskillen in the early 19th century. Her name is commemorated in the *title* of our coffee shop and is *intended* as a tribute to all those who worked and traded in the Buttermarket.' (The italics are mine; the word order is not—vv).

Reading all this gibberish, I start seriously doubting the statement of the Irish Booker-Prize-winning writer John Banville: 'The British gave us the English language, and we Irish are making pretty good use of it.'

I sit in the coffee shop, 'entitled' Rebecca Dick, and leaf through today's issue of *The Impartial Reporter*, Enniskillen's local newspaper. One of the main rules of newspaper journalism is 'never make a judgment in a headline' (I once found a classic breach of the latter in *The Folkestone Herald*'s headline, 'Evil Baxter Kicks Sheep').

The Enniskillen paper seems to be breaking this rule in its very masthead by judging its own reporting as impartial.

On page one, *The Impartial Reporter* duly (and 'impartially', no doubt) tells the story of yet another paedophile priest: 'Tragedy of

Abuse Victim Revealed', supporting Pete MacCarthy's observation
that each Irish paper (North or South) runs a daily column on the
subject.

'Mother accused of using son to steal from shops in "Fagan-
type" way', runs the second-page headline. I read on, hoping that
'Fagan' is a misprint of Dickens' 'Fagin': 'Mr Liam McNally, R.M.,
referring to the character in the Charles Dickens' novel *Oliver
Twist*, said: "Fagan-type". Both Mr Liam MacNally and the editor
of *The Impartial Reporter* must be forced to re-read *Oliver Twist.*

'Police looking for prowler find man with stolen ladies'
underwear,' the headline on page three informs me. The piece
quotes the hapless prowler's defence lawyer: 'While the offences
were distressing for the women involved they were at the lower end
of the scale of theft.' Interesting. What would be at the higher end
of 'the scale of theft'—hats and overcoats?

By page four, I start feeling nostalgic for the old Skibbereen
*Eagle*, with its impeccable English and dry sense of humour...

Anne, my guide, arrives shortly, and takes me on a quick tour of
the town. She tells me that, unlike the South, Enniskillen was
blitzed during World War ii.

Another difference with the South (and this one is an echo of
the Troubles) is that the Victorian town hall has a security lock
attached to its elaborately carved front door. Anne enters the code,
and we go inside to have a look at the plush Council Chamber,
which resembles the parliament chamber of a small nation (I saw
a very similar—only much more modest—one in Andorra).

We then drive out of town—past the oblong building of the
former RUC, now PSNI (Police Service of Northern Ireland), still
enclosed by a massive steel-and-concrete fence, yet no longer
wrapped up in barbed wire—as every police station was during
the Troubles.

A narrow dirt track leads us to the river bank, from where we
can see Devenish Island, where locals used to bury their family
members during the Great Famine. The scenery is peaceful and
romantic, and it is hard to imagine flocks of black-clad grieving
people carrying coffins along the forest path towards the river.
They would then load their loved ones' remains onto a boat to take
them to the island...

This is Ireland: grief, suffering and beauty—all at the same time and on the same spot!

The new memorial to the Famine victims (in Cornagrade) consists of two erect columns and a table, with empty copper plates, in between. Anne tells me it was designed by Eamonn O'Doherty, who also designed a Great Hunger memorial in Westchester, New York.

My main point of interest in Enniskillen, however, is Portora Royal School for Boys, where Oscar Wilde, one of my all-time favourite writers and personalities, studied in 1864–71.

To me, Wilde is more like a close personal friend. I am sure I wouldn't have survived my latest personal crisis (of many), had it not been for a postcard, pinned to the wall above my writing desk, with just one sentence on it: 'We are all in the gutter, but some of us are looking at the stars.'

One of the most beautiful things ever written (or said), this sentence is worth volumes of insipid modern prose and poetry.

And about ten years before—recovering from yet another massive setback—I was eventually able to replace Prozac with the following hourly mantra: 'A society can forgive a murderer, but never a dreamer.'

God knows, how many times—facing a pile of unpaid bills, feeling cornered or suffering from writer's block—I was taken out of limbo and forced to smile by recalling my friend's sardonic pronouncements of the type: 'I was working on the proof of one of my poems all morning, and took out a comma. In the afternoon I put it back again.' Or: 'History is an account of events that did not happen written by people who weren't there.'

Having my morning espresso and a cigarette outside Caffé Napoli in Dublin's Westland Row, I look at the windows of the fine Georgian house across the road and can almost discern the silhouette of little Oscar at number 21, the house in which he was born, wearing—in full accordance with Victorian children's fashion—a blue velvet dress (wasn't it from this that Wilde's obsession with velvet began?), peeping out from behind the curtains. What he saw was probably not that different from the present-day scene, except for the cars, Caffé Napoli and me.

The first work of Oscar Wilde that I read was probably *The Canterville Ghost*. Later—at school—we studied (as a 'scathing satire of the capitalist society', of course) *The Importance of Being Earnest*. Interestingly, in the Soviet Union, the play's title was translated as *The Importance of Being Serious*. The word 'earnest' (read 'honest') in the title of a popular play that was constantly performed in many a theatre and hence featured prominently on posters all over the country was deemed too subversive by the ever-vigilant (and ever-so-dumb) Soviet censorship authorities.

In a small leafy park opposite his Merrion Square house, Oscar himself—a self-absorbed and decadent aesthete, clad in his favourite velvet smoking jacket with floating tie—reclines comfortably against a rock. In this exceptionally brilliant sculpture by Danny Osborne (the eccentric charm of which is strangely enhanced by the fact that it was commissioned by 'Guinness Ireland Group'), my friend appears extremely relaxed. So natural in fact that I am tempted to write and remember: 'I can resist anything but temptation'?—that he looks as if he is about to step off the pedestal and dash off for a pint of Guinness—just 'to keep body and soul apart,' no doubt. In reality, he is probably not that relaxed, for 'being natural is simply a pose'…

He sits under a branchy rowan-tree (in autumn, the berries on it become a deep purple, the colour of freshly spilled human blood, which, according to an old Russian superstition, foretells a cold winter) inside 'a little tent of blue that prisoners call the sky'. Oscar earned the right to coin such seemingly 'sentimental' metaphor after two years in Reading gaol.

There is another Oscar 'home' in North Dublin, although he never lived in it. I mean the small and cosy Dublin Writers Museum in Parnell Square.

Unlike his two other Dublin abodes, his quarters here are cramped. The space allocated to him in the Museum is tiny—and not just in proportion to his own ego. He shares one and the same glass case with Bernard Shaw. Why? And why was Oscar's 150th birthday hardly noticed and commemorated in Ireland in 2004? A possible explanation can be found on the interpretation plate above the exhibits:

'He (Oscar—vv) never took Ireland as his subject and for that reason is usually classed as an English writer.'

What a load of nonsense!

Firstly, geniuses are by and large stateless: they belong everywhere and nowhere—all at the same time. And Oscar, like no one else, would hate the idea of being labelled, or 'classed'. Secondly, he was born and grew up in Ireland and therefore can be safely regarded as Irish by definition. I am sure he would have much preferred that to being branded as belonging to the country that actually destroyed him.

At first glance, Bernard Shaw appears a suitable 'neighbour': a fellow playwright and wit, he was born just two years after Oscar, in 1856, yet outlived him by fifty years and died at the 'venerable' age of ninety-four in 1950.

'He whom the gods love goes young.'

Can you imagine Oscar living into his nineties? You can't? And neither can I. Unlike, it has to be said, Malcolm Muggeridge: 'I have little doubt that if Oscar Wilde had lived into his nineties…he would have been considered a benign, distinguished figure suitable to preside at a school prize-giving or to instruct and exhort scoutmasters at their jamborees. He might even have been knighted.'

'Sir Oscar Wilde, OBE'…How incongruous! One thing I am sure of, however, is that, unlike the elderly Bernard Shaw, Oscar would never have been duped by Stalin into believing that communism was the best thing since sliced bread.

One other writer, playwright and wit strikes me as being the closest to Oscar—in life, in literature and even in death: Anton Chekhov. The two never met of course, but the coincidences are striking. They lived at almost exactly the same time, albeit in different countries. Chekhov was born six years later and died at forty-four in 1904—four years later than Oscar.

Chekhov was a practising physician, and Oscar, although not a doctor himself, was the son of Ireland's best-known ophthalmologist.

They both worked in the same genres, although Chekhov never wrote poetry.

Even their sexual preferences were, allegedly, not that dissimilar.

Like Oscar in English, Chekhov is by far the most quoted writer in the Russian language. 'I dreamt that what I had thought was reality was a dream, and what I had thought was a dream was reality,'—this entry from Chekhov's 'Diaries' can easily be nominated for an Oscar, i.e. pass for something Oscar Wilde has written or said.

Their tragically parallel lives ended on largely the same note— a joke.

Looking at the particularly naff and faded wallpaper in need of replacement in the Paris hotel room, where he was dying, Oscar said: 'One of us will have to go...'

Chekhov on his deathbed asked for a glass of champagne. 'Champagne, *Ich sterbe*[17]...' were his last words.

They both wrote their lives and lived their writing. I am sure they would have enjoyed each other's company.

Oscar's Enniskillen 'home'—his *alma mater*, where he spent all his 'formative years', from ten to seventeen—sits on top of a hill overlooking the town. I approach it with trepidation—as if about to visit a dear, long-lost friend.

Wilde and his older brother ended up studying and boarding here because their father was friendly with Portora's drawing master, who promised to keep an eye on the boys.

Oscar's nickname at the school was Grey Crow—most likely because he was different from other boys. To begin with, he did not like sports. Most certainly, he was bullied and that must have helped to mould his writer's personality. Creativity is often a product of suffering and injustice.

Walking Portora's dark and echoey corridors, ascending the worn-out (by Oscar's feet, too!) marble grand staircase and lingering in the gloomy vaulted dining room, I can almost sense the pain, frustration and claustrophobia Oscar must have experienced within these walls.

In a sense, the bullying of Oscar went on in Portora long after his death—until the 1930s, when the modest memorial plate—OSCAR WILDE, 1854–1900, WRITER & WIT was replaced on the assembly hall's wall, having been angrily taken off, due to the 'scandal' of his homosexuality. Murray, too, must have been affected by the stigma: he never mentions Wilde (or Portora) in his *Handbook*.

Oscar would have been pleased to know that his old school has now become one of the venues for Enniskillen's annual Oscar Wilde Festival. This reminds me of the story the great Russian ballet dancer Rudolf Nureyev recounted to me in one of his last interviews in 1993. Like Oscar, Nureyev was mercilessly bullied— by pupils and teachers alike!—at school in the Soviet city of Ufa because of his passion for dancing. Just as in late-19th-century Britain, homosexuality was a serious crime in the USSR. When Nureyev visited the school in the early 1990s on his first and only trip to his motherland after his defection (he was 'allowed' to return for a couple of days to attend his mother's funeral), he was amazed to see that the building now housed a ballet school.

Art always triumphs over prejudice in the end.

The long and forbidding corridors of Portora are overhung with portraits of obscure long-dead graduates and sombre head-masters, but Oscar's refined face is nowhere to be seen. This is bizarre, for, even if to forget his greatness as a writer, he was a Royal Scholar, with exceptional academic achievements. On the faded Royal Scholars board in the assembly hall I finally find Oscar's name. Restored in the 1930s (after being painted over in the wake of his infamous trial), it stands out on the board and looks fresher and more prominent than the rest. And in the corner of the school library (former dormitory), under Portora's new Anti-Bullying Charter' (what an irony!) on the wall, I spot a glass case containing several dog-eared books that used to belong to Oscar. Among them, *The Analogy of Religion* by Joseph Butler, 1868, and the Bible, which contains the dedication: 'This prize and Holy Scripture was given by the Rev. W. Steele to Oscar Wilde, midsummer, 1869'.

My guide Anne tells me that Reverend William Steele was the headmaster, whose own son drowned in Erne Lake three days after finishing school and being accepted to Trinity College Dublin.

I finally find Oscar's portrait, too. It is locked away in a smallish side-room of the former headmaster's residence. With a cigarette in his mouth, my friend looks lost and anonymous. There are no names under the painting—neither of Oscar nor of the artist. Next to him hangs a pompous portrait of a 'Mr Justice George Wright'.

A school brass band is rehearsing behind the wall, the discordant funereal sounds adding to Portora's depressing atmosphere on this dull winter afternoon.

As I smoke outside the main entrance door, several uniformed freckled boys in their early teens run out of the building. Waiting to be picked up by their parents in shiny cars (the school is no longer a boarding one), they keep yap-yapping happily into their mobile phones.

Oscar would have been amused…

## Day Three
# Omagh–London/Derry

*'The Town itself contains little to detain the tourist. It has the usual county town structures—a Court House with good Doric front, Lunatic Asylum, Gaol, barracks, a Church with a lofty spire which looks very well from the Railway, and a new R.C. Church.'*
('A HANDBOOK FOR TRAVELLERS IN IRELAND', MURRAY, 1912)

*'Omagh...has tolerably well-kept streets, lighted with gas; houses generally of stone, and much improved of late years...About a mile from the town there is a large lunatic asylum of recent erection, intended for the incurable lunatics of the Northern counties.'*
(THE 'IMPERIAL GAZETTEER', W.G. BLACKIE, ED., 1855)

On the way to Derry (or 'Londonderry' for the British and the Loyalists),[18] I stop in the town of Omagh, Co. Tyrone —the site of the Troubles' biggest atrocity in 1998, when twenty-six people were killed on the spot (three more died later of their wounds) and over two hundred were injured. It has been argued that the terrorists, the Real IRA, deliberately gave a misleading warning that made lots of people—mostly morning shoppers—rush in panic towards the 500-pound car bomb.

Parking in the main street, I notice that my car, hired in Dublin, is the only one around with Republic-of-Ireland number plates, making it look distinctly foreign and me feel uneasy, for reasons that are hard to explain.

What strikes me most about Omagh is how ordinary it is. The main street, that was largely devastated by the bomb, is now lined with the usual—British—cheap, poorly stocked retailers: 'Shoe Zone', one-pound bargain stores, all sorts of charity outlets etc. The locals look sullen, scruffy and pale, as if malnourished. The general feel of the place is sombre and depressing, as if it is still reverberating from that massive explosion of seven years ago.

Inside Eanetta's Bistro, everyone—men, women, tea-sipping old ladies—is puffing away forgetfully, as if smoking in this catering establishment is a must. A baby, wrapped not so much in a cheap cotton-wool blanket as in clouds of cigarette smoke, is coughing timidly in his sleep. A wild-looking man with a badly scratched face at the table next to me is mumbling to himself.

Nursing my life's worst 'cappuccino', I leaf through today's issue of the *Irish News*. Among the lead stories is a report about an Omagh family who lost a son during the 1998 bombing, and who have just lost another one in a car crash.

I leave the café and wander into the Sacred Heart Church on top of a hill. It is dark inside. The stale air smells of incense. A sad-faced elderly woman, dressed in black, is kneeling on the floor. In the far corner, next to the altar, a group of girls are rehearsing their First Communion.

My heart fills with sudden affection for this subdued, down-to-earth and so very *vulnerable* Irish town—an easy target for the cruel fanatics calling themselves 'dissident Republicans', the best place for whom would be Omagh's old 'asylum for incurable lunatics of Northern counties', mentioned above by Blackie and Murray.

When I return to my car, I discover it has been parked on double yellow lines. However, the numerous traffic wardens (all young, fat females) milling all over the street, did not issue me with a ticket. I should be feeling lucky, yet, for some reason, I don't. Their uncharacteristic leniency is perhaps a repayment for my gust of affection. Decent Omagh.

I stop for a picnic lunch on the grounds of the Ulster American Folk Park, outside the town. Having popped into the Park for a quick look at the exhibition, I end up spending several hours in that spectacular open-air museum, telling the story of Irish emigration to America with tact, ingenuity and plenty of imagination. You first walk through the 'Old World' part of the display, recreating an impoverished early-19th-century Irish village (you can enter authentic shops and houses and even meet the residents and craftsmen, played by gregarious and knowledgeable 'impersonators' in period costumes); then you get on board the USA-bound vessel to endure all the hardships (as well as smells and sounds) of the crossing, and finally emerge into the 'New World' —an Irish/American town, where refugees from Ulster have started their new American lives. The fact that 'period smells' (of sea, horse manure, timber, printing presses etc) are recreated in the Park gives it a touch of authenticity: smells are extremely powerful ambassadors of time. I can still remember Chekhov's doctor's suitcase in his house, now a museum in Melikhovo, near Moscow. It was still faintly reeking of medicines, when I examined it eighty odd years after its owner's death.

I find the subject of the Park close to my heart and wish I could stay there longer. It brings about memories of my visit to Cobh in Co. Cork—by far the most beautiful Irish town I have seen, and by far—the saddest...

It was from Cobh, formerly Queenstown, that over three million Irish migrants left their country in search of better lives. It was there that they had their last simple meal in Ireland, the so-called 'American wake', before boarding 'coffin ships' to the USA, Australia and Europe. It must have been heart-breaking to be leaving behind all this beauty that many of them were not destined to see again.

On the wall of St Patrick's Cathedral in New York I once saw a plate dedicated to St Frances Xavier Gabrini, the patron saint of emigrants (and immigrants). It was shortly after I myself had to defect from the Soviet Union with my family. I stood there for a long while, and, not being a believer, silently begged St Frances to extend her divine helping hand to us in our new emigrant life.

Indeed, emigration, even if successful, is seldom a bliss. And at times it becomes a misery bordering on grief. A rather morose Russian friend of mine once compared it to a dress rehearsal for one's own funeral.

The 'skeleton' nature of my route, however, requires me to carry on. As a memento of my visit, I buy a copy of the 1847 'Notice to Passengers' from the recreated workshop of 'R.J. Blair, Printer & Stationer' (a real person who ran his printing business in Ulster in the 1870–80s). The poster, printed on an old press in front of my eyes says:

> 'NOW IN PORT. Notice to Passengers. Those passengers who have taken their Passages for New York by the LADY CAROLINE, captain Carlton, are required to be in Derry on Monday, the 14th of July, 1847, pay a remainder of their Passage Money, and go on Board as the Vessel will sail first fair wind after that date. A few more Passengers will be taken, on moderate terms, if immediate application is made to Mr David Mitchell, Dungiven, or the owners, J.&J. Cooke. Derry, June 28, 1847.'

At the bottom of the poster, below the drawing of the *Lady Caroline*, straddling the waves, her sails full of wind, is a note: 'The cargo of the *Lady Caroline* just arrived, from NEW YORK consisting of Indian Corn, Indian Meal, Flour, &c., for Sale, on moderate terms'.

I roll up the poster and tie it with a rope, weaved in the neighbouring weaver's shop—the way they did it in 18th-century Ulster. The touch of this rough dishevelled rope is like the touch of Time itself. I can suddenly clearly see the ship, and the passengers, with all their kids, bags and baggage; and the world-weary captain Carlton sucking his pipe on the bridge...

My intention is to frame the poster and put it on wall of my study at home. The immediate problem is that I don't really know where 'home' is...

With the timeless mud from the Park's dirt tracks of the past on my boots, I drive on to London/Derry.[19] I notice that, unlike their Southern counterparts, drivers in the North are extremely polite: they always give way and never get aggressive.[20]

Approaching London/Derry, I observe that every single road sign that carries the British version of the city's name has the

'London' bit either scraped off or painted over. Can it be the work of the IRA's special road-sign task force operating under cover of darkness and armed with torches, ladders and special paramilitary 'scratchers'? Again, I am reminded of the 'regional centre of N.': 'When the moon rose and cast its minty light on the miniature bust of poet Zhukovsky, a rude word could clearly be seen chalked on the poet's bronze back. The inscription had first appeared on June 15, 1897, the same day that the bust had been unveiled. And despite all the efforts of the police...the defamatory word had reappeared each day with unfailing regularity.'

'Nationality—'Northern Irish' says my pre-printed registration form when I check in at The Tower, the only hotel within London/ Derry's 17th-century fortification walls '1 m in circumference and perfectly preserved', according to Murray. I can't help being amused by this, yet another 'nationality' of mine (on top of Ukrainian/Russian/British/Australian).

I find that, as a traveller, I sometimes attract trouble. Czechoslovakia's former President Alexander Dubcek died in Bratislava when I was on a two-day newspaper assignment there, and I was able to file an unexpected report on his dramatic funeral. Similarly, my arrival in Newry had coincided with a paramilitary shooting. The very hour I arrive in L/D and am cruising the city centre looking for my hotel, a bomb explosion—the first one in many years—shatters the city walls. Surprisingly, I don't hear it myself, even though it is just several hundred yards away and only learn about it from the evening news.

It appears that it was a 'controlled' explosion of a hoax device, hidden in a wheelie bin that was in turn concealed inside a white van, hijacked at gunpoint and parked near the city's police headquarters. The surrounding area is still cordoned off, and police patrols are on every corner, when I go out for dinner with local contacts.

It is an 'Old Firm' evening, when Celtic play Rangers in Glasgow, both teams having ardent supporters in Northern Ireland. Stroke City's pubs are brimming with groups of Celtic and Rangers supporters—each in its team's colours and in its own designated

'Catholic' or 'Protestant' watering hole, of course. Each equally drunk.

I once attended an Old Firm match in Glasgow and was amazed how deeply the fans were split along sectarian lines. Both at Celtic Park and outside its grounds, Celtic and Rangers supporters never mixed and were kept apart by the police at all times. Yet both parties were equally plastered, despite the fact that, to reduce the drunkenness, the kick-off had been set at midday. The fans had simply started drinking the night before. Empty whisky flasks crunched under my feet as I walked towards the stadium. They covered the ground like a huge glass carpet and were sparkling in the sun like fresh snow…

'We don't shoot each other like they do in Ireland, because we spend all our angst on football,' one of the Celtic supporters told me after the game…

In London/Derry—until recently, at least—they did both: spent their 'angst' on football and murdered each other, too…

My friends, whom I am visiting in Derry, and I dine at a bistro where they serve giant tiger prawns that I am tempted to brand 'Celtic Tiger prawns'. The restaurant is full of young people and could be anywhere: London, Melbourne or New York. We are served by two waitresses: one, smiley and efficient, the other, sullen and clumsy. It is like the old good-/bad-cop method of police interrogation: after being handled by a 'bad cop', the suspect is more likely to spill the beans to the 'good' one. Has the restaurant adopted a similar approach on the psychologically correct premise that tips for the 'good' waitress, when contrasted to the 'bad' one, are likely to be higher than normal? They could share the proceeds afterwards…

A particularly large 'Celtic Tiger' prawn gets stuck in my throat when one of my fellow diners assures me that there is not a single Protestant in the bistro. 'They have their own haunts,' she insists and adds that, even now, the city has only one 'integrated' (i.e. mixed Catholic and Protestant) school, whereas all the rest are still 'segregated'.

As I walk back to my hotel, a dead-drunk Celtic supporter in a striped shirt falls out of a 'Republican' pub and promptly goes to sleep on the pavement.

# Day Four
# London/Derry

*'Striking and beautiful views of Derry and its setting can be seen from the surrounding hills.'*
('ULSTER HOLIDAY GUIDE', 1949)

Stroke City's morning newspapers are full of speculation about yesterday's blast and its perpetrators. The Unionist *Londonderry Sentinel* blames 'Republicans', the Catholic *Derry Journal* doesn't blame anyone in particular, yet accuses '... the British Army of 'inappropriate handling of the controlled explosion'.

In the brief morning sunlight, I can clearly see what a beautiful city this is. The cosy narrow lanes of the Old Town wind up and down the hills, and truly 'striking' (for once, my euphoric *Ulster Guide* was right) views of the hills and the river open up from the ramparts. I come to enjoy the city's ambience: the locals in coffee shops, where they sell 'Segafredo Zanetti', my favourite brand of espresso, are invariably friendly. They say 'No bother', instead of 'You are welcome'—just like in the South. It is hard to believe that this was the venue of Bloody Sunday in 1972—the watershed of violence in Northern Ireland, after which, as one of my local contacts remarked yesterday, 'even very peaceful people became fighters'.

It takes a much closer look to spot police patrols in the streets (the aftermaths of yesterday's explosion); watchtowers sticking out here and there; double fences, with CCTV cameras on top, around some 'troublesome' residential areas; traces of bullets on the walls of the Orange Hall—scars on the city's mutilated body. It is obvious that London/Derry is still divided—and not just by its two 'official' names.

From one of the bastions, my guide—one of my dinner

companions from last night—points down at the Catholic suburb of the Bogside across the river and then at a fence-enclosed 'Loyalist enclave'. I soon lose track of who is where and what and why…

We drive down the hill to the city cemetery. 'You shouldn't park your car with the Republic of Ireland number plates, in some places here,' warns my escort as we pass through the city's drab western suburbs.

The cemetery on the West bank of the Foyle is massive. I prudently park in its Catholic part, among the 'IRA graves', decorated with Republic of Ireland flags. On some gravestones, life-size statues stand, of masked men in sunglasses (!) and para-military berets, submachine guns in their gloved hands. Why would a dead man need sunglasses, particularly if he is a statue? They would be of as much use to him as skis to a camel. Or as a fifth leg to a dog, as they say in Russia.

The answer is obvious: to inspire fear. Even from the grave…

REMEMBERING OUR COMRADES AND FRIENDS KILLED BY THE BRITISH ARMY is carved on tombstones, next to KILLED IN ACTION, 1971, KILLED IN ACTION, 1983, KILLED ON ACTIVE SERVICE, 1973. So, the 'action' (read war) was here then. And, as I have just been made aware, probably still is…

We drive on to the Bogside, a segregated Catholic suburb, and my escort briefs me on its tempestuous history. In the 18th century, Catholics, who were not allowed to live inside the Walls, were banished to that marshy West-Bank area. Many of the houses they settled in were still in use in the 1960s. The dwellings had no inside water supply, toilets or bathrooms. It was the protests against such subhuman conditions that led to the riots of 1968 and 1969 (the so-called 'Battle of the Bogside'), after which the British Army agreed not to enter the area. The beleaguered Bogside residents then barricaded the suburb and started calling it 'Free Derry'. The no-go-area status of the Bogside was ended by the Bloody Sunday massacre in January 1972.

YOU ARE NOW ENTERING FREE DERRY, announces the sign painted on the gable end of a house. The Bogside these days looks like an open-air Museum of the Troubles. The walls of standard council houses are covered with belligerent murals, drawings and graffiti: REAL IRA—OUT!, SDLP—OUT!, and so on. Most of the murals—like the one depicting Bernadette Devlin addressing a rally—are painted skilfully, even artistically. I am not at all surprised to see the sign THE BOGSIDE ARTISTS' STUDIO on one of the area's shabbiest sheds. Like the graffiti-covered remains of the Berlin Wall, these awe-inspiring murals and other forms of rebellious street art must be preserved for posterity—as a memory, or rather—as a warning.

I can bet that both Murray and Baedeker—in their striving to be as apolitical as possible in their handbooks—would have avoided any mention of places like the modern Bogside. This realisation brings me one step closer to understanding why Baedeker chose *not* to write about Ireland.

For a change of pace, I go for lunch to Austins, London/Derry's answer to Harrods and Britain's oldest independent store, having just marked its 175th anniversary. Until now I thought that the oldest family-owned supermarket was Jenners in Edinburgh, yet Declan Hasson, Austins' Finance Director, who joins me for lunch, says that Jenners is independent no more, having just been bought by House of Fraser.

'Austins has survived the Boer War, both World Wars, the Troubles and numerous attempts by High Street giants to acquire us.'

'Are you successful?' I ask him.

'Well, we are still here, and this in itself is not a little thing, by modern standards.'

After months of enforced shopping at Dublin's rip-off Spar and Centra outlets, it is nice to be inside a store that has not—yet—been swallowed by one of the Orwellian community-destroying conglomerates. I know only too well how hard it is to stay independent these days—be you a retailer, a publisher, a journalist, or simply a decent human being—and sincerely hope that Austins' independence will last much longer than that of 'Free Derry'. And although shopping tips did not feature in any form in Baedeker's and Murray's classic handbooks (unlike in most modern guide-books in which shopping—on a par with eating—is the single most important element of travel), it occurs to me that Murray himself might have popped into Austins to purchase a new pair of boots, or, say, a raincoat, in 1912.

With the gruesome atmosphere of the cemetery and the Bogside still with me, I pick up a glossy flier advertising a 'Bra Fitting Evening' at Austins and wonder whether I'd be allowed to attend. Not as a participant but as an 'impartial' (*pace* the Enniskillen rag)...observer? And when inside one of the store's bathrooms I see the sign: WELCOME TO THIS FACILITY! IF YOU SMOKE IN THIS TOILET, YOU WILL SET OFF THE FIRE ALARM!, my mood improves considerably. It is somehow reassuring that political correctness has permeated even one of the world's least politically correct places—Northern Ireland. Unlike most other parts of the Western world, it has been in desperate need of it.

In the afternoon, I have a meeting with Gerard Diver, a city councillor and Programme Coordinator of Youth Bank/Impetus, both initiatives for young people. His offices are in the Activity and Reconciliation Centre in St Columb's Park, to where I drive reluctantly, having negotiated several major—almost Celtic-Tiger-like—traffic jams.

Gerry is a legendary figure in L/D. Working for a strictly non-partisan organisation, he nevertheless professes admiration for John Hume. 'I am a nationalist politician living in the midst of a Protestant community,' he says. 'Some people are eager to put me in a box because of my political views, but I try to keep my work separate from politics by not treating it in a partisan way.'

On the very day he was elected to the city council in 2001, a fire bomb was planted under his door. Miraculously, neither Gerry nor his family members were hurt.

He tells me that yesterday's 'controlled' explosion, the first major blast in L/D since 1985, brought him back to the past. 'I had this semi-forgotten feeling of panic, and my immediate concern was whether somebody I knew was there...It used to be like that every day here in the 1970s. Now we are enjoying what we call a "low level of violence".'

The project he is in charge of involves bringing together children from both sides of the Catholic/Protestant divide. As he explains, 'Derry is very polarised. If you want to get a true story, you have to read both Nationalist and Loyalist newspapers. Most people from the city's almost exclusively Catholic west would not meet anyone Protestant until the age of 16. Even school uniforms are an issue. Students from Protestant schools would never venture to the predominantly Catholic city centre in their uniforms. Some of them say they were spat at when wearing them.

'Our project encourages the two groups to interact. We stage plays on the issues that worry both communities, like sexual health, say. We organise joint conferences and trips, and I have to say that Catholic and Protestant youths get along very well within our framework. We have travelled a long way to achieve this kind of co-operation, which was totally impossible ten to fifteen years ago.'

Gerry's words make a lot of sense: an age-long prejudice in people's minds can only be successfully challenged during their formative years. It takes a good deal of patience and time to see the results, but this is the only option.

Back at the hotel, I look at today's issue of the Catholic *Derry News*. It is full of scorn about the fact that Union Jacks were flying at half-mast, alongside the Irish Tricolour, in L/D as a tribute to Edward Heath, Britain's former Prime Minister, who passed away yesterday, calling it 'a disgrace' and an 'insult' (Heath had been Prime Minister at the time of Bloody Sunday). The horrible sectarian games continue...

This evening, I pop in for a drink to The Talk of the Town—a Republican watering hole, where I chat with a guy called Seán. He assures me that until recently I wouldn't have been allowed inside this pub unless I made a 'Republican sign' on entering. He doesn't specify which sign I'd have to make.

'It's all very different now,' he says. 'Even five years ago people used to walk the city streets with their heads down. Not any more...'

Maybe the efforts of Gerry and his colleagues are bearing fruit, after all?

By his third pint of Guinness, however, Seán's optimism seems to be running out. He tells me about a ride he took yesterday in a cab in the aftermath of the 'controlled explosion'. When the driver was stopped by a policeman on patrol, the following dialogue took place:

> Driver: 'We're in a hurry.'
> Policeman: 'You can thank the IRA for the delays.'
> Driver: 'It wasn't the IRA. The IRA would have done it properly, unlike you guys in the RUC.'
> Policeman: 'We are no longer the RUC. We are the PSNI!'
> Driver: 'Listen, I have a mongrel dog. I can, of course, call it an Alsatian, but it will still remain a mongrel!'

According to Seán, the policeman swallowed the abuse and walked away.

We leave the pub together and shake hands before heading in opposite directions. I look back at Seán's receding figure. He is walking away unsteadily, trying hard to keep his head up.

Day Five

# London/Derry–Portrush

*'Londonderry…stands on an oval-shaped hill; the buildings rising tier above tier in a very picturesque manner…On the opposite bank of the Foyle is a large suburb, called the Waterside, which is connected with the city by a magnificent wooden bridge 1068 ft long. Some of the streets are very steep, and, though lighted with gas, so few of them have an elegant appearance, that Londonderry may emphatically be called a town of back streets.'*
(THE 'IMPERIAL GAZETTEER', W.G. BLACKIE, ED., 1855)

I am having morning coffee with Tommy Carlin, my tour guide for the day, in the lobby of my hotel. Tommy's mission is to show me L/D, where he has spent all his life, but before we start I ask him how come the city's long-suffering centre looks so architecturally graceful and harmonious? My initial thought is that —in the tradition of Baedeker and Murray, who tried to stay away from politics, and similar to my guide in Enniskillen who staunchly refused to talk about the Troubles—Mr Carlin, being a tour guide himself, is going to be reluctant to come up with an honest answer, but he proves me wrong.

'It is the bombs that have helped to make Derry lovely,' says he. 'By 1975, three-fourths of all the buildings inside the Walls were destroyed—either bombed or fire-bombed, and it looked as if nothing could save the city. In 1978, two bishops—Catholic and Protestant—sat together and formed an organisation called the Inner-City Trust, whose main task was to repair damages to the buildings while the bombing campaign was still on…'

'But what was the point of the repairs when the same building could be bombed again the following day—like often happened in Belfast?' I ask him, resorting to my favourite interviewing technique—playing devil's advocate.

'For the repairs, they recruited young people from both communities, having taught them some building skills. The point was: if you build something yourself, you are unlikely to destroy it. It worked. And not just for the structures ruined during the Troubles. The old fort that used to house an ammunition depot blew up in the early 19th century, and the youngsters of the 1980s built an exact replica of it. It is still there, round the corner from your hotel which is, incidentally, the first new hotel built inside the Walls for two hundred and fifty years.'

'When did the bombings come to a stop?' I ask, trying to forget the other day's explosion, even if 'controlled'.

'The last significant bomb went off in 1985—two civilians were killed…that was the point when locals, particularly, women, had had enough. They approached the IRA and persuaded them to stop. No terrorist organisation can exist without the support of the population. Yet Bloody Sunday is well remembered. I bet very few local people will be wearing poppies in their lapels here today…'

It is Remembrance Day, of course. 'The sectarian problem is still here, of course,' he continues, 'but it is no longer as acute as in Belfast. There is a positive feel now, and our biggest problem is unemployment…'

Our tour of London/Derry can be summed up as ticking off the landmarks of the Troubles. Murray's *Handbook* in my hand (a *handy* book indeed!), I try to pinpoint some sights, mentioned by Murray, while Tommy supplies his laconic comments. It all looks like a bizarre touring dialogue, with the interlocutors separated by ninety-three turbulent years:

> MURRAY: 'We reach the *Royal Bastion*, modified by the erection of Walker's Monument, 90 ft. high, a fluted Doric column, surmounted by a statue of the hero (Rev. George Walker,[21] killed in the end of the city's siege by King James's Irish army in 1690—VV) with Bible in hand. It was completed in 1828, and was 2 years in the process of erection.

It contains the names of other leaders and a spirited inscription.[22]

TOMMY: 'The Monument was blown up by the IRA in 1973...' One of the images on the Monument is that of the treacherous Governor Lundy.

MURRAY: 'Lundy...made many attempts to give up the city into the enemy's hands, and only succeeded in evading the rage of the garrison by escaping in the guise of a porter.'

TOMMY: 'The image of Lundy gets burned every year...'

MURRAY: 'Ship Quay presents a large open space, and contains some fine buildings.'

TOMMY: 'Four car bombs exploded in Ship Quay in 1970.'

MURRAY: 'Castle Gate and Castle Street...have undergone but little change since their original construction...'

TOMMY: 'Castle Street was the scene of two car-bomb explosions...'

These cross-references by my two esteemed guides make me feel like a true time traveller. No wonder that at some point I mistake a medieval grate for a security fence. London/Derry appeals to me more and more. It is no longer the town of 'back streets', as Blackie put it, but a city of 'elegant' side lanes. Looking at once-ravaged buildings, lovingly restored using old photos, I can't help admiring London/Derry's resilience and stamina. True, its face is heavily pockmarked by years of barbaric and pointless mutilation, but it is still truly beautiful—in the way only scarred faces can be. Stroke City teaches you the lesson of optimism and survival, and I feel sad at having to leave it soon.

Before driving on, I check my e-mails in the city's busy public library. While doing so, I watch my fellow web-surfers out of the corner of my eye. Open, simple faces. There's no way I can tell which is a Protestant and which a Catholic. If the two communities mix freely somewhere, it must be here—in the Internet room of the public library. Cyberspace is a great leveller, incompatible with feuds and bombs.

I Google 'Londonderry' and find a fascinating news story: Derry's old cannons (culverins, falconets, minions etc.) from the time of the great siege are being restored and will soon be put back onto the bastions—'for tourism purposes only'. I hope these ancient cannons will serve as silent guardians of peace in the long-suffering Stroke City, no matter by which of its two current names it will continue to be known.

———

*'Thus one comes to Portrush, of which one scarcely knows which is the more famous—the Golf links or the Blue Pool. When both are so good, there is no need to quarrel over pre-eminence.'*
('ULSTER HOLIDAY GUIDE', 1949)

*'Portrush\* (pop. 1941) is every year becoming a more favourite spot, both from its attractions as a marine residence and its proximity to the Causeway. The sea rolls in here in full strength and splendour, and the air is singularly bracing and invigorating.'*
('A HANDBOOK FOR TRAVELLERS IN IRELAND',
MURRAY, 1912)

*'Portrush—a small seaport…It is much resorted to for sea-bathing; has an extensive soap and candle manufactory, a well-protected harbour, and an active intercourse with Londonderry, Liverpool and Glasgow. Pop. above 800.'*
(THE 'IMPERIAL GAZETTEER', W.G. BLACKIE, ED., 1855)

'There is no need to rush, when you drive to Portrush,' I keep humming, as I make my way to the next stop on my skeleton route, Portrush, Co. Antrim.

The main points of time-travelling interest in the town are neither the sea nor the golf links about which the Ulster Guide was so enthusiastic, but the railway station (if it is still there) and the establishment that Murray called simply 'Hotel'. The latter, in particular, receives such an uncharacteristically glorious description in the *Handbook* that it makes me wonder whether a generous commission could have changed hands:

> 'The old Northern Counties Railway did much to develop the place. The Railway Station is a fine new structure, with clock-tower, refreshment rooms, and tea pavilion, while their Hotel, erected at a cost of 40,000 pounds, and now the property of the Midland Railway Company (Eng.), is a first-class establishment; it is thoroughly equipped, has a fine system of baths, and offers every convenience for the comfort of visitors.'

And, if this eulogy (by Murray's standards) was not enough, in the 'Index-Directory' section of the handbook, the Hotel ('first class, bath-house on beach') tops the list of recommended places to stay in Portrush. In Murray's time, when 'class' meant much more than it does now, the word 'first-class', used twice in the description of the Hotel, was not just a rating one step above 'second-class' dinginess. It meant 'more than excellent', even, 'perfect'.

What happened to the hotel in the years following Murray's visit is clouded in mystery. The last reference to it I was able to find is in the ads section of my 1949 *Ulster Holiday Guide*. Among other features, it mentions the 'Finest Ballroom in Ireland'. My 2004 *Rough Guide to Ireland* stays mum about the hotel.

Forecasts of stormy weather seem to be coming true. As I approach Portrush along the coast, my car is shaking under powerful gusts of wind. The town itself appears frozen—both in the wind and in time.

Any sea resort in winter is full of sadness and nostalgia. Portrush is also full of wind. Everything in the deserted town is rustling, fluttering and vibrating. Yet nothing rushes in Portrush (if not to count a lonely beach jogger in a woollen cap) on this sunny December afternoon. Nothing, except for the wind…

The wind whistles through empty amusement arcades, rattles shop signs (the only outlet that is open is 'Mr Chips'). And the air is certainly crisp and 'bracing' (*pace* Murray).

Portrush is pretty (in a slightly tacky, provincial-lass sort of way), yet clinically dead. No one seems to be tempted by the High Street clothes store's generous offer of a 'Free shirt with every tie purchase'. At least, it is not the 'Three shoes for the price of two' deal that I once saw advertised in Tasmania.

I hide from the wind inside the town library and find it full of intelligent-looking kids playing computer games.

In the Portrush entry of his 1912 *Handbook*, Murray mentions 'a good Town Hall, with reading rooms for the use of the public for nominal rate.' I pay £1.50 for thirty minutes on the Internet (not very 'nominal') and, on top of that, fill in a lengthy questionnaire which looks more like a job application form:

'Which books have you been looking for in the library?'—I write: N/A—Internet.

'Did you find the book you were looking for?'—N/A again. Then comes the 'equal opportunities' (for choosing a book?) section, where I am asked to state my ethnic origins, age, religion etc. I write 'N/A' in all the spaces (including 'age') and recall how, years ago, when asked to fill a similar form at a Soviet library, I put down 'Scythian' in the 'nationality' column, and a friend of mine registered his as 'Etruscan'. I doubt very much that Murray had to fill in the 'equal opportunities' form while using the Town Hall 'reading rooms' ninety-three years ago…

The Comfort Hotel where I am staying is precariously close to the roaring sea. It is a standard family establishment, with some pretty stringent regulations, e.g. 'No alcohol is permitted in guest bedrooms from carry-outs or off-licences' (according to a 'guest information' leaflet that I pick up at reception). I wonder whether such anti-alcoholic zeal is the sad (and boring) legacy of two 'temperance hotels' that used to be in Portrush in 1912, according to my omniscient Murray.

The hotel's principal attraction is a young Eastern European female receptionist, who is extremely nice and helpful (and good-looking too!). She keeps obsessively calling me 'Sir', runs upstairs to check the heating in my room and smiles beguilingly at the sight of me. At one point I even start entertaining a delusion that she fancies me (this is what staying at a family hotel on one's own can lead to). I try to sort out in my head which country she may be from. Definitely, not Russia or the former USSR—much too nice and courteous. Poland? She doesn't look Polish. Finally, I ask her, and the mystery is solved: from the Czech Republic, of course. I should have guessed! My own and other people's (mostly males') experience shows that Czech women are naturally the nicest in Europe. In *Czechs and Balances*, a witty and clever book by Benjamin Kuras, a London-based modern Czech writer, he explains why:

> '...let's face it, boys. Where else do you find a beautifully feminine, gentle, sexy and caring female with a university degree who takes you lovingly into her home, gives you breakfast in bed, irons your shirts, goes off to work smartly dressed, comes home to you cheerful and unaffected by stress, cooks you dinner, massages you from head to toe, bonks you blind, blows you back for another round when you thought you were finished for a week, does not get tired, does not fake orgasm, keeps telling you how wonderful you are, and does not want to change you—and manages to be all that on an average income of 200 dollars a month?'

In the absence of sleeping pills and due to the ban on other (more natural) sleep-inducing substances (see above), I use my 1949 *Ulster Holiday Guide* as a nightcap. In its habitually ecstatic chapter on Portrush, it quotes a 1761 advertisement for a local hotel that I find rather charming:

> 'At the house commonly called Bushfoot, where John Dunkins, Esq, usually lived, there will be lodgings kept for bathers or those who have in mind to drink the salt water (a popular medically approved panacea in the 18th and 19th centuries—vv), by Edward Fayth. Any gentlemen or ladies who will favour him with their company may depend on clean and orderly attendance with a reasonable charge, his wife being an Englishwoman. Also he will keep a cakehouse for those who pass or repass to the Giant's Causeway with cider and mead, and a fish dinner will be dressed for any that inclines to dine, and those who come to bathe are

desired to give a week's warning to your most obedient
humble servant, Edward Fayth. N.B.—He intends keeping
of goats.'

Appeased by the visions of the smiling Czech receptionist and of
goats 'bathing' in the sea, I soon go to sleep.

## Day Six
# Portrush–Ballycastle

Having a solitary breakfast at the hotel restaurant where I am surrounded by screaming babies and their subdued (after a sleepless night?) parents, I look through the morning papers, all carrying photos of the storm in Ballycastle—my next destination. Outside the restaurant window, the wind is tossing about torn newspapers and plastic bags. It is also raining, so 'bathing', even if not in the sea, is not entirely out of the question.

My umbrella cracks under the wind the moment I step outside to start my search for the railway station and the Hotel. The next powerful gust breaks it in two, and I deposit it into the nearest rubbish bin, already full of wind-broken umbrellas.

Across the road is a small surfing shop. Shall I buy myself a wetsuit? It would do fine in this weather. The memory of my only attempt at surfing in Cornwall, however, is too fresh.

The wetsuit I was given on the beach, after a twenty-minute crash course for beginners, was wet and extremely tight. It took me forty minutes to put it on. I was fumbling with it (or rather with my own body, that staunchly refused to be squeezed into the suit) while other people from our party were already riding the waves for all they were worth (frankly, they were not worth a huge deal). When I finally succeeded, I realised with awe that I had mistakenly put my hands through the trouser legs, and my legs—through the sleeves. That was why it had taken such an effort! It took me another forty minutes to liberate myself from the slimy suit's rubbery embrace, and by then the surfing time allocated for our group had run out...

Instead, I take shelter in a café called The Scullery. 'If you want to smoke, you can do so upstairs, although it is a no-smoking building,' a woman behind the counter whispers conspiratorially, and I am again reminded that it is the North, not the South.

The rain and wind soon die down, and I resume my quest. Finding the station proves harder than I thought, and before I finally get steered in the right direction, I have to endure several pointless dialogues with rare pedestrians—all involving the same scenario:

'How do I get to the railway station?'

'Well, you can try to go that way…'

'Is the station there?'

'No.'

I walk past the Murray-recommended Eglinton Hotel. It is closed, and green stucco is peeling off its tattered façade. Above the permanently locked door, there hangs an angry sign: TOILETS FOR CUSTOMER USE ONLY. Inside, a young female receptionist is sitting behind a computer. I knock on the window trying to attract her attention, but she pretends not to notice me. She is Polish perhaps. Definitely not Czech. I am pleased I am not staying there.

Billboards on many street corners announce, ALCOHOL-FREE AREA (one hangs straight across the road from an off-licence). Another legacy of the bygone temperance days? Or else, there must be a serious drinking problem in Portrush.

In the harbour area, many buildings are enclosed with high fences and barbed wire, making this peaceful seaside town look like a fortress.

I finally stumble upon a modern concrete cubicle, the new railway station. The only platform is deserted and resembles a long, rain-polished conference table. The station master directs me to the old station building next door. 'It now houses shops and bars. Only the old station clock is left,' he adds with a yawn.

Only one outlet is open in the imitation Tudor building that was Murray's 'fine new structure', the Station Bar. It is decorated with a poster asserting that it is 'The busiest little bar in town.'

The 'busiest little bar in town' is empty, and it is almost painful to think of the ambience in Portrush's less busy watering holes. Inside, I find a small collection of the usual railway paraphernalia:

a map of the Midland Railway, an old conductor's punch, several model steam engines. The golden age of the railways is obviously over in Portrush.

As for the 'first-class' and 'excellent' hotel, it is impossible to find: no one seems to have a clue as to its existence. I am about to give up, when, browsing through old local-history folios in a small second-hand bookshop, I find a photo of the grand Portrush establishment and—from the buildings around it that seem familiar—manage to pinpoint its exact location.

What a blow! When I get there, I find a huge gap is in its place. And the space is fresh, for immobile bulldozers and excavators are still on the site. The 'thoroughly equipped' hotel must have been demolished very recently. Most likely, to clear space for yet another amusement arcade. I wish they had pulled down the Eglinton Hotel instead…

Unlike the main building, the bath-house of the hotel has survived and now houses the Portrush Countryside Centre. Whatever they may be up to in the Centre these days, I am sure it has little to do with 'bathing' and/or drinking of 'salt water'.

Before leaving Portrush, I briefly consider abandoning my car here and, following Murray's advice, visiting the Giant's Causeway by 'electric tramway—the first if its kind in the United Kingdom.' Describing this technological miracle in the section 'Portrush to the Giant's Causeway by electric tramway', Murray—again, uncharacteristically—delves into technological detail: 'The electricity is generated by machinery worked by the water of the Bush River, 1 m. from the town of Bushmills. The current is conveyed along the rail to the cars by means of brushes which rub against its surface. Tickets of admission to view the machinery at Bushmills are given by the manager at Portrush.' And so on. Having read the last sentence of the section, I change my mind: 'Owing to the accidents which have occurred on the line from the electric current, a change has been called for by the Board of Trade.' And, in any case, the 'electric tramway' is no more, which leaves me with only one conventional means of travel—by road, or as Murray would put it, 'by motor-car'.

While loading my bags into the boot, I am approached by a

couple of locals, who say hello and apologise for the weather...I
grant them an apology and start the engine.

On my way to the Causeway, I detour to Mussenden Temple, the
eccentric creation of the no-less-eccentric Bishop Francis Hervey,
about whom I heard a lot from my London/Derry guide Tommy
Carlin during our city walk. The Church of Ireland Bishop of
Derry between 1768 and 1803, he was prone to travelling and used
to spend most of his summers in Italy, mostly in Rome, where he
was once (in 1803) discovered *in flagrante* with two 'ladies of ill
repute' (he was 'entertaining' them inside his carriage, parked in
the very centre of the Italian capital!) and was sentenced to three
months imprisonment.

On his way back to Britain after serving his stretch, Hervey was
caught in a snowstorm in the Alps and sought shelter in a roadside
tavern. The innkeeper refused to let the 'heretic' inside and put
him up in the stable, where he died of gout by morning. Hervey's
adventures did not end with his death: Italian boatmen would not
carry the body of the 'heretic Bishop', so his friends packed
Hervey's remains in a wooden box, labelled 'Marble Statue' (!) and
filled with ice and had them ferried back to his home in England.

What a life! Or rather: what a death!

A great admirer and a connoisseur of Italian architecture,
Bishop Hervey built the first proper bridge across the River Foyle
in Derry. The structure was erected not so much for the benefit of
the city's residents as to facilitate the Bishop's own trips to see Lady
Frideswide Mussenden, his cousin and lover, who lived thirty miles
north at Downhill. There, he built a large house and next to it, on
the edge of a cliff overlooking the Atlantic, an exact replica of the
Temple of Vespa in Rome—the city that he adored. Unfortunately,
Lady Mussenden herself died before its completion. She was only
twenty-two. After her death, the grieving Hervey dedicated the
Temple to her memory and, having turned it into his library, often
came there to look at the sea and to read. Later, with an astonishing
lack of prejudice, the outlandish Protestant Bishop allowed a
weekly Catholic mass to be celebrated in the Temple, for the village
of Downhill had no church then—an act of amazing courage not
just for those times but for modern Northern Ireland too.

Now you will understand why I couldn't miss this place.

I am standing in the rain among the ruins of the Bishop's house, next to the meaningless sign which declares that the HOUSE IS ALWAYS OPEN. How can one 'close' a ruin, with neither ceilings nor doors? Not a single living being is in sight, yet the place feels alive. Why? Partly because of the tireless wind whooshing through the mouldering stones and the heavy rolling of the troubled sea down the hill. And partly, because of the presence of the eccentric Bishop, who had the misfortune to be born well ahead of his time. The Temple itself is about half a mile away across muddy fields. I venture towards it, but soon retreat, driven back by the wind and rain. Instead, I try to visualise the Bishop trudging to his sanctuary through the mud, his black robes flying in the wind.

I wander on the grounds of the former Bishop's house—in search of that one significant detail that would bring Hervey's restless spirit back to life. And I find it. A shabby stone hut with a cellar, next to a semi-ruined dovecote. A weather-beaten sign above the gaping cellar entrance informs me that it used to be an ice house, an 18th-century version of a fridge, where precious ice used to be kept. It curiously echoes Hervey's final journey home— packed in ice and labelled as a 'statue'! I can't say that the sight of the ice-house has brought him back to life (that would be an unfortunate metaphor), yet it has definitely provided a direct link to the tragicomic circumstances of his death two hundred years ago.

I thank the Bishop for my successful spiritualism session and get back into the car, parked near-by and rocked from side to side by the unceasing wind.

As I drive along towards the Giant's Causeway, a World Heritage Site, as asserted by numerous roadside signs, large flakes of white foam from the turbulent sea—about fifty yards away—keep falling on the windscreen like snow.

Having passed by the spectacular ruins of Dunluce Castle, I soon arrive at Bushmills, the town that boasts the world's oldest whisky distillery. Or rather—whisk*e*y distillery, to stick to the Irish (and American) spelling of this gaelic word.

Lots of cars are parked at the distillery's entrance. No wonder: in Russia we used to call such rainy and windy days, 'vodka weather'; in this case, it is certainly 'whiskey weather': there's nothing much else to do but visit a distillery, with a warming whiskey-tasting session at the end. To me, however, the distillery is also a test of my recent decision to go on the wagon.

My innate ability to attract trouble and/or change manifests itself again. I learn that Bushmills has just been bought by Diageo, the world's largest multinational drinks cartel, and because of this —as with any major corporate takeover—the staff appear confused and uncertain. They can't even give me a promotional brochure, because—as the lady at the reception explains, their old pamphlets are no longer relevant, and the new, Diageo, ones have not been printed yet.

I go on a tour of this 'distillery on the periphery of Europe', as it is put in the promotional video reel, in the company of some elderly, yet joyful and noisy, American tourists (aren't all American tourists elderly and noisy?) during which I learn several useful facts:

1. The difference between the making of Scotch and Irish whiskey (or shall I say 'between making whisky and whiskey') is that to make the former barley is dried over peat fire, and for the latter, barley is dried by clean hot air.

2. In Ireland, they distil whiskey three times ('triple distillation'), in Scotland—twice, and in America—once.

3. The whiskey lost to evaporation is called 'Angel's share' (I rather like this term).

4. Before being filled with whiskey, empty bottles are rinsed with…whiskey (I am not sure whether this procedure is endemically Irish).

Having successfully avoided the tasting, I drive on.

———

*'Ballycastle…consists of one principal and several smaller streets; houses well built, chiefly of sandstone; supply of water ample.'*
(THE 'IMPERIAL GAZETTEER', W.G. BLACKIE, ED., 1855)

*'Ballycastle is famous as a tennis centre...It has good
golf links, bathing, boating and fishing—and life has
few more pleasant things to offer than a day along the
Cary or the Shesk rivers with or without a rod.'*
('ULSTER HOLIDAY GUIDE', 1949)

The first thing that strikes me in Ballycastle is the number of ice-cream shops around the Marina. On a windy winter evening, they do not appear particularly tempting.

In the lobby of my Murray-recommended Marine Hotel on the seafront (or rather its brand-new namesake that has replaced the original), I pick up a leaflet advertising 'The Humour of the Troubles'—'playwright Martin Lynch's hilarious new one-man show rampaging through the funny side of Belfast life during the Troubles', due to start in half an hour. What a coincidence! I am due in Belfast the day after next, and this sounds like a great introduction to the city.

The show takes place in the drab modern Sheksburn House that looks like a typical 1970s' town hall from the outside. From the inside, it turns out to be exactly that—the town hall.

There's a small crowd at reception, yet no one seems to be buying tickets to the show priced at £8 each. Instead, the receptionist is handing out some printed 'invitations'. This reminds me of Ilf and Petrov, who once wrote about getting into a popular Moscow theatre in the 1920s: 'Only courting couples and wealthy heirs go to the box-office. The other citizens (they make up the majority, you may observe) go straight to the manager...' Neither a part of a courting couple, nor anyone's wealthy (or poor) heir, I decide to pay for my ticket: Martin Lynch has to earn a living too.

Both the invited non-paying spectators and the very few paying ones are offered red or white wine in plastic cups that they are encouraged to take to the auditorium. I refuse the wine and opt for a cup of orange juice. A man next to me is hastily mixing his red wine with...orange juice (an Irish cocktail?) which reminds me of a London neighbour of mine, who used to mix vodka with milk. The scene also conjures up uneasy memories of a wine-tasting I attended in Norway, when some tasters poured all their wines into one large beer glass and downed the lot in one go, whereas others dipped bread into their glasses and mopped it up like a soup. One guy (not me) was drinking out of a spittoon bucket...

As I witnessed the scene here, I felt sorry for Martin Lynch. Once, a reading at Hay-on-Wye Literary Festival, to publicise my book about the drinking cultures of Eastern Europe, each member of the audience was supplied with a plastic cup, filled with vodka. It was one of the most difficult talks in my memory: few things are as hard as addressing an audience of two hundred tipsy people... Unless you are a bit tipsy yourself, of course (which I wasn't).

The show starts twenty minutes late, and I wonder whether it is because Martin Lynch needs time to achieve the same state of inebriation as his audience. When he appears on stage, however, he looks Hemingway-like, yet perfectly sober, though the moment he begins speaking with a thick Belfast accent I start wishing he were not, for I can hardly understand a word. Had his speech been a little slurred—and therefore not so fast, I might have grasped more.

As it is, I can only decipher some snippets. The rest of the audience, however, doesn't seem to have a problem with his accent and keeps giggling into their plastic cups. I should have probably had some of the 'Irish cocktail', too.

Martin, who had lived through the Troubles, shares his experiences with the audience. Among other things (that I fail to understand), he talks about his Belfast mate called Frantsie (or 'Fatsie'—I can't be sure), who 'once applied for a BBC job, but didn't get it because he was a Catholic'. According to Martin, when Frantsie had three pints of Guinness in him, he said everything twice. Once ordered by a British officer to identify himself, he said; 'It's me! It's me!'

I write down certain expressions that I do manage to comprehend. When I re-read them later, in the discomfort of my hotel room (blasted by loud music from the restaurant until 1 a.m.), I realise that they draw a gruesome picture of life in Belfast during the Troubles:

When the Troubles began in 1969, it changed people's lives. People retreated to sectarian ghettoes. They built barricades to protect themselves. One man went to work with his whole family in tow for he was afraid to leave anyone at home. At the time, Martin lived in Turf Lodge—the 'safest' Catholic part of Belfast, with no Protestants around. They formed the Turf Lodge Citizens' Defence Committee. Black taxis replaced the buses that were systematically bombed. The fare was half that of a bus. Before the Troubles, Belfast had only twenty black cabs, and during the Troubles, there were thousands of them, each packed full.

The atmosphere was one of fear and intimidation. British patrol helicopters were constantly hovering above their heads and the British Army searched the city district by district, house by house, blocking out whole areas. People were routinely arrested for looking like Gerry Adams, and Martin himself was briefly incarcerated in Castlereagh (the high-security police detention centre in east Belfast). 'Rotten food, green eggs—I still ate everything…'

Despite Martin's horrifying portrayal of Troubles-torn Belfast, I walk back to my hotel exhilarated. The very fact that people can now see humour in the Troubles is reassuring.

'Laughing, mankind says goodbye to its past,' wrote Polish satirist Stanislaw Jerzy Lec.

Day Seven

# Rathlin Island– Carnlough

*'Rathlin, or Raghery Island, the Rikina of Ptolemy, is of considerable extent, measuring from E. to W. about 6m, of the shape of a finger, bent at right angles (or, as Sir W. Petty quaintly describes it, of an " Irish stockinge, the toe of which pointeth to the main lande")...The population is about 350; the inhabitants are a simple quiet race, who chiefly gain their subsistence by fishing, gathering kelp, and growing barley.'*
('A HANDBOOK FOR TRAVELLERS IN IRELAND', MURRAY, 1912)

*'Out at sea is Rathlin, where Robert Bruce took refuge...and no doubt Rathlin still shelters descendants of the spider, which taught him to "try, try again".'*
('ULSTER HOLIDAY GUIDE', 1949)

A handful of sleepy morning commuters and a black retriever dog are the only passengers on the tiny Caledonian MacBrayne ferry called *Canna*, taking me to Rathlin— Northern Ireland's only populated off-shore island, six miles across the sea from Ballycastle.

One young man's luggage consists of several dozen toilet rolls and a baby car seat—a load that makes him look like a Soviet train passenger returning from a shopping trip to Moscow (toilet paper was always in short supply in the USSR, and triumphant pedestrians carrying dozens of toilet rolls on crude ropes, wound around their bodies like bands of machine-gun bullets, was a common sight on Moscow streets). Supplies must be not that brilliant on the island…

'Listen carefully to the safety announcement,' crackles the ferry's intercom, yet no announcement is forthcoming.

I come out onto the deck, from where I can see the whole of Ballycastle harbour, enclosed by a fence with barbed wire on top—a detail I was unable to spot from the shore. This makes me wonder whether I am going to find any barbed wire on Rathlin. From my printed travel companions (old and modern guide-books), I know that the island's population has been going down steadily—from 753 in 1855 (Blackie), 350 in 1912 (Murray) to 'around seventy' now (Caledonian MacBrayne 'Sail Away to Rathlin Island' brochure). Such steady decrease is due not just to 'traditional' Irish reasons: poverty and the Famine (in fact, during the Great Famine, the islanders may have fared better than most, with the abundant harvest from the sea around them)—but also due to centuries of ravaging clashes over the island between the English and the Scots.

There is one vehicle travelling on the ferry's car deck—an old battered jalopy without number plates. The skipper tells me that cars on the island are only allowed by special permission and can only be driven by islanders themselves. I wonder who may need a car on six-mile-long and one-mile wide Rathlin? Is it, like Sherkin Island with its abundance of cars to travel three miles, just a reflection of a new, Celtic-Tiger-inspired, reluctance to walk or cycle that I have observed all over Ireland, particularly in the South?

The small ferry is rocking violently, and I get worried that the car will end up overboard. Looking at it makes me dizzy: I must be experiencing the onset of sea-sickness. Luckily, there's not enough time for it to get worse, for one of Rathlin's lighthouses is already coming into view.

A red Royal Mail van is waiting for the ferry on the pier. The few passengers disembark and walk or drive away. Completely alone, I walk along the shore, past a children's playground under the sign:

ADULTS ARE NOT WELCOME UNLESS ACCOMPANIED BY A RESPONSIBLE CHILD, and come to the oblong barn-like building that is the Richard Branson Activity Centre. Branson crash-landed on the island (or rather *splash-landed* in the sea few miles away from it) in his hot-air balloon thirty-one hours into his trans-Atlantic flight in July 1987. The islanders ferreted him out. Several months later, Branson returned to Rathlin to donate £25,000 to the restoration of the Manor House—the same building that now houses his own Activity Centre. I wonder what sort of 'activities' the Centre is involved in, but there's no one inside (or around) to ask.

Richard Branson was not the only famous island's visitor to drop by (in his case—almost literally). In 1898, Guglielmo Marconi and his assistants, Kemp and Glanville, set up the world's first radio transmission across the water from Rathlin to Ballycastle. The ghost of Marconi, it seems, accompanies me on my Ireland journeys, almost Murray-like.

I pass by the island's only red phone box. As a mobile-phone *refusnik*, I find it hard not to use a public phone (there are not many of them left—in Ireland or in Britain) whenever I see one. I drop a coin into the slot, and—to my amazement (I am always surprised by a public phone that actually works) hear a loud buzzer. I call my best friend Sasha, who lives near Bratislava in Slovakia, and tell him I am calling from a tiny island in the Atlantic. There's nothing much else to say, so I put the phone down, but hearing my friend's voice—as clearly as if he were standing in the booth next to me—makes me feel less lonely.

I soon wander into Craig's Bar, on the sea front. The only other patron is a grey-haired old woman silently sipping coffee and periodically nodding off in her chair. A podgy ruddy-faced man, an archetypal little-island pub owner, is behind the bar. I think this must be Craig himself, but the publican says his name is Bertie.

I introduce myself and ask him to tell me about life on Rathlin. Bertie grabs this unexpected opportunity to talk.

'I grew up on the island. When I went to school in the 1960s, there were two hundred and fifty people here. Lighthouses then had to be manned, you see...We had fifty or sixty pupils at the school, and now they have only three...'

With a distinct Northern accent that I find a bit more comprehensible after Martin Lynch's one-man show, he recalls Rathlin's biggest moment of fame—Richard Branson's splash-landing.

'After rescuing Richard, boys from the island went in a boat to pick up the balloon, but failed—it was too big, massive—like an elephant...'

I ask him whether Rathlin was ever affected by the Troubles.

'Nah. We're too far away. The closest the Troubles came to us were a couple of little bombs in Ballycastle—that was all...'

The pub is getting busier: three sullen men with beefy wind-beaten faces come in and install themselves at the bar. It is obvious they will not be leaving soon. The coffee-sipping granny is sleepily pulling the handle of a fruit machine in the corner.

On the walls are old photos of island life and maritime paraphernalia: bits and pieces from the ships that crashed near Rathlin. Also—the stuffed head of a bull. The head looks ragged, with tufts of brown hair peeling off here and there. He doesn't look very happy.

'Yeah, it does look a bit tired,' Bertie cackles. He has just finished serving the grim newcomers. 'The Lord of the Manor once got cross with the bull and shot him. Then he repented and had his head stuffed...'

A poster for Famous Grouse whisky hangs on the wall next to one for Guinness, and the TV is tuned to BBC1, which is broadcasting the Remembrance Day parade from Westminster.

Outside stands a marble sculpture of a chair facing the sea. THE WRITER'S CHAIR. UNDERTAKEN BY BALLYCASTLE WRITERS, says the faded plate on it that also carries a poem by Seamus Heaney:


> 'When you sat
> Far-eyed and cold
> In that basalt throne,
> The small of your back
> Made very solid sense.'

The poem brings about a pang of remorse at wandering on a wind-swept little island, instead of sitting in my 'writer's chair' and penning a great Russian (English? Irish? Australian?) novel. Most writers are familiar with this feeling: missing the process of writing when you are not writing and hating it when you are. Just like the proverbial seaman's nostalgia for *terra firma* when at sea, and for the sea when on land.

The more I explore Rathlin, the more I like it. I have a solitary picnic outside Richard Branson's manor house, munching away synchronically with the cows grazing behind barbed wire twenty metres away. It is soothing to realise that, unlike elsewhere in Northern Ireland, the only barbed wire on Rathlin is to stop the cows from escaping their pastures.

The already familiar Royal Mail van pulls over next to me, and the postman peeps out of the window. 'You must be the writer researching a travel book on Ireland,' he smiles. 'Welcome to Rathlin!'

He must have been tipped off by Bertie. Rumours travel fast on the island.

'Do you always work on Sundays?' I ask him

'Unofficially,' he winks and drives away.

Further down the road, I come across a small general store called Island Treasures. Behind the counter is a young woman who was among my fellow passengers on the ferry this morning. She recognises me too. 'You must be the travel writer,' she says, and I am again amazed by the speed of Rathlin's wireless verbal telegraph. The heritage of Marconi?

Her name is Katrina. Born on Rathlin, she now lives in Ballycastle, but comes here daily during the season and on Sundays in winter to run the shop.

The stock of her 'treasures' is small, yet versatile—from socks to picture postcards. There are also British tabloids, which Katrina herself brings from the mainland, and amateur photos of Rathlin (£1 each) which, she assures me, are rather popular with visitors.

Katrina seems to share my love of islands: 'I don't like places where you can't see the sea,' she smiles while wrapping a loaf of bread for a little girl, squeezing coins into her tiny tanned fist.

'There's now only one teacher on Rathlin,' she continues. 'He commutes from the mainland and so does the island's only policeman and the Protestant priest.'

Katrina and her husband left the island several years ago, because he couldn't find a job here, but she always brings her ten-year old son to Rathlin with her. When he is not at school, of course.

Through the shop window, I see a little boy playing with the black retriever from the ferry. After a couple of hours on the island, I can recognise not just people, but animals, too!

The pair is playing next to another shop—a tiny grocery across the road. Its windows are boarded up, and the doors are locked, yet the hand-written sign above the entrance reads OPEN.

'The owner of that shop died last year,' Katrina sighs, 'and her son can't be bothered.'

I ask her about the man who was carrying the toilet rolls onto the ferry. 'He moved here with his girlfriend several years ago. They only recently got married. His wife is an artist, and he works from home too.'

Katrina seems to know everything about the island. In this little world, every minuscule detail suddenly acquires considerable importance, and the mainland, with all its conflicts, worries, troubles and The Troubles, fades away and appears increasingly insignificant. A very calming sensation. Like meditation that becomes life itself.

Before leaving Island's Treasures, I buy a pair of warm woollen socks, perhaps attempting (subconsciously, no doubt) to smuggle out some of the human warmth that I feel so strongly on Rathlin. As on every island that I visit, a fleeting thought of making it my home crosses my mind, but quickly vanishes—like a seagull dashing past the shop's dusty window with its piercing, almost human-like, scream.

As I walk back to the harbour, I am overtaken by a shabby island jalopy without number plates. The toilet-roll carrier from the ferry and his wife are inside. They wave to me like to an old acquaintance.

The last ferry of the day is chugging away from Rathlin as I approach. It turns out she was just changing piers—like a steam engine on a turntable—before mooring again.

This time the *Canna* is full of kids on their way to secondary school in Ballycastle for the start of a new week. Among them is a plump teenage boy on crutches who looks like a smaller copy of Bertie, the publican—most likely, his son (or grandson?).

Katrina is also on board, with her boy and the sad-looking dog. 'He doesn't like the noise of the engine,' she says stroking the retriever gently.

The almost familiar island is receding as the ferry makes her way through the burning sunset. I stand on the deck thinking of the rather clichéd story of Robert the Bruce's short exile on Rathlin. Having been defeated in battle, he (allegedly) fled to the island and hid in a cave where he took to watching a spider trying to climb up his thread. The spider kept falling down, yet persevered in its attempts until finally—on the seventh try—it succeeded. The sight of the stubborn spider (again, allegedly) inspired the beleaguered king 'to try, try and try again'—to the extent that he returned to Scotland and won his next battle with the enemy.

It occurs to me that, naff as it may be, the story serves as a good example of the spirit of Rathlin itself: ravaged, devastated, abandoned by so many islanders, it nevertheless maintains its own slow and laid-back life.

'Faith is the refusal to give up,' this quote from Jonathan Sachs, Britain's Chief Rabbi, hangs above my writing desk. I've been trying to follow it all my life.

Despite the presence of two churches—Protestant and Catholic —on Rathlin, it is 'the refusal to give up' that seems to be the islanders' main faith. This is probably why I feel almost at home here…

I take out my notebook and re-read the notices copied from the island's notice board:

RATHLIN FILM CLUB—EVERY WEDNESDAY.
COTTAGES TO RENT…(I wrote down the phone number—just in case).

And the most evocative one:

HAVE YOUR VHS OR VIDEO TAPES CONVERTED TO DVD. CONTACT DAVE.

No contact details follow…

In the afternoon, I drive through the Glens of Antrim to Carnlough. The one-lane road winds along the coast, and I soon get firmly stuck behind the world's slowest car, the driver of which seems to be enjoying a motorised evening walk. There's ample time to study the mysterious 'R' plate on the mechanical snail's rear window. What can it stand for? 'Retarded'? 'Retentive?' Or—most likely—'Reptilian'!

I finally overtake him precariously, but soon pull over to consult a map. As I am doing so, the ambling motorist chugs past me triumphantly, and I end up stuck behind him again! This time all the way to Carnlough.

————

*'Carnlough* * *(pop. 1056), a pretty and cheerful-looking watering-place, with a fine Strand…It has the recommendations of lovely scenery, smooth beach, and general cleanliness.'*
('A HANDBOOK FOR TRAVELLERS IN IRELAND', MURRAY, 1912)

*'There are few pleasanter places than Carnlough…for the seeker of a quiet holiday, especially to those still given to the use of their legs…'*
('ULSTER HOLIDAY GUIDE', 1949)

My destination in Carnlough is the Murray-recommended Londonderry Arms Hotel—one of the quirkiest in Ireland. It was built in 1848 as a coaching inn by Frances Anne Vane Tempest, Marchioness of Londonderry, and her great-grandson Winston

Churchill inherited it in 1921.

The plunge from the pristine emptiness of Rathlin into the Georgian and early-Victorian splendour of the lavishly decorated hotel lounge makes my head spin. On one of the walls is a mini-display dedicated to the Londonderrys. The couple did a lot for Carnlough, particularly during the Great Famine.

Frances Anne was a lady of exquisite beauty. And this is not hearsay: a copy of her portrait by Sir Thomas Lawrence adorns the lounge. The Russian Emperor Alexander I fell in love with that portrait and sent the Marchioness a set of Siberian amethyst jewellery in the beginning of a long and devoted, yet (allegedly) totally platonic relationship.

Frances Anne's splendour and intelligence caused a good deal of envy among London high-society ladies. In the display, there's an extract from a letter written by Princess Lieven, the wife of the Russian ambassador to London, a former mistress of Metternich (not an exclusive club, that) and a future *saloniste* in Paris. She acerbically described the stunning Marchioness as 'one of the effigies you see in Greek churches, with no colour or shading but loaded with enough jewellery to buy a small German principality.' Bitchiness was obviously alive and well in the first half of the 19th century.

They tell me I am the hotel's only guest tonight. Walking up the grand staircase with my suitcase, I nearly get a scare being suddenly surrounded by dozens of suitcase-dragging strangers all of whom—on closer inspection—turn out to be one and the same person—*moi*, reflected in the hall's countless mirrors.

I begin to understand why members of Victorian nobility were so fascinated with mirrors—to beat the loneliness of their huge and empty mansions.

I am accommodated in the hotel's grandest room—the Churchill Suite, where the great man himself used to stay when visiting his domain. The 'Suite' consists of just one spacious and dimly lit room, crammed with Georgian and Victorian furnishings and knick-knacks to the point that it feels puny.

The 1860s–70s was the time when the living room assumed the function of a museum of *objects d'art*. Here, in the Churchill Suite, I find an impressive array of Bristol candlesticks, Sèvres vases,

Bohemian lustres, bleak mirrors, decorative wall plates and massive clocks (none of which seems to be working). This is very nice, of course, but when I decide to sit down and make some notes, I can't find a place to do so: the massive mahogany dressing table, next to the ornate behemoth of an oak wardrobe with very little space inside, is not suitable, being too high. Numerous minuscule stools on bent wobbly legs are superfluous and useless. They are only strong and large enough to hold a half-empty box of Kleenex tissues (their legs would be bound to break under the load of a full one). I end up kneeling in front of the enormous—not Queen- or King- but Churchill-size!—bed. The scale is similar to the one I once saw in an Italian restaurant in France where pizza portions were graded into: standard-, large-, giant- and 'Pavarotti'-sized.

It is on that gargantuan bed that I have to eat my picnic-style supper (having covered the bed with bath towels first). Churchill would have been distressed by the sight...

This immersion into the Victorian environment, albeit uncomfortable, is useful for my time-travelling purposes. It provides first-hand experience of the Victorian epoch's grandeur and beauty combined with a total lack of practicality. Appearances mattered more than convenience in those days, and Victorians were prepared to suffer for their sake.

The room is also freezing. One smallish antique radiator, assisted by a feeble electric heater in the corner are unable to warm up this high-ceilinged gallery of Victorian furniture and myself, who has become part of this junk for the night, tossing and turning in the Churchill/Pavarotti (Churchillotti?)-size bed until the early hours of the morning.

I know I am alone in the house: the staff have all gone home. The old floorboards squeak, triggering thoughts of ghosts and apparitions (if they do exist, this hotel should be their favourite haunted haunt), and I can almost hear the voices of the hotel's Victorian guests and servants:

'Sir, this room is very clean; the furniture is handsome and new; and there is a fine mirror over the chimney-piece.'

'Is the bed good?'

'The mattresses have just been newly stuffed, and are very soft.'

'How often do you change the sheets?'

'Every fortnight; and your towel will be changed once a week.'

'Does the chimney smoke? We shall soon have winter, and it will be necessary to have a fire. It is beginning to be cold already.'

'It does not smoke at all.'

'Can I have warm water to wash with, when I want it?'

'If you give a trifle to the housemaid, she will wait upon you attentively, and will also clean your shoes and boots.'

'As this is the case, I will take the room for three months...'[23]

I sleep fitfully and dream of Churchill playing chess with Bertie, the Rathlin publican, inside an igloo.

## Day Eight
# Carnlough–Belfast

I wake up shivering and covered in goose pimples. The sea outside the window is covered in goose-pimples too.

It is bitterly cold in the downstairs restaurant, where I eat a solitary breakfast. I ask for a copy of *The Guardian*, and the receptionist brings it to me on a tray in a couple of minutes. She went to a newsagent's across the road to buy it! It does make me feel a bit 'churchillian'. And a bit warmer too...

Having returned to my room, I read the paper on the loo—the ultimate Victorian decadence.

The weather is certainly getting colder, and, before leaving, I ferret out of the suitcase my old anorak with its fake fur collar. My only worry is that its lining is bright orange and I am not sure how safe it will be to wear this colour in Belfast. It looks like—after a week on the road—I have started taking the Mickey out of myself. This is what loneliness may lead to.

As I drive out of Carnlough and see it in broad daylight for the first (and last) time, I can't help noticing how pretty it is: houses of white limestone, crescent-shaped streets. Across the road from a school is a private nursing home of the same architectural design. The symmetry of life. Another Victorian feature?

As I pass under a viaduct, built under the supervision of the compassionate Marquis and his lovely wife, a complete stranger waves goodbye to me...

I drive down the Antrim coast road, originally built as a military road in the 1840s to open up this particularly inaccessible part of the country. Near the southern end, I pass through a place called Ballygalley which echoes Delhi-belly—and reminds me of a particularly nasty stomach bug that I once contracted in India.

In Carrickfergus—a drab suburban town near Belfast—I get out of the car to stretch my legs and wander past endless car parks with no cars and ugly supermarkets without customers. The town's complete lack of grace is particularly striking after last night's and this morning's cool (in the true sense of this word) Victorian experience.

There is nowhere to have lunch: everything in Carrickfergus, including the town itself, is shut. A permanently closed 'More' store with boarded windows in one of the main streets should have been renamed 'No More'...

The only objects in town that move are the Union Jacks flying and fluttering from every roof and lamp post. The passion for British flags seems obsessive here. I should be safe in my orange-lined jacket, after all.

————

'*Belfast, like Britain, can stand up to its enemies and the destruction and disaster.*'
('ULSTER HOLIDAY GUIDE', 1949)

'*The situation of Belfast is well adapted for commercial purposes, and as an industrial centre it ranks first among Irish cities.*'
('A HANDBOOK FOR TRAVELLERS IN IRELAND',
MURRAY, 1912)

A plain WELCOME TO BELFAST road sign makes me instinctively press the brake pedal and slow down. This is because during my first visit to Belfast in 1994—when I was driven from the airport by my host, a young Queens University lecturer in Politics—a metal barrier popped out of the ground in front of our car as were entering the city. The lecturer explained that the barrier was activated by remote control from one of the British Army watch towers in the vicinity to allow them more time to check our car's number plates. There was one more man travelling with us, and my host also said that three men travelling in one vehicle were regarded as highly suspicious in Belfast.

This time, nothing pops out of the ground as I cautiously move towards the Madison Hotel in the city centre. The traffic is dense, yet all the drivers appear relaxed and extremely courteous.

My hotel is on Botanic Avenue, not far from Queen's University, where I stayed last time. Except I can hardly recognise the streets. Eleven years ago, they looked dull, and pedestrians walked with their heads down—like in a Soviet town. Also, there were no ethnic faces in the crowd.

It is very different now. The afternoon throng is colourful and seemingly laid-back—like in any other large British or Irish city. Casually dressed youngsters are sitting at *al fresco* tables outside coffee shops. The on-going Peace Process seems to have changed Belfast (or at least this area of Belfast) for the better.

My hotel has no car park, and I have to look for a home for my car in the back streets off Botanic Avenue. I find a dark and littered little lane, fenced off on both sides. Every square inch of the concrete fences is covered with unintelligible, yet obviously wild and aggressive, graffiti.

'Is it safe to leave the car here overnight?' I ask a woman passer-by.

'I wouldn't recommend it,' she says. 'There's a lot of roughness going on, as you see.' She points at the graffiti. 'It's OK during the day, but not overnight...'

The problem is there's no other place to park for miles around, so—reluctantly—I have to leave the car in Graffiti Lane squeezed between the two desecrated fences.

In the evening, I walk the streets of the University quarter—all lively and upmarket. Numerous pubs and bars are full of friendly and peaceful people. I remember my last visit, when I was having an evening drink with the BBC Northern Ireland correspondent in one of these pubs, and a man was shot dead in the pub next door.

Photos of houses priced at over a half a million pounds are displayed in the windows of real-estate agents. Belfast is definitely on the up.

A well-dressed young man (probably a student) is begging half-heartedly in front of a Centra shop on Botanic Avenue—a habitual Dublin sight (In Dublin city centre, I was once approached by a smartly dressed man who asked me to spare him 'eleven euro for a cappuccino'. And a woman from the corner of Pearse Street and Westland Row would yap-yap on her swish mobile phone in the intervals between pleadings for money).

The Irish, it seems, have no qualms about street begging.

I pop into the Mogul Indian restaurant and buy what turns out to be my worst ever Indian take-away—another similarity to Dublin, where Indian (and most other) restaurants are notoriously unremarkable and remarkably pricey.

On the evening TV news there's a report of a male body found in a Belfast house stating that a sectarian motive behind the murder has not been ruled out. This somewhat spoils my otherwise positive first-day impressions of the transformed, peaceful Belfast.

## Day Nine
# Belfast

*'Belfast, owing to its extremely low position, has from a distance, nothing imposing to its appearance; but, on a nearer approach, is found to improve considerably. The houses, mostly of brick, are well built, many of them very handsome; the streets are regular, spacious and cleanly, well macadamized and lighted, and the whole general aspect of the place eminently calculated to make the most favourable impressions, not a little strengthened by the cheerful stir and activity which prevails in the mercantile quarters and which, associated with an enterprising spirit, have obtained for Belfast the reputation of being the first town in Ireland in commercial prosperity, and second to Dublin only as port.'*
(THE 'IMPERIAL GAZETTEER', W.G. BLACKIE, ED., 1855)

First thing in the morning, I venture into the dark lane to check out my car, half-expecting it to be either stolen or—in the best of scenarios—covered with vicious graffiti. To my surprise, the vehicle is intact, except for a couple of fresh bird poo spots.

I won't need the car today, for I am going on a guided black-cab tour of Belfast.

Before the tour, I need to send a couple of letters.

In front of the closed post office on Botanic Avenue, I find the most docile and patient queue I've ever come across (and I have seen a lot of them in the former USSR, I can assure you). 'They have their training on Tuesdays and will be open in half an hour,' a woman in a kerchief tells me amicably.

The letter-posting has to be postponed, for my cabbie-cum-guide must be already waiting at my hotel's reception. And he is.

Peter is a stocky middle-aged man. He has been a taxi driver for over twenty years and now works for 'Black Cab Tours'—the company that specialises in taking flying visitors (like me) around the city's sites and numerous trouble spots. Belfast Black cabs were made famous (or rather notorious) during the Troubles, as the only available means of public transport in the areas like the Shankill Road.

Peter tells me he grew up in Belfast and as a boy used to play with Gerry Adams. 'We didn't get on very well,' he adds hastily.

We jump into the waiting cab. Peter plunges into the tour the moment his car starts moving. He is a fast talker. Sitting in the back and trying to make notes, I strain my eardrums to hear what he is saying into the microphone and have to ask him repeatedly to speak slower—a request he ignores.

'This is the Opera House, built in 1894, that was almost destroyed by the bomb…'

'When?'

'Can't remember: too many bombs…'

We leave South Belfast and drive across the city centre.

'On your right is the Europa Hotel—probably the most bombed hotel in Europe,' he crackles into his mike, with some fiendish pride in his voice.

'You mean it was bombed during the Troubles?'

'The Troubles and the Blitz too. During the Blitz Belfast was a prime target as a major port. My mother told me all about it…The Blitz plus the Troubles probably killed more people here than anywhere else…'

I am not so sure of the historical validity of his last remark.

'A lot of visitors expect to find high security and ruined buildings here, but in fact, Belfast is rather peaceful and quiet these days,' he carries on.

We pass by City Hall, a building that appears to be modelled on London's St Paul's Cathedral.[24]

'The locals call it the Dome of Pleasure,' comments Peter. 'It is full of political dinosaurs—all about point-scoring...'

We head towards Queen's Island, the home of the once-famous shipyards. The shipyard area looks abandoned. There are no people around, only rusty 1960s' cranes—like some tarnished relics from the past—stick out of the ground here and there.

'The yard is in decline. It used to employ thirty thousand people and now only about two hundred. There hasn't been a ship built here for seven years...'

We stop near Dry Dock No 3, where the *Titanic* was built. THE TITANIC WAS BUILT IN BELFAST! asserts a large banner on a near-by warehouse. I am tempted to retort: 'So what?'

'It was actually not one *Titanic* but two,' says my knowledgeable driver. 'The *Titanic*'s twin ship was called the *Olympic*. It was only a bit smaller and plied the seas until 1936...[25] Do you know that one of the four funnels of The *Titanic* was a fake? Yes, it was painted on the canvas to give the ship a bigger and better look...'

'Why are people so fascinated with the *Titanic* disaster?' I muse aloud.

'The public feels good about the fact that all that wealth can suddenly sink. No one is safe...' Whoever said that all cab drivers were clandestine philosophers was right.

The area around the port looks bleak: ugly 1970s office blocks and lots of empty spaces piled with debris.

'We call this area the Titanic Quarter,' Peter says. 'This is what we do in Belfast: we take a disaster and make it work for us.'

Whatever he means, I cannot see in what way the 'Titanic Quarter' can fit in with Belfast. But maybe he meant something else? At least, there are no fences or barbed wire in sight.

'They removed all the security barriers from the port area in the 1990s, because it is now a protected heritage site,' explains Peter.

I like the logic (or rather the lack of it) of his last statement. At times, it seems, to protect a site, barriers have to be taken away.

We are off to look at other Belfast sites—'protected' and 'unprotected', and I wonder whether a repetition of my London/Derry 'parallel tour', where the words of the modern guide were interspersed with those of the 93-year-old Murray, can work in Belfast. Initially, it all looks fine.

Of Donegall Street:

> MURRAY: 'This thoroughfare is a construction of the last quarter of the 19th century, and is a great improvement to the city, occupying, as it does, the site of some of the oldest and narrowest streets then swept away. It is of fine proportions, and the general effect is pleasing from the variety of its architectural buildings...'
>
> PETER: 'This is Donegall Street, Belfast's mini Fleet Street, with offices of such newspapers as the *Belfast Telegraph*, which is Unionist, the *Irish News*, which is Catholic and the *News Letter* which is Loyalist...' Hearing this, Murray would have raised his bushy Edwardian eyebrows.
>
> MURRAY: 'St Anne's Cathedral, designed by Sir Thomas Drew...was opened for service in 1904...'
>
> PETER: 'St Anne's Protestant (*sic*—vv) Cathedral took eighty years to build, because it kept running out of money. The final touches to it were made in 2005...'

We proceed towards North Belfast and our tour becomes more and more absurd, the interaction between my two guides—real and imaginary—becomes more and more stilted. The reason is simple: Murray did not mention many of the 'historical sites' we are passing. No wonder: the last entry in his essay on Belfast history is about King Edward and Queen Alexandra's visit to the city in 1903, 'when the fine statue to Queen Victoria was unveiled by His Majesty.'

So Murray has to stay mum as we drive along Clifton Street— 'the main road for the Twelfth of July Orange Parade' (Peter) and past the dilapidated high court building in Crumlin Road that 'used to have bullet-proof rooms, where people were tried without a jury, although the IRA never recognised these courts which were also opposed by local lawyers...', according to Peter. He is frantically trying to appear non-partisan, yet his attempts at impartiality are becoming increasingly unsuccessful. Soon he gives up all pretence and starts openly professing his Catholic/ Republican sympathies.

Only once does the silenced Murray get a chance to put in a

couple of words. When Peter, in the usual cab-driver fashion, starts castigating Belfast's chaotic and irregular public transport, the famous guide-book writer butts in: 'The tramway service…in the city is excellent; the lines traverse the principal streets in many directions, while connecting the docks with several railway termini…' It is now Peter's turn to stay silent, for there's no modern version of the 'excellent' and long-defunct Belfast 'tramway' in Northern Ireland's modern capital.

His silence, however, does not last long, for we soon arrive at the Shankill Road area. I suspect I won't be able to hear another word from Murray until the end of the tour.

Black cabs still seem to be the main form of transport on the Shankill Road: dozens of them are moving in both directions.

'People are used to them,' Peter shrugs.

Almost all of the buildings are in desperate need of painting, with patches of peeling stucco concealed under aggressive murals. The area is dissected by security fences. It is obviously not 'protected' in the sense that the old port neighbourhood is.

'The ethnic cleansing still goes on here today!' Peter blurts out all of a sudden. He doesn't expand, and I don't ask him to.

We enter the Loyalist quarter. I deduce this from the changed character of the murals, the themes of which now fluctuate between THE SIEGE OF DERRY and THE PERSECUTION OF THE PROTESTANT PEOPLE BY THE CHURCH OF ROME, 1600.

'Are the Loyalists going to disarm?' I ask my driver.

He presses the brake, pulls over and turns towards me: 'You have to be careful saying things like this here!' he hisses. I can see that he is genuinely scared, despite the fact that we are sitting inside his cab, with the doors and windows closed!

'There's a transition into a gangland culture here,' he whispers, 'but anyone who says this aloud is in danger of being shot.'

So much for the Peace Process…

'They [he means Protestants, of course] had a very good life in Belfast and still do,' he carries on in a half-whisper, before re-starting his car.

Huge letters UDF, UFF, PUP and UDU can be seen on every other house. The ubiquitous 'u-s' in them make the graffiti sound accusatory.

'"Mad Dog" Adair lived in the street down there,' Peter waves his hand towards a large gabled house in a seemingly quiet side-lane. 'And in that house over there Stevie "Top Gun" was murdered. He actually had a drug overdose but the question was whether or not he had administered it himself. That man killed more Catholics than anyone else. There were rumours that Adair fancied his wife...Mad Dog now lives in hiding under threat of death, and they [again, he means the Loyalists] all fight among themselves: UDA against UFF, UFF against UDU and so on.' The playful word 'PUP' does not just denote a small dog, but is also an abbreviation for 'Progressive Unionist Party', whatever it stands for.

We get out of the car to have a look at a memorial plate that says: LIEUTENANT JACKIE COULTER, KILLED IN ACTION.

'See, they even use British military ranks, not like the IRA, who call their fighters volunteers,' says Peter looking around nervously, like a big troubled bird. 'Here they are more loyal to the Crown than anywhere. They adore Cromwell, who actually hated the very monarchy they love so much...'

What a mess our tour that started so peacefully has become! There's so much hatred here that I can almost feel it in the air. Every structure in the vicinity seems to be involved in the ongoing conflict—directly or indirectly.

'This tower was only demilitarised in the last six weeks...The British army had a post on the roof of that house...These gates and crossing points close at night automatically...These traffic lights mark the dividing line between UDF and UDV, whose disagreements are not ideological, but purely territorial...' Peter keeps commenting.

It gets madder and madder by the minute.

We pass by an oblong primary school building, next to a mural of King William of Orange ('He was OK: on the Pope's payroll and had no problem with Catholics...')

'This is a Protestant school. Segregated education is our main concern. Until we change that, nothing will get better. This is where it all starts...' Peter says.

Two Chinese women are crossing the road as we stop at the

traffic lights. Looking at them, I remember again that there were no foreign faces in Belfast in 1994, although there were some foreigners. After delivering a lecture at Queen's, I was introduced to a young man from the former Soviet Union. He told me that 'Russians' were among very few foreign residents in Belfast. 'It is so quiet here compared to Moscow,' he said. 'And finding a job is easy. As long as you don't poke your nose into politics—you are safe.'

I remember thinking then that it was almost impossible to live in Belfast without poking one's nose (or else having it poked) into politics. So, no matter how horrible the present-day reality of North Belfast, things must be improving even here.

Another little sign of changing times is a charity shop in support of the poor in Romania and Albania. After everything I've seen so far, the shop looks out of place, for this area of Belfast needs plenty of 'support' itself.

We drive along the Shankill Road Wall, separating the Catholic area from the Protestant one (at least, they don't check your passports at this crossing…not yet). It can be regarded as a junior sister of the Berlin Wall. Unlike the latter, however, it is still standing strong.

'It all started in 1969. A crowd came from the Protestant side and burned all our houses, That was the onset of the Troubles. The police could not separate the two communities, and this wall had to be built…'

To me, dividing walls were always a sign of weakness, the last (at times, the only) and not particularly convincing argument of an ailing and morally bankrupt system (or country) in its favour. Yet here, in Belfast, they seem to mark the divides between religious and historical grievances.

'When this wall is removed, I will know that peace has come to Northern Ireland,' concludes Peter.

I stare at the wall that looks as impregnable and as intimidating as ever and recall another one that I happened to stumble upon in the South, in Dublin, to be more exact.

On the morning of 7 October 2004, I heard on the news that Dublin City Council had overnight erected a concrete barrier to block the only access road to one of the Travellers' halting sites. It was done under the laughable pretext of eliminating 'considerable dumping of commercial waste' which didn't make sense, for even one of the City fathers admitted that the 'illegal dumping was significantly from outsiders'.

And how on earth could a wall, erected clandestinely—under cover of darkness—prevent 'illegal dumping' or any other illegal activity for that matter?

Walls and barriers of all sorts are useless and counterproductive by their very nature. Instead of resolving an 'issue', they create many new ones on top of it, with the initial 'problem' remaining unsolved.

'Force breeds counterforce'—this, Newton's Third Law of Motion, can be applied in equal measure to social structures. The stronger the barriers—the harder people try to break through. The classic proof is the infamous Berlin Wall, the final collapse of which I was able to observe in Berlin in 1990.

One thing that truly stunned me in Ireland was how quietly and matter-of-factly the ongoing oppression of Travellers was taken by many of those regarding themselves as liberals and intellectuals.

'We in Ireland know…about the traveller problem,' Kevin Myers claimed in his column, entitled, 'I'm Irish, I know about the gipsy problem' (!) in London's *Daily Telegraph* on 8 October 2004.

In it, he branded Travellers 'a socially-dysfunctional minority who believe that they should be allowed to do as they want' and characterised 'traveller life' (yes, conspicuously—with a small 't') as 'patriarchal, caste-based, dirty, diseased, alcoholic, illiterate, violent, misogynistic, low-achieving…and, most of all, short' (as if the Travellers' untimely deaths were their own fault, too!). 'Only multicultural mumbo-jumbo at its most fatuous crowns this dismal tribal phenomenon with the title "culture", he concluded.

I hate political correctness, invented by mediocrities in an attempt to paint the whole of our colourful world grey. I think that, in its worst forms, PC represents the greatest danger to human civilisation since communism. There's only one thing worse than PC: total *indifference* to human suffering, exacerbated by patronising upper-class *arrogance*—of which the above-quoted rant is a shining example.

There's one meaningful Russian borrowing in the English language, the tongue-breaking word 'intelligentsia'. It denotes a hard-to-define concept that has little, if anything, to do with intellect, intellectuals and/or erudition. The best (to my mind) definition of it was coined by Chekhov, who described members of 'intelligentsia' as the people who feel personal guilt for every single injustice in world.

Kevin Myers is certainly not one of them.

I will always remember the crack of dawn on 14 October 2004, when—from under an umbrella—I watched the collapse of the Dunsink Wall. It was the second major human divide to crumble apart in front of my eyes.

A photographer from the magazine for which I worked and I were the only members of the media witnessing this truly historic event.

Walls and barriers are only built to be demolished...

In contrast to the stealthy construction of the ill-fated wall in the middle of the night, its demolition was conducted in the open. Only there was hardly anyone to see it: a nasty drizzle must have deterred Irish 'watchdogs of democracy', read journalists, from turning up *en masse*. Pity, for it was democracy as such that was at the centre of the Dunsink Lane confrontation.

Diggers, bulldozers and pneumatic drills were painstakingly tearing through the wall that—in the treacherous light of dawn— was coming to resemble a black rotten tooth. I was thinking of all the wasted effort that had gone into erecting it in the first place and was now going into pulling it down.

In Berlin, they decided to keep a graffiti-covered chunk of the Berlin Wall intact as a memorial. Perhaps it would have made sense to preserve a slab or two of reinforced concrete from the Dunsink Wall and to put them on display in the centre of Dublin as a monumental reminder of human prejudice, cruelty and outright foolishness...

The time was approaching 9 a.m., and soaked Traveller kids were trickling through the growing gap in the wall on their way to school.

'Are you a Traveller?' a dust-covered foreman in charge of the demolition asked me worriedly.

'Yes, I am a traveller,' I replied.

_____

Back in Belfast, we cross into the Catholic area on the other side of the Shankill Wall and, having driven along Bombay Street ('totally burnt out in 1969'—Peter), stop at the entrance to Clonard Martyrs Memorial Garden—a small Republican cemetery squeezed between bleak and unseemly apartment blocks.

Peter takes a key out of his pocket and unlocks the gate, topped with a sculpture of a phoenix.

We look at a large plaque, divided into two parts, a 'Roll of Honour'. On the left: IRA VOLUNTEERS, KILLED BY THE BRITISH ARMY; on the right, CIVILIANS MURDERED BY LOYALISTS AND BRITISH FORCES. Among the latter, women and children, some as young as four and five. The dates of their deaths vary—from the 1920s and the 1940s to the 1960s.

In a separate section of the Garden we find the graves of the CLONARD MARTYRS, 2ND BATTALION, BELFAST BRIGADE, KILLED BY CROWN FORCES AND LOYALIST MURDER GANGS.

'They separate the IRA fighters from civilians here to beat the claims that only IRA members were targeted by the British,' Peter comments sullenly.

The fact that graves can be used for political purposes is truly horrifying. It is here, in Clonard cemetery, that one comes to realise the real depth of Northern Ireland's continuing divide.

The place puts Peter in an aggressive mood, with all his feeble attempts at political correctness well forgotten: 'Discrimination against Catholics was always here,' he states defiantly. 'Until recently, the police force only had seven percent Catholics. As for BBC Northern Ireland, it employed no Catholics at all…'

As we leave the cemetery, Peter re-locks the gate and carefully puts the key back into his pocket.

Our black cab cruises along Odessa Street and Sevastopol Street —all quiet and deserted. It is ironic that so many streets and lanes in the Republican part of Belfast are named after places on the Crimean peninsula and the Black Sea coast. A famous Russian/Ukrainian holiday spot, where I spent lots of memorable summers, the Crimea is also the place where the British army suffered a number of defeats before eventually winning a partial victory in the war of 1854–6, shortly before these west-Belfast streets were built.

Our final stop in the area is outside Sinn Féin headquarters on the Falls Road. It is a modest office block, with a mural of Bobby Sands above the entrance and a small gift shop at the side.

Peter, who was born in this area, doesn't try to conceal his affection for the party. 'It is a model small party—anti-racist and internationalist,' he says.

'In what way are they internationalist?' I enquire.

'They have very strong links with Palestinians and the Basque Movement. The Basques come here in large numbers.'

He tells me how in 1992 a policeman, whose best friend had been killed by the IRA, entered the Sinn Féin office, shot dead two party officials and then committed suicide.

'Five families were devastated as a result,' he adds. 'It is a domino effect—like dropping a pebble into the water…'

I venture inside the gift shop and leaf through *Poems from Prison* by Bobby Sands and several books by Gerry Adams. Having noticed my interest, a shop assistant gives me a leaflet, an invitation to attend Gerry Adams' book signing. By the time of the event, I will already be back in Dublin.

Apart from the books and posters (containing slogans such as, 'Re-Route Sectarian Parades!', 'Disband the RUC!'), the shop stocks a large number of tacky Irish souvenirs, crucifixes and cheap jewellery.

I pick up a green bookmark with 'I wake up every morning and thank God for being Irish' printed across it.

After what I've seen today, I wouldn't put my name under these words.

On the way back to the city centre, Peter grows silent. Looking at his stiff back, I can feel he is preoccupied with something.

'I want to ask you a favour,' he mutters finally without turning back. 'People still get killed here for expressing their opinions. So when you write about the tour, can you please change my name?'

I promise him that I will.[26]

'Watch your tongue and never say what you think, if you don't want to get yourself and all of us into trouble,' my parents told me when I was seven years old. It was a cruel thing to say to a child, but, with memories of the Stalinist terror, when people were imprisoned and executed for 'expressing their opinions', still fresh in their minds, they thought it was a warning they had to make for my own good. Here I have to say that I always found it hard to watch my tongue (and my pen) hence the various trials and tribulations I have had to go through in my life…

In 1966, when I was twelve, we were asked at school to write an essay on our favourite literary hero. Instead of writing (as we were all expected to) about Pavel Korchagin, the clichéd protagonist of Nikolai Ostrovsky's daft and nauseatingly pro-Soviet novel *How Steel was Tamed*, I chose to do my essay on Ostap Bender, the aforementioned 'smooth operator' from *The Twelve Chairs*. An hilarious and vitriolic parody of Soviet officialdom and bureaucracy, the novel sparkled with caustic anti-totalitarian humour. Like many of my compatriots, I read the novel dozens of times and knew it almost by heart.

I was living with my grandparents at the time, and my grandfather, an old Bolshevik and a revolutionary in his youth, who became profoundly disillusioned with communism by the end of his life, was summoned to the school headmistress, a bluestocking and virago, and reprimanded for his grandson's 'dangerous literary tastes'.

He came back home very upset. But instead of telling me off (as I expected), he said: 'I am deeply ashamed. Not for you but for your teachers. They want you all to like the same books. They want you to have the same tastes and thoughts. If this is what we fought for in the Revolution, then I am ashamed for myself, too.'

I will remember this first real lesson of freedom of speech, taught by my granddad, for as long as I live.

My Belfast driver's words therefore sadden me considerably. They show that—contrary to my hopes and initial impressions—Belfast has not yet become a part of the free world. Things have certainly improved since 1994, but Freedom is a peculiar substance that cannot be rationed or cut into pieces. It is either there or not there—there is no middle ground. One cannot be half-free, twenty per cent free or even three quarters free. There is only one option:

you are either a free person or a slave. 'We must squeeze slavery out of ourselves drop by drop,' Chekhov once wrote.

Many 'drops' of slavery will still have to be 'squeezed out' of Belfast before it becomes free.

At lunch I leaf through today's copy of *The Guardian* (unlike in the South, it is on sale in every newsagent's here). Coincidentally, I find in it an article on the brutal murder of North Belfast youngster Craig McCausland by Loyalist paramilitaries only a couple of months ago. Craig's mother was also killed by them eighteen years earlier, when she was only twenty-three. 'So has anything changed in Northern Ireland?' asks the newspaper. Having also looked through today's issue of *The Belfast Telegraph*, reporting (rather matter-of-factly) on a series of fresh killings by both Loyalists and Republicans, and still reeling from this morning's revealing black cab tour, I can answer a resolute 'No' to that largely rhetorical question...

On the way to my hotel after lunch, I notice that they are putting up a Christmas tree near Belfast City Hall, and to keep pedestrians away the spot has been encircled with yellow police tape making it look like a murder scene. Or is my vision of things still blurred by my gruesome impressions of the tour?

The entrance to the recently robbed branch of the Northern Bank is patrolled by at least a dozen armed policemen—a classic example of locking the stable door after the horse has bolted.

In the afternoon, I visit the famous Linen Hall Library, containing the world's largest collection of material relating to the ongoing Northern Ireland conflict from all sides of the divide— comprising altogether over 250,000 units of storage. In the words of John Gray, the Linen Hall's respected Librarian: 'We have enough within these walls to offend absolutely everyone.'

Not counting the young curator, nodding off at his desk, I am alone in the room full of books, posters, newspapers, postcards, drawings, catalogue boxes and whatnots—face to face and ear to ear with the images and voices of the Troubles.

'After 3,168 deaths and 25 years of terror, the IRA says IT'S OVER!' the headline of the *Belfast Telegraph* of 31 August 1994 shouts joyfully. The issue carries the IRA statement about its 'cessation of military operations' as well as numerous photos of the dead and wounded during the conflict.

This triumphant mood is in contrast to the more sombre one in the same paper one-and-a-half years later, on 10 February 1996, the day after the IRA bombing of Canary Wharf: 'TRUCE LIES IN TATTERS. IS THE PEACE OVER?'

It takes almost another year-and-a-half to get the answer to that question: 'IRA CALLS CEASEFIRE' ( 'The IRA today announced an unequivocal restoration of its ceasefire') on 19 July 1997 and at last: 'IT'S YES!'—on 23 May 1998 ('70% of voters backed the Stormont Agreement…').

As we know now, that was not the final call either.

Remembering Martin Lynch's one-man show in Ballycastle, I am drawn towards a display entitled, REAL HUMOUR OF THE TROUBLES. The exhibits are evenly (and cleverly) spread on the walls and bookshelf tops all over the room, as if to balance the otherwise sombre mood of the collection.

Among those that make me smile (uneasily) are:

– A wad of spoof £10 and £20 banknotes with the faces of Gerry Adams and Martin McGuiness printed on them, with the legend, 'I promise to rob the bearer on demand of the sum of £26,500,000 sterling [the amount stolen from the Northern Bank]' 'guarantee' at the bottom.
– Tins of 'King William's Orange Conserve', a part of the 'Orange Jam Series'—all showing King William on a horse and produced by the Ulster Society. The tins are displayed next to an array of phallic-shaped rubber bullets that strike me as unexpectedly huge.
– A bar of Drumcree Chocolate with, WE DEMAND THE RIGHT TO MARCH printed on the wrapping.
– A coat hanger bearing a caricature of David Trimble, a snake-like garrotte around his neck.
– A baby's bib in the shape of Ulster with orange footprints all over it.
– A collection of tea, coffee and beer mugs on a separate shelf: an SDLP tea mug, a Gerry Adams coffee mug (with his mug), a UVF

FOR GOD & ULSTER tea cup, a NORTHERN IRELAND ASSEMBLY and a (mysterious) ULSTER SAYS NO (to what, I wonder, before later learning that it was to the Good Friday Agreement) mugs next to each other.

– A set of cards, wishing me a 'Merry Christmas from the UDA', each featuring a gun-wielding snowman.

The curator wakes up and tells me that the Derry branch of Sinn Féin established its own Christmas card series in 1970s. They even had their own crudely printed stamps. The Belfast branch followed, producing a different set of anti-loyalist stamps each year. The spoof Christmas-card tradition was soon picked up by other parties and groups from both sides. A Christmas card of the Northern Ireland Civil Rights Association shows Santa facing a brick wall with his back to helmeted and gun-totting British soldiers. On another, Santa carries a gift bag loaded with ammunition and a grenade launcher on his shoulder.

'We keep getting humorous stuff like this regularly,' says the curator.

My favourite exhibit is definitely a beer mug with the inscription BIGOTS BEER—A SUBTLE BLEND OF PREJUDICE & DENIAL—the words that, to my mind, sum up this collection and the whole of Northern Ireland conflict—rather nicely.

It is a good sign that the warring parties are trying to make fun of their opponents. Yet, to my mind, the real breakthrough in the conflict will only occur when they are also able and willing to laugh at *themselves*.

On my last evening in Belfast, I try to walk off the Troubles' overdose in the graceful Regency crescents of the Queens Quarter —a stark contrast to the aggressive ugliness of the Shankill Road area. My car is still intact on Graffiti Lane, confirming that Belfast is indeed a very safe place for cars, if not yet for people.

I wander into an empty second-hand bookshop on Botanic Avenue. 'Are there any books upstairs?' I ask the sales lady. 'No,' she replies. 'Only stranded customers.'

One thing is certain: despite many years of the Troubles, Belfast humour is alive, which means that Hope is alive too.

# Belfast–Downpatrick

'*Downpatrick*[*] *(pop. 2993)…is well built and has some handsome county buildings such as the Court House, Infirmary, and Gaol, the cost of this last being 63,000 pounds. The Large Lunatic Asylum stands E. of the town, and has been erected at a total cost of about 100,000 pounds sterling. Approaching either by rail or road, the tourist has a good view of the Cathedral…*'
('A HANDBOOK FOR TRAVELLERS IN IRELAND',
MURRAY, 1912)

'*Battles and burnings through the centuries have left very little surviving of the old Downpatrick.*'
('ULSTER HOLIDAY GUIDE', 1949)

'*Downpatrick…is divided into the English, Irish, and Scotch quarters and consists of four principal streets, meeting in the centre, and intersected by several smaller…The houses are, in general, substantial and well built, and the streets well paved, with an ample supply of water.*'
(THE 'IMPERIAL GAZETTEER', W.G. BLACKIE, ED., 1855)

A fter my 'skeleton tour' of Belfast which has revealed lots of skeletons—metaphorical and real (in the cab, if not in the cupboard)—I need some cheering up. All the way to Downpatrick I play a solitaire word game—my favourite way of de-stressing. I come up with a logo for Downpatrick—'the town that is forever Down' and conjure up in my imagination its more cheerful sister town called 'Uppatrick' somewhere in the South, or possibly in Australia.

But Down in this context has nothing to do with direction or mood. It is simply an anglicised form of the Gaelic word *Dún*, meaning a fort. So it's cognate with the Dun in Dundalk, just across the border to the south, or with Scottish place names like Dundee or Dunfermline. Indeed, the Dun prefix is not just confined to places where Gaelic was once spoken. You'll find it as far south as London: thus Dunstable, near Luton, for instance, although I think that the root of that Dun is Anglo-Saxon rather than Gaelic. At any rate, there have been a lot of Duns about in various tongues, adding to the joyous confusion of languages that are such a pleasure to me.

Place names, too, offer endless potential for pun and games. I remember filming once in the Tasmanian town of Penguin and copying shop signs of the type 'Penguin Pizza', 'Penguin Shoes' and 'Penguin Butcher' into my notebook. When a local woman approached our crew with the question: 'What are you doing here, mates?' our Irish film director, Richard Lightbody, replied that we had come from Penguin's British sister town called Duck, to study Penguin's shop signs. The lady seemed happy with that answer and left us alone…

Trying to find my Murray-recommended Denvir's Hotel, I open a map of the town, kindly provided by Down Tourism Office, and notice the existence of a suburb called 'Down Heights'—a name that sounds almost Kafkaesque and resonates with *The Yawning Heights*—a dystopian novel by Russian émigré writer Vladimir Zinoviev.

Denvir's is an ancient structure. Built in 1642, it looks as if it has remained untouched since then: oak beams, stone floors, meat hooks hanging from the ceiling, a large open fireplace in the lounge, and a courtyard so tiny that I can hardly squeeze my car into it. The receptionist tells me that the top of the hotel's bar is crafted from the timbers of ships sunk in the nearby Lough. She also says that I am the hotel's only guest today—the fact that makes me feel a bit uneasy, as if I were the only passenger on a sinking boat.

This feeling grows when I come to my room—tiny to the point of claustrophobic—and filled with massive furniture of indeterminate make. The bed is painted green, and there's no-where else to sit down.

Luckily, there's an ensuite bathroom (I thought there wouldn't be any after spotting a blue Victorian wash tub with a jug in the corridor).

In the huge oak wardrobe I discover a pair of rumpled black trousers and scruffy black shoes to match them. My first thought is that these items are provided for the hotel's guests for free—like the slippers and bathing robes in some 5-star Hiltons. But how would they know my size? More likely, they were left behind by a previous tenant. I try to think who he could have been and come up with four following possibilities:

1. An IRA informer kidnapped in the middle of the night before he could put his trousers on.
2. A confused and forgetful travelling scribe like myself.
3. A fleeing lover caught *in flagrante delicto.*
4. St Patrick himself!

The last supposition may sound blasphemous to some. Yet, if we remember that Armagh City, caught in the age-long dispute with Downpatrick over the Saint's burial place, supports its assertion by seriously claiming some of Patrick's possessions,[27] why can't Downpatrick respond with some items of his attire, i.e. trousers and shoes?

I come close to claiming this ground-breaking discovery. It is only Murray's mention of Downpatrick's renowned 'Lunatic Asylum' (from what I know, the institution is still there) that stops me from making the claim out loud.

I take the relics down to reception, and they pledge to try and trace their forgetful owner.

JEANS SALE NOW ON—FROM £10 runs the banner above a makeshift market stall near the entrance to the St Patrick Centre—a modern, almost futuristic, steel-and-glass building. I wonder what St Patrick himself would have thought of a 'sale' going on right next to his temple. Mind you, if the pants left in my room were indeed his, he might have been quite pleased to get himself a pair of fake Levis for a tenner. After all, he was a modest man.

This is what my 2004 *Rough Guide* has to say about the St Patrick Centre: 'Downpatrick thrives upon its association with the saint, and the new and extremely expensive St Patrick Centre, just off the main drag, Market Street, aims to recount his life and influence in extensive detail. Its hagiographic, multimedia approach is pretty arid, however, and by the time you've been round its maze of interactive displays and sat through the five-screen 180-degree virtual helicopter ride through Christian history, you might even wish you've never heard of the saint...'

One of the bookshelves in the Centre's gift shop is designated 'Chargeable Literature', which leads me to wonder if they are talking about a new literary genre—books that can be electronically 'charged' with whatever emotion the reader opts for: fascination, excitement, boredom? The shop also sells 'St. Patrick's chocolate bars' and the usual array of tacky Irish souvenirs.

Next to the gift shop is a wall panel with 'How to Use the Exhibition' instructions that include suggestions such as: 'Enter the spirit of St Patrick and wear the clothes of the time; 'Pay particular attention to Sound Cones' (??), and 'Do not touch the screens;'

I am about to 'enter the spirit', in full accordance with the Instructions, when a very young man in a green sweater materialises from behind a curtain and introduces himself as Stewart (or, maybe, Stuart—I shy away from asking him to spell his name lest he take me for an American tourist).

'It is all very high-tech here,' says Stew/ua/rt, his eyes sparkling. 'Plenty of light and sound effects. Very interactive and hands-on...'

The first part of the exhibition deals with Patrick's 'formative years' as a boy and a Roman slave. 'When at school, Patrick used an abacus like this to do his sums,' says a sign above a wooden abacus. 'Have a go at the sums below using the abacus.'

In actual fact, 'when at school' I used 'an abacus like this to do my sums' too, but have completely forgotten how to do it. It is pleasing nevertheless to have something in common with the Saint.

The abacus, sadly, marks my one and only similarity to Patrick. 'He prayed a hundred times every day and almost as often at night,' asserts another interpretation notice which strikes me as baloney. Praying 'almost' two hundred times a day—I calculate that even if Patrick never ate, slept or went to the loo he would have had to start a new prayer every six minutes, without having a single break in-between, not even for a second!

The more I explore the Centre, the harder it is to suppress associations with another temple-cum-museum I visited on a compulsory school pilgrimage many years ago. That one was located in Ulyanovsk, formerly Simbirsk, a town on the banks of the Volga River, where Vladimir Lenin (whose real last name was 'Ulyanov), 'the great leader and teacher' of workers, peasants and executioners of many countries, was born and grew up. The museum portrayed Lenin (who, in reality, was a mentally disturbed child, prone to tantrums and hitting his head against the wall), as an extremely 'modest' and compulsively 'honest' person never capable of telling a lie (that didn't stop him from ordering the execution of millions innocent people at a later stage of his life). Among the exhibits were the pen that little Lenin used at school, his watch and a photo of a 'tea spoon that Lenin used in exile'. The tea spoon itself was probably deemed too precious to be displayed to the public.

These associations keep growing as I wander deeper and deeper inside 'the spirit of St Patrick', with push-button screens and interactive displays glowing in the 'spiritual' dark.

I am alone in the state-of-the art (or '5-star', as it is advertised in the Centre's glossy brochure) multi-screen panoramic cinema, watching a promotional movie about St Patrick that starts with the warning, 'You may experience motion sickness'. As the movie unveils, with an angry Ian Paisley-like voice droning about St Patrick's 'legacy' and 'greatness', I do start experiencing pangs of nausea. It is not 'motion sickness' though, rather 'emotion sickness', for the words and the manner of presentation are all so painfully familiar. Similar, if much less technologically advanced, devices were used in my long-suffering mother country in reference to Lenin, Stalin, Brezhnev and a number of other 'great leaders and teachers' at the time of their officially approved 'greatness', normally followed by officially engineered oblivion and demotion.

Don't get me wrong: St Patrick, if he existed at all, was undoubtedly a much, much better person than any of the blood-thirsty Soviet dictators. Also, I am sure, he wouldn't have approved of all this pomp. The mechanism of the personality cult is always the same, its main purpose being to brainwash the 'populace' into unquestioning obedience and to distract them from the real problems of everyday life.

As another voice (thankfully, not Ian Paisley's) thunders from each of the multiple screens: 'Patrick crosses borders, reaches out to everyone!!!' the only thing I can hear is: 'Lenin is always alive. He is always with us. He is still the most alive person among all the living!!!'

Unable to bear it any more, I hastily leave the movie theatre and Centre.

The jeans sale outside is over, and the sellers are packing their goodies into large cardboard boxes before putting them into the back of a waiting white van. Only now do I notice that the Centre stands right next door to a large shopping mall.

It is getting dark. I try to find St Patrick's grave but get lost in a vast car park next to St Patrick's Cathedral and start walking back to the hotel, past 'Down High School'. This time, feeling pretty down myself, I don't even smile.

Before falling asleep in my hotel room, I read a couple of pages from Filson Young's *Ireland at the Crossroads*: '...But the facts remain; and the lives of men and women continue, in spite of any individual influence, to be darkened by the crushing rule of the Church. How like its spirit to that vain worship of which it was said, that its teaching is only the commands of men; how different from that of the band of plain men who wandered by the summer shore of Galilee, mad with the inspiration of their joyous gospel.'

I lie in my bed sleepless until the early hours of the morning, listening to all kinds of ghostly noises behind the walls of my room: squeaking floorboards, snores and muffled voices. This is spooky, for I am sure I am alone at the hotel. Unless I count Lenin, who 'is always with us', of course.[28] And, possibly, the 'Spirit of St Patrick'...

Day Eleven
# Downpatrick–Armagh City

Some crazy church bells wake me up at 7 o'clock in the morning. I linger in bed for some time listening to amplified street sounds, which my room seems to attract like a radio receiver.

I have breakfast at the hotel's bar, cave-like fireplaces and faded wall mirrors being my only company, and keep wondering about the source of last night' spooky noises. They reminded me of another inexplicable event I was confronted with a couple of years ago.

I came to Dublin from the UK, where I was then based, to visit my son, who was living in Dublin, and to mark my 50th birthday with him. On the eve of my first jubilee, we sat over a Russian meal of borscht, pickles and meat dumplings late into the night. When the clock struck twelve, my son raised his glass to wish me a happy birthday. It was right at that moment that the old telephone on the mantelpiece gave out two short piercing rings…

Now, a telephone ringing at midnight isn't much of a story, had it not been for one simple fact: there was no actual telephone line in the house of my son, who relied solely on his mobile. The disconnected antediluvian 'apparatus' itself was a useless piece of furniture—a leftover from some previous tenants. There was no cable, no number, no nothing.

And yet it did ring precisely at the moment when I turned fifty!

My son dropped his glass and grabbed the receiver. Of course, there was nothing but silence. The phone was dead.

The next day we called (from my son's mobile, no doubt) the

telephone exchange and were assured that there was no cable connection at my son's address and therefore the phone could not ring.

The problem was that it did!

'You were contacted by the other world,' some of my metaphysics-prone friends suggested thoughtfully on hearing the story.

That midnight phone call from nowhere was by far the spookiest thing I had experienced so far. And it happened in Ireland, which is often perceived as a 'haunted country' But is it really?

'In Ireland, they seem to seriously believe in the paranormal,' said my old friend Kevin Dawson, a BBC Radio 4 producer, with whom we had dinner shortly afterwards.

Kevin and his crew had just returned from Co. Offaly, where they recorded 'Excess Baggage', a weekly travel programme from 'the most haunted building in Europe'—Leap Castle, a former stronghold of the O'Carrolls.

They spoke with the Castle's current owner—musician Sean Ryan and with photographer Simon Marsden, both of whom confirmed the strong presence of 'the elemental' on its grounds.

To balance the programme up, they also interviewed Patricia Lysaght, Professor of Irish Folklore at UCD, who explained that in Ireland there existed 'an alternate reality', nurtured by Irish folk tales and accepted by almost everyone as fact.

Everything went according to plan. The laser disks, with voices and sounds recorded on them, were brought back to London ready for editing. It was then that the incomprehensible happened. While putting the programme together in the studio, Kevin heard a blood-chilling *inhuman* voice whispering 'Hello' (it sounded more like 'H-oo-ou—lou-oo') and 'I…died…' on one of the disks. No one in his crew had the slightest idea of how it ended up there. The disks were all properly stored and safely guarded…

Let me tell you straight away that, having travelled the world with Kevin, I know that he is simply incapable of telling a lie.

To highlight his own bewilderment, Kevin put the intrusive voice of the 'ghostly something' on the programme's website.

Coincidentally, on my flight back to Dublin, I found an article on Ireland's haunted castles and houses in Cara—Aer Lingus's inflight magazine. Written by Nikki Walsh and aptly titled 'Jeepers Creepers!', it offered detailed, if somewhat tongue-in-cheek, descriptions of the ghosts to be found in the five weirdest Irish dwellings (excluding Leap Castle, for some reason). They ranged from a man with 'lifeless eyes' watching the news on TV at Glin Castle, Co. Limerick of an evening (don't we all have rather 'lifeless' eyes when watching TV?) to a headless (and topless!) woman, harassing guests at Wicklow Head Lighthouse, and a self-moving linen chest in Renvyle House, Co. Galway.

The latter brought back associations with someone else's black rubbish bags, mysteriously appearing in front of my Dublin house overnight. Could they be self-moving, too? A mystifying case of a litter poltergeist?

Still under the impression of Kevin's truthful story, I was nevertheless inclined to take Nikki Walsh's lively article, clearly targeting potential visitors to Ireland, with a large grain of salt. In her own words, it was all about 'a giddy sort of eccentricity that drew guests like a magnet'.

There is no denying the fact: 'Haunted Ireland' has become a lucrative trademark to attract tourists, and ghosts themselves (if any) have evolved into a big commercial venture. I once boarded 'the world's only ghostbus' for the famous 'Dublin Ghost Tour' intrigued by the Tour's own webpage promising to 'put you at your unease…and introduce you to the dark romance of a city of gaslight, ghosts and chilling legends'. The interior of the double-decker was made to look like the insides of an oversized coffin and the passengers, including myself, giggled nervously, when frightened—over and over again—by Brent Hearney, a talented actor turned scare-mongering ghost-tour guide.

On one of many 'Ghostly Ireland' websites, I found a 'Buy a Ghost' link, where you could acquire not just a 'Ghost dress' and a 'Ghost Voice Message Recorder '(the fateful BBC laser disk?), but also an enigmatic 'Ghost in the Shell' (£22.49). And while there's nothing seriously wrong with marketing this country as a 'haunted land', one has to be careful not to overdo it, as they did in Romania. Or in Transylvania, to be more exact. Their over-the-top PR campaign ended in spectacular failure. It succeeded only in frightening the few potential tourists away *before* they had a chance to visit 'Dracula Land'.

A lesson for 'Haunted Ireland' to learn...

Apart from ghosts of all shapes and sizes, Ireland seems to be obsessed with superstitions, some of which (like fear of Mondays and black cats, say) are similar to the Russian ones: as in Ireland, there has never been a shortage of either imagination or insecurity in Russia.

I was rather amazed, however, by such archetypal Irish beliefs as unlimited faith in all sorts of healers (particularly, in the healing powers of the 'seventh son of the seventh son') that can be explained by total lack of trust in (and more recently, inaffordability of) official medicine, as well as by the church-inspired stigma that used to be attached to left-handed people, regarded as 'sinister' and hence devil-possessed. A woman from a Co. Clare village told me how her left-handed son was routinely punched by his schoolteacher every time he tried to grab a pen with a 'wrong' hand...

Irish superstitions, just like those in Russia—a country with similarly tragic history—strike me as being mostly negative and bad-omen-type.

But how about Irish luck? Is it just an oxymoron—like 'Jewish luck'? And does it really exist?

Luckily (*sic*), while in Cobh, Co. Cork, I stumbled upon a real-life story that combined ghosts with an extraordinary stroke of good fortune.

Ireland's main emigration point, Cobh, was also the last port of call of *Titanic* before it sank. And the Cunard liner *Lusitania* was torpedoed just twenty-five miles off its coast in 1915. A real 'fatal shore'...

It was only logical for ghosts to be swarming all over the town. And they were—as testified by a 'Ghost Walk of Cobh' flier that I picked up at the town's Visitors Centre:

'Explore the sinister side of Cobh at night in the darkened streets of the town. Tales told of Haunted buildings. Ghosts and Apparitions. Booking essential.'

Six of those 'ghosts and apparitions' (aren't they synonyms?) —of Margaret Rice and her five children who sailed together on board *Titanic*—were discovered (and 'confirmed' by a clairvoyant!) by Vincent Keaney, a successful local restaurateur, inside the former Scotts building that was a one-time point of departure for *Titanic* passengers. It was now housing Vincent's own *Titanic Bar* and restaurant.

A native of Cobh, Vincent left Ireland in 1971 in search of better luck overseas, not realising that luck had been waiting for him back at home. His expedition proved a complete disaster, apart from the fact that he had acquired a family on the road. Having returned to Cobh with three young children in tow years later, Vincent was penniless and had to go on the dole.

On a Saturday (mind you: not Monday or Friday!) in 1995 he spent his very last pound on a Lotto ticket, won the jackpot and became a millionaire. Having bought the Scotts building, he renovated it and turned it into *Titanic Bar*. While restoring the building he found a booking form for Mrs Margaret Rice and her five children in the attic...

Inspired by Vincent's example, I started purchasing Irish Lottery tickets.

Despite occasional ethereal voices and dead phones ringing at midnight, Ireland proved a lucky country for me. For what is luck? It is but another superstition, or even a ghost, if you wish—only a positively charged and a smiley one.

Believe it or not, but I have already guessed two numbers right. Twice.

On the subject of 'myths', I meet Ken, a local Downpatrick writer, amateur actor and part-time guide, at the bar and question him about St Patrick.

'A lot about St Patrick is mythological, and it is only an educated guess that he was born here,' he shrugs. 'It is like the belief that St Columba is buried on the island of Iona, say.'

He tells me that Downpatrick, Armagh, Glendalough and Kildare compete for the title of 'the saintliest place in Ireland'. I have been able to witness some events in the ongoing marketing Olympics between these places during my travels in Ireland. The rivalry has all the elements of a major advertising campaign, with St Patrick, St Columba and St Brigid the 'target products'.

My next question is about the local Lunatic Asylum, described (if not exactly 'recommended') by Murray.

'There is a strong tradition of mental hospitals here,' Ken says and promises to show me the building during the tour of Downpatrick on which he is about to take me. Before we start, he shares with me an interesting fact about my hotel. According to Ken, the inn was used for years by top legal figures who came to the Murray-praised Court House across the road: barristers, solicitors and journalists covering the cases. And outside the hotel, there used to be a 'debtor's haven'—a spot where the debtor was legally out of reach of creditors. London and Dublin had a number of them in the Middle Ages.

We begin by visiting the grave of St Patrick, driving towards the grey bulk of St Patrick's Cathedral. The saint's alleged grave is on a hillock behind it. The tombstone carries just one word, PATRICK, drawn across it graffito-like. Actually, not just one word. Having squinted at the plate, I discern the following 'credits' in the corner: 'Down District Council Recreation/Tourist Department, Sep. 1985'.

The hardly visible 'small-print' puts everything nicely into place, for this is what it is all about: 'recreation'! My opinion is confirmed when Ken tells me that, in fact, the grave site is merely where 'oral tradition tales' tell us where St Patrick could have been buried. I like his quiet scholarly scepticism.

A stunning view of a Lidl supermarket opens up from the grave spot.

We enter St Patrick's Cathedral and meet a curator called Joy.

'I saw you yesterday wandering in the car park in the dark!' she tells me gleefully. 'Are you a journalist? Are you taking down names and addresses?'

She has an engaging smile, and I decide to share with her my concerns over the opulence and pomposity of the St Patrick Centre.

Unexpectedly, she totally agrees with me: 'It is more about commerce than Christianity,' she says.

We continue our trip, driving through some deprived areas of the town. 'Downpatrick is not particularly sectarian and wasn't heavily affected by the Troubles,' Ken says. Nonetheless, the poverty of some of the town's quarters makes me think that the millions wasted on the lavish St. Patrick Centre, with all its electronic contents and its openly totalitarian message, could have been better spent on improving the quality of life in Downpatrick.

We stop near a small old church in the outskirts. THE SITE OF THE FIRST CHRISTIAN CHURCH IN IRELAND, BUILT ON THE SPOT WHERE ST. PATRICK BEFRIENDED A LOCAL FARMER, says the disproportionately large interpretation sign. This reminds me of a caption I once saw in the North Korean glossy propaganda monthly *Korea Today*: 'Great leader Kim Il Sung befriends an old peasant woman and offers her a lift in his car.'

Inside, the church is dark, echoey and empty. Ken's mobile rings piercingly breaking the silence. Through a dim little window, I can see a huge statue of St Patrick on top of a hill in the distance. It totally dominates the surrounding landscape bringing to memory a Brezhnev-era Soviet poster of the giant face of Brezhnev hovering above tiny ant-like 'workers' swarming underneath, and the caption: ALWAYS AMONG THE PEOPLE!

'I wrote a play about Patrick,' Ken says suddenly. Then adds after a pause: 'Not about St Patrick, but about Patrick Kavanagh…'

Ken is not sure how to get to the Lunatic Asylum (I tell him this is a good sign). We finally find it on top of yet another hill. The red-brick castle-like Victorian building is indeed 'large' (Murray). The sign at the entrance designates it as MENTAL HEALTH DIRECTORATE. DOWN & DOWNSHIRE HOSPITAL—probably a politically correct modern equivalent of 'Lunatic Asylum'. I can see why the great guide-book writer singled it out from other Downpatrick buildings: in size and splendour, it is second only to the cathedral we've just visited.

I find this observation vaguely significant.

When I pop into Denvir's to pick up my bags, the receptionist tells me triumphantly that the absent-minded owner of the trousers and shoes has been tracked down, and the items are about to be reunited with him.

'I hope he has a spare pair of both to wear in the meantime,' I say.

So, the pants and the shoes were not St Patrick's, after all. This means that, unlike its rival Armagh, Downpatrick won't be able to own the saint's possessions and will have to be satisfied with claiming just his burial place, also disputed by Armagh.

————

*'Hillsborough\* (pop. 617), is an English-looking little town on the side of a hill, containing a well-preserved Fort, built by Sir Arthur Hill in the reign of Charles I, and still kept up as a hereditary garrison under the Marquis of Downshire, who enjoys the titles of Marshal of Ulster and Hereditary Constable of Hillsborough...'*
('A HANDBOOK FOR TRAVELLERS IN IRELAND', MURRAY, 1912)

*'Hillsborough...a pretty and interesting village of outstanding importance.'*
('ULSTER HOLIDAY GUIDE', 1949)

On the way to Armagh, I stop at the charming English village of Hillsborough. Don't worry: I have not been affected by the lunacy of Downpatrick's splendid 'Asylum': Hillsborough, with its quiet winding streets lined with solid Georgian houses, cosy tearooms and antique shops, has 'a chintzy Middle-English ambience', according to my observant 2004 *Rough Guide to Ireland*. The 'ambience' must have been there for a long time, for Hillsborough's 'Englishness' was also noted by Murray (see above). It is therefore little wonder that Hillsborough Castle—a mini-Buckingham Palace (complete with wrought-iron gates and a small sentry booth, marked 'EIIR 1952', at the front) was chosen by the British monarchs as their Northern Ireland residence and the place to accommodate visiting foreign dignitaries (the latest being George W. Bush). It is like the reincarnation of C. S. Lewis's wish, expressed in one of his letters, 'to have the dreaming spires of Oxford on the hills of Down.'

The village was built by many generations of the Hill family (hence the name), and Hillsborough Fort is still owned by one of them—the latest in the long line of Marquises of Downshire, to whom the community still pays an annual rent of a pair of white doves. I learn this curious fact from the small local tourism office, probably the most well-stocked and helpful in the whole of Ireland —North and South.

Walking around Northern Ireland's 'Best-Kept Village' (if we are to believe the street signs, and there's no reason not to!), makes me feel as if Belfast, London/Derry and the legacy of the Troubles are thousands of miles away. Nothing here reminds of the on-going conflict. Except, perhaps, for just one detail—short stretches of barbed wire on top of the splendid Castle gates.

I lunch on cream tea and scones in a homely 'English tea room', browse the Cheshire Cat toy shop for presents for my kids (yes, my journey is now almost complete!) and resist the temptation to have my hair cut at 'Shane Bennet, Northern Ireland Hairdresser of the Year', purely for reasons of my modest time-travelling budget.

It is like a detour to a different world—Ireland's Little England, with bits of barbed wire on its gates…

―――

*Armagh\* (pop. 7588), finely situated cathedral town and the seat of the Primate of All Ireland…There seems to be little doubt that St Patrick founded the… Cathedral Church in 444–5…'*
('A HANDBOOK FOR TRAVELLERS IN IRELAND', MURRAY, 1912)

My hotel—the City Hotel—in Armagh is easy to find. I literally stumble upon it when approaching the city. It is discreetly tucked away in a quiet oasis of nature a short walk away from the centre.

My room has a balcony overlooking a rugby field where local teenagers are practising tirelessly.

My last overnight abode on this journey, this is easily the second-best hotel I have stayed while in Ireland (the very best one, of course, was Newry's Canal Court—see 'Newry'). The room is spacious, full of light and newly decorated. Everything works. Even the electric switches, the bane of my travelling existence, are very easy to find.

I walk down to the hotel's gym, but am denied access on the grounds that I don't have a swimming cap and swimming trunks. They offer to sell me a set for £15. Pondering this lucrative proposition, I look through the glass door leading to the gym and spot a very fat man lying on the floor and trying to kick a huge rubber ball with his feet. His face reflects such indescribable suffering that I decide to give the gym a miss. And to save fifteen quid as well.

Back in my comfy room, I dine on room-service chicken tempura (starter) and grilled salmon (main) and then sit down to watch the news. The first item on the bulletin is the seizure in Armagh of 'millions of cigarettes linked to dissident Republicans.' How interesting. I used to think that cigarettes were mostly linked to cancer…

Having had a self-rolled and hence not linked to anyone (or to anything—so I hope) cigarette on the balcony, I climb into my bed and quickly fall asleep.

Day Twelve

# Armagh City–Newry

'*Armagh is the most beautiful inland town in Ireland; there is history in its every stone... The City today has an atmosphere all its own. Fine modern shops line the main streets...*'
('ULSTER HOLIDAY GUIDE', 1949)

'*Armagh is the city of great antiquity. The houses are of a hard reddish calcareous stone, and generally slated. A number of the public edifices are of hewn limestone, of a vivid colour, and are, for the most part, advantageously situated. The town is well supplied with water, by pipes from a reservoir on an eminence in the neighbourhood.*'
(THE 'IMPERIAL GAZETTEER', W.G. BLACKIE, ED., 1855)

'*No person of taste, who had travelled much, would consider it an exaggeration to give the City of Armagh a leading place among the most delightfully situated inland towns of the United Kingdom... The religious, educational and other attractions make Armagh a favourite place of residence for cultivated people...*'
('THE BOOK OF COUNTY ARMAGH', GEORGE HENRY BASSETT, 1888)

I start the last morning of my journey with a cup of excellent espresso, served by a smiling Polish waitress, in the hotel's restaurant. Sipping the coffee, I brace myself for yet another 'St Patrick' experience.

Armagh's main St Patrick shrine is called 'St Patrick's Trian Visitor Complex'.[29] Combining three different exhibitions ('The Armagh Story', 'St Patrick's Testament' and 'the Land of Lilliput') under one roof, it is complex indeed! And, just like the Downpatrick Centre, it is totally deserted. At least, unlike countless Lenin museums in the USSR (every city and town had at least one!), it is not full of school kids on compulsory excursions.

'We say we are more important than Downpatrick, because Patrick lived here,' a woman at reception tells me. I decide not to challenge her statement.

The Complex, built in 1992, strikes me as a bit more modest and less technologically advanced than its Downpatrick counterpart. I am lucky to be assigned a knowledgeable guide—a soft-spoken English lady, who claims she is a 'cosmopolitan'.

'St Patrick's Confessions were written in Latin—in very poor Latin, mind you, for he was not a scholar,' she tells me with a smile.

This unexpected touch of realistic modesty makes St Patrick look more human and less intimidating in my eyes. It brings him back to life much more effectively than all the interactive displays of the 'Complex' and the 'Centre' combined.

'St Patrick should have been a great uniting force for Protestants and Catholics, but, sadly, it is not the case,' she sighs. 'Our two bishops have tried very hard to patch the divide in the community, but have succeeded only partially. At least here we all go to the same shops—unlike in Belfast…'

We walk past an enormous statue of Gulliver at the entrance to 'The Land of Lilliput'.

'Swift was a Dubliner, but came to Armagh at the end of his life,' my guide explains. 'He stayed at Gosford Castle and did corrections to the first London edition of *Gulliver's Travels*. That book, with Swift's notes in the margins, is kept at our Public Library, and you can have a look at it, if you wish…'

A young woman in Victorian costume—part of 'the Land of Lilliput' exhibition—is standing forlornly near Gulliver's statue.

'What is your role here?' I ask her.

'I entertain school children by impersonating a contemporary of Jonathan Swift,' she says. 'I know my costume should be

Georgian, not Victorian, but we don't think the children will be able to tell the difference…'

Like Downpatrick, Armagh has two St Patrick's cathedrals: the Church of Ireland and the Roman Catholic one. Each claims to have been founded by St Patrick.

DONATIONS MIN. £2 says the printed sign on the door of the Church of Ireland Cathedral. It is like a hand-written note I once saw displayed by an ingenious street beggar in Rome: 'I only accept banknotes of €5 minimum'.

Visitors to the Cathedral are clearly not in a hurry to part company with their honestly earned 'min. £2'. In fact, there is not a single person inside, except for a woman at the tourist information desk. A large wooden 'Abbots & Bishops' board of the type one often sees in schools' assembly halls, with lists of best students and former headmasters, is on one of the walls. The list of bishops starts with 444—PATRICK and goes all the way to 1986—ROBERT HENRY ALEXANDER EAMES.

'Both Protestants and Catholics claim Patrick as their own,' the woman tells me. I thank her for this valuable bit of 'tourist information' and head for Armagh's second St Patrick's Cathedral —this time the Catholic one. It is perched on top of yet another hill (every local tourist brochure says that Armagh stands on seven hills, 'like Rome'), and is much grander than its Protestant namesake. This is probably why there are no demands for donations on its doors.

The second St Patrick's Cathedral is as empty as the first one. I sit down on a pew and start making notes. One of the habits I have acquired in the course of my travels around Ireland is popping into churches to make notes in peace—my own little ('Vitalist'?) liturgy. Whatever religious branch they represent, inside, Irish churches are normally quiet and peaceful…

Before leaving Armagh and heading back South, I have an appointment with Jonathan Swift, who called himself 'a word-besotted traveller' in the epitaph that he had written to himself! Our meeting place is at Armagh's Public Library. The first London edition of *Gulliver's Travels*, proof-read by Swift, is kept in the Library's rare books section.

'I have come for Jonathan Swift', I say to the intercom. Buzzer, click—and I am let in.

Again, just as in the two cathedrals, I am on my own in the shrine. Only here I don't feel alone, for I have the company not of a mythical saint, but of a flesh-and-blood and larger-than-life Irish satirist, poet and writer. There couldn't be a better finishing point for my time travels in modern Ireland.

With care and trepidation, I turn over the yellow-ish crispy pages:

'Travels into Several Remote Nations of the World. In Four Volumes. By Lemuel Gulliver. Vol. I, London 1726.'

Some of Swift's neat corrections, or 'proofing' to use a modern publishing term, are marked in black ink on the text:

'Lilliputia' Chapter: p.79. '*bending*' instead of 'binding' ('binding the extremities into a hook'); p. 145. '*Blefuscu*' instead of 'Lilliput' ('Emperor of Lilliput'); 'Laputa' Chapter: p.71. '*Books*' instead of 'Both' ('Both in philosophy, poetry, politics, law...');

'Voyage' Chapter: p.88. '*posterior*' instead of 'inferior' ('...and the inferior for ejection'—the misprint almost as bad as the common modern boo-boo of confusing 'posterior' with 'posterity'. 'I am writing for the posterior', an aspiring, yet unsuccessful, writer friend of mine used to tell me proudly).

As I read the corrections, I can feel Jonathan Swift sitting next to me squinting at the text from under his lush curly wig...

Altogether, there are not too many misprints at all. The quality of publishing in 1726 was clearly much higher than two hundred years later. In his 1930s' *Notebooks*, Ilya Ilf has a humorous entry about a publishing house that decided to eradicate all misprints from their books. They wrote memos to the staff, conducted countless meetings, and still, when the next edition of their Encyclopaedia came out, it had '*Encyclopoodia*' printed on the cover!

I gently stroke the ink marks, made by one of Ireland's greatest writers nearly two hundred years ago.

*When I see (and touch) these faint, yet curiously assertive, marks of time, I—for a fleeting moment—am teleported back in time...*

This last sentence repeats my feelings in the introduction to this book, almost word for word—a sure sign that my journey and the book itself have travelled the full circle and are both close to conclusion.

As always, rain catches up with me as I approach the North/South border.

Driving through Newry, one of my favourite places in Ireland, I suddenly realise I don't have any change in euro for the first Celtic-Tiger road toll station across the frontier.

I park near Dunnes Stores and spend half an hour trying to change pound coins into euro—all in vain, until a young lady from the store's newspaper kiosk simply gives me two euro coins and refuses to accept anything in return.

What a reassuringly optimistic last touch to my trip! I now wish I had succumbed to the demand of a 'min. £2' donation at Armagh's St Patrick's Cathedral this morning to balance this unexpected and unasked-for gift...

I pull over at a currency-exchange outlet marking the unmarked North-South divide and get out of the car.

The rain has stopped.

A huge juicy rainbow, with one end in Ireland and the other—in the other Ireland, is effortlessly bridging together two parts of the same small nation, dissected by the non-existing frontier.

*Dublin–London, 2006–07*

# Confused Sunflowers

A Short Postscript

While in Ireland, I observed the sunflowers which had been planted near the entrance to Toscana Italian restaurant in Sandycove, near Dun Laoghaire, for many months.

The sunflowers' behavior was highly unusual. Due to the near-permanent absence of sunlight, their seeded, bright-yellow heads, genetically designed to turn towards the sun, were confused. They all pointed in different directions, at times staring at each other in a rather discombobulated way.

Modern Ireland reminds me of a confused sunflower, not entirely sure of where to look: at its gruesome past; its materially prosperous, yet spiritually vacuous, present; or its largely uncertain future. It is unsure of whether to turn towards Britain, Europe, or further afield—to the USA.

That very uncertainty, to my mind, characterises the Celtic Tiger Land more than anything else.

The beautiful, if somewhat withered by the cold winds, sunflower called Ireland desperately needs a luminary to turn to.

Perhaps it doesn't have to look too far: the confused flower itself is in the shape of the sun.

APPENDIX I
# Cork City

> '*Cork is a mixture of some fine streets, broad*
> *quays, and many ill-paved lanes, the whole being*
> *set off by a charming frame of scenery that*
> *compensates for many a defect.*'
> ('A HANDBOOK FOR TRAVELLERS IN IRELAND',
> MURRAY, 1912)

> '*The general appearance of the city [of Cork] is*
> *cheerful and picturesque, although its suburbs,*
> *and many of its lanes, present appearances of the*
> *most wretched poverty.*'
> (THE 'IMPERIAL GAZETTEER', W.G. BLACKIE, ED.,
> 1855)

Cork City was unlike any other place in Ireland—still 'cheerful and picturesque' 150 years after W.G. Blackie of Glasgow put together his famously irreverent Gazetteer. The rebellious and freedom-loving spirit of the city impressed me so much that I wanted to write about it in a way that was different from the rest of this book. Just for once, I decided to put on the denim 'mantle' of a modern guidebook writer—as opposed to time-beaten togas of Baedeker or Murray—and to produce an imitation (or spoof) mini guide-book.

After all, as claimed in the 'Cork 2005 European Capital of Culture' brochure, 'We Corkonians are constantly open to surprise. As a matter of principle we are always open to the unexpected—after all, that is why we live in Cork.'

Here's the surprise (see below):

## A TOUGH GUIDE TO CORKONIA

### General Information

Corkonia (or—for brevity—'Cork') is a semi-independent country to the south-west of Dublinia, sometimes referred to as 'Ireland'.

The natives are a fiercely patriotic lot, defining themselves as non-Dubliners first and only then as Corkonians. The capital is Cork City, also known as Festival City, City of Making (no one knows exactly of what), Rebel City (no relation to Fallujah) and—more recently as 'ECOC' which stands for 'European Capital of Culture', or, according to other sources, for 'Extraordinary Capital of Corkonia'.

There is no consensus as to either the size of the city's population (the estimates vary from thirty-three to 250,000) or the exact number of bridges across the River Lee (from none to twenty-eight).

Cork's national colours are red and white, also known as 'blood-and-bandages' (see 'hurling' in 'Sports and Pastimes' below). The national symbol is an eleven-foot salmon, also known as the 'Goldy Fish' (see 'Food'). The Corkonian pro-independence movement is represented by a popular underground website *www.PeoplesRepublicofCork.com* and by the masthead of the official national broadsheet *The Corkman*.

### History

The formative event in Corkonian history, the so-called 'Cork Gunpowder Explosion', took place on 3 November 1810, when twenty-two people were killed and more than forty injured as a result of the carelessness of a drunken gunpowder factory worker, who tried to dry stolen gunpowder (before selling it to some powder-hungry quarrymen) by holding a burning candle to it.

Cork became the hub of the initially successful Temperance Movement, led by Father Theobald Matthew, that resulted in lower production of whiskey in the 1840s, yet failed to affect the natives' ongoing love for their own brews of stout—Murphy's and Beamish (see 'Where to Drink', or simply drink without looking).

The next significant event occurred in 2004, when Cork won the World Cup in hurling (see 'Sports and Pastimes'). And the latest notable date was, of course, year 2005, when Corkonia's main city was designated 'European Capital of Culture' and thus turned all remaining parts of Europe (including Rome, Paris, Berlin and Broomhead) into EPOCS—European Provinces of Culture, albeit temporarily. The event has left no imprint whatsoever and by now is all but forgotten.

## Geography
Corkonia's flood-prone capital lies on an island, formed by the River Lee, and is connected to the rest of the nation—the deprived North and the more affluent South—by bridges (for the exact number of bridges see 'General Information'). At the moment of writing, the locals are campaigning to name one of the bridges 'Roy Keane Bridge' in memory of the famous Corkonian warrior and national hero, who, incidentally is still alive.

Access to Corkonia by land is largely blocked by the insurmountable Kinsale Street Roundabout, which Corkonians lovingly call 'The Magic Roundabout' for its pivotal role in the country's relative isolation from the rest of the world.

On 8 November 2004—to Corkonians' considerable dismay— the Monasterevin by-pass, cutting the journey between Dublin and Cork by thirty minutes, was opened. 'Dublin Has Moved Closer to Cork', as it was put by Cork's main broadsheet 'De Paper' (at times incorrectly referred to as *The Irish Examiner*) on the same day.

## Local Time
Unspecified and variable—as reflected in the nickname of the city's best-known clock, 'The Four-Faced Liar'.

## Language
'To understand the people of Cork, one must know their language,' noted Sean Beecher in the introduction to his hard-to-obtain (outside Cork) *Dictionary of Corkonian*.

Corkonians speak 'Gammin'—their unique language—with an inimitable singsong drawl (not dissimilar to Liverpudlian Scouse), swallowing vowels (of which there are twenty-six in the Corkonian alphabet) and consonants (of which there are two), too. A first-time foreign visitor may be led to believe that they all have little church spires inside their mouths which—on inspection— usually proves untrue.

Below are some useful words and expressions:

'Dead man'—empty glass
'Gauzer'—good-looking girl
'Gowl'—fool
'Hack'—fun
'Magalorim'—drunk
'Mombolised'—very drunk
'Gawked up'—drunk out of one's mind
'Langer'—a polysemantic term with no exact equivalent in English
'Langers'—a plural of 'Langer' (see above); also—drunk.
'Belt away'—carry on with what you are doing
'Fair Dues'—well done
'Over there la'—over there
'Great Tack'—great stuff
'Alright boy'—hi, langer (see)

Apart from the above-mentioned dictionary, another highly recommended manual of Corkonian is *Dowtcha Boy* by Morty McCarthy, a native linguist who recently emigrated from Cork to Stockholm to teach English. The country is now bracing itself for the invasion of Corkonian-speaking Swedes.

## Getting there

Visitors to Cork normally do not require a Corkonian visa, unlike those from Dublinia, who do not need visas either.

Aer Arann has daily flights between Dublinia and Cork International Airport. Do not be surprised by the following onboard announcement before landing: 'Cork airport authority requires all mobile phones to be switched off until you are well inside the terminal'. The reason is that, on top of the smoking ban, Cork airport has recently introduced a talking ban (Corkonians have a reputation of one of the world's most garrulous people).

Make sure you do not speak to anyone (including yourself) until you leave the terminal building.

## Getting around
Unless you want to spend the whole of your visit admiring the Magic Roundabout (see 'Geography'), do not use buses or cars while in Cork. Do not ask local bus or taxi drivers for directions: their sense of time and distance is distorted by being permanently stuck in traffic jams. When walking around, watch your step: just like prior to the ECOC 2005 season (see General Info), the country is still in the throes of frantic road works. Before leaving your hotel, consult the popular 'Pothole of the Week' section at *www. PeoplesRepublicofCork.com* for the latest road re-developments.

## Sports and pastimes
Corkonia's most popular national sports are 'pickey' (a street version of hopscotch), 'up against the wall' (a street version of soccer, normally played at the National Football Stadium), go-carting or 'steerning' (usually inside a supermarket), taxi racing (use of blinkers and honking are not allowed), street boating (at the time of floods), hurling (balls, stones, bottles etc), road bowling (see above for 'Pothole of the Week') and road crossing— the latter being the most dangerous of all (see 'Getting Around').

The favourite Corkonian pastimes, apart from the one mentioned below (see 'Where to Drink'), are 'slocking (stealing apples), 'Doing pana', i.e. wandering up and down the permanently dug-up Patrick Street without any purpose and (more recently) 'ECOC-ing', i.e. complaining of the waste of city resources associated with the ECOC period (see above).

## Food
Corkonian mouth-watering culinary specialities include: *tripe* (cow's stomach), *crubeens* (pigs' feet) and *drisheen* (blood sausage) A more recent one is 'Kalina Jagerspeck'—a German-manufactured Russian specialism: pure lard with tiny insets of smoked pork. The latter can only be acquired at 'Staraya Rus' (Old Russia), a Russian/Lithuanian shop on North Main Street.

**NB:** Do not ask for 'Russian boots'—a Corkonian term for 'Wellingtons'—at Staraya Rus. Also, not to upset the natives, do not try to consume 'Goldy Fish' (see 'General Info')—one of the country's symbols, even if you manage to remove it from the spire of St Anne's church in the Shandon area.

**Where to Drink**
At Preachers, The Thirsty Scholar and pretty much anywhere else —as the natives do.

**Where to Eat**
Anywhere, except for the places listed below (see 'Where Not to Eat').

**Where Not to Eat**
A Taste of Thailand on Bridge Street, where 'Thai' food has the unmistakeable flavour of Cork (and of cork); Staraya Rus (see 'food', and this includes seafood!); The Kylemore restaurant at Cork International airport, where they charge international prices for local-sized portions.

**Where to Stay**
Cork City Gaol, according to *www.cork-guide.ie*, has 'cells, furnished with life-size figures, souvenir and refreshment areas, friendly staff and good facilities…'

**Where to Shop**
For European Capital of Culture 2005 memorabilia (badges, pamphlets, wines, notebooks etc) try the former ECOC Headquarters (50 Pope's Quay), where they are all still stocked in a little side room next to reception. Make sure you don't confuse the unwanted ECOC brochures with paperback copies of the *Da Vinci Code* (Waterstone's bookstore, 69 Patrick Street)—the best-selling thriller by Dan Brown (not a native of Cork), for they have almost identical black-amber colour schemes on their covers.

## What to Do
See 'Getting Around', 'Where to Eat', 'Where Not to Eat', 'Where to Drink', 'Where to Shop', 'Where to Stay' and 'Sports and Pastimes'.

## What Not to Do
Do not run the risk of trying to trace down the people behind *www.PeoplesRepublicofCork.com*—a highly conspiratorial underground organisation of 'People's Republicanism', striving for Corkonia's complete independence. The exact strength, composition and whereabouts of the organisation are closely guarded secrets—to everyone, including its own members (if any). Among their revolutionary activities are: campaigning for the relocation of the Government from Dublin to Cork, cleaning road signs and secret patrolling of the country's border, to search cars for such subversive (from the People's Republicans' point of view) foreign goods as Dubliner CDs, Brennan's bread, cans of 'Guinness' etc—and to confiscate them. To be on the safe side, do not bring these goods to Corkonia.

Some experts believe that the organisation is funded by the proceeds from selling 'Peoples' Republic of Cork' T-shirts that are safe to buy and to wear outside Corkonia.

## Sense of Humour
Corkonians are renowned for their peculiar, self-deprecating wit (no wonder, therefore, that Cork City was recently twinned with Shanghai!). A good example of it is the sign in the windows of some of the country's newsagents: 'Sober or Blotto—Remember the Lotto' (Corkonian National Lotto has a prize-fund of 40 billion shandons. **NB**: Shandon—'$n'—is a local currency unit. One Euro buys $n10 billion at the current exchange rate).

## On a more serious note
If Culture indeed needed a capital, the Rebel City would have been one of the main contenders. But, luckily, it never did and never will. After all, who needs a Capital of Culture when we already have the Capital of Corkonia?

As they say in Cork, 'fair dues' and 'belt away'!

# On Irish Humour

*'Satiric touch…No nation needed it so much…'*
(JONATHAN SWIFT)

The Christmas gift that I had bought in Dublin for a Scottish friend of mine proved a disaster. It was a kitchen clock, but one of its hands was permanently twisted so that whenever the big hand pointed at twelve, the small—limping—one was stuck halfway between two other digits. To my considerable embarrassment, the incurable defect became obvious only *after* the present was unwrapped. No matter how hard I tried to persuade my friend that even faulty clocks showed the right time twice a day and that my gift was still OK for, say, hammering nails into walls, her verdict was simple: 'You've given me an Irish clock!' I got a bit offended by such blatant negative stereotyping of my newly adopted nation. Why was it that, in jokes all over the English-speaking world, the Irish were invariably portrayed as dumb? I was about to retort to my Scottish friend that it was better to be perceived as being sheepish than as being greedy—a common stereotype of the Scots, but then remembered that the most poignant jokes about the Irish come from the Irish themselves!

Wasn't it in Ireland that I myself heard frequent references to 'Irish timing' when someone was running late? Wasn't it the maverick Irish wit Brendan Behan who famously said that if it was raining soup, the Irish would be out with forks?

As for negative stereotyping—well, a nation with enough self-respect can always cope with it, can't it?

My observations show that every country in the world targets residents of one particular area—be it a province, a state or a neighbouring nation—upon which to exercise its wit. In Australia, it is Tasmanians; in Canada—Newfoundlanders, or 'Newffies'; in

Russia—Georgians and, yes, Ukrainians; in Ireland—the Kerrymen. Even in tiny Malta they routinely crack jokes about the Gozitans—the inhabitants of the island of Gozo, famous for its goat's cheese (something to the effect of them being 'cheese-headed'). Ukrainians are probably the most hard-done by, for they are stereotyped as both stingy (like the Scots) and dumb (like the Irish).

It is only the Irish and the Jews that are targeted more or less universally. And I think I know why. Whereas Australians, Americans, Scots, Ukrainians or, say, the French seldom, if ever, direct their wit at themselves, Irish and Jewish jokes are almost always self-deprecating. Not only are these two much-persecuted nations capable of satirising themselves, they also don't really mind other people's gags about them and are always ready to join in.

Self-deprecating humour is often a recipe for self-preservation. Peter Ustinov first became a mimic and a wit as a schoolboy—in response to Westminster School bullies, who kept harassing him for his innate 'rotundity' (he once told me that being born 'rotund' was like winning prize number 274 in the lottery of life). Instead of sulking or bursting into tears, he chose to start laughing at himself, and the bullies—not sure how to react—eventually left him alone. In this respect, we can safely call late Sir Peter a truly 'Irish' humorist.

I heard my ever first Irish joke in Moscow in the mid-1980s, the one I mention in my introduction to the Skeleton Tour of the North, about the competition, sponsored by Northern Ireland Tourism Board, whereby a winner would be entitled to a one-week free holiday in Belfast and the runner-up—to a two-week holiday (I didn't know then that it was coined by Brendan Behan). On hearing it, I laughed almost to tears. Or was it through tears? 'Laughter through tears', an expression, coined by a 19th-century Russian literary critic Alexander Belinsky, had always represented an archetypally 'Russian' (or Soviet, if you wish) attitude to life—on a par with 'hope against hope'. The parallels between Northern Ireland at the height of the Troubles and the chaotic pre-perestroika Soviet Union were close enough for this yarn to ring the bell among Muscovites.

At the time of hardship and uncertainty, self-directed laughter becomes the best available remedy for tears. The most popular gags in the Soviet Union of the 1970s–80s were a series of question-answer mini-dialogues, purporting to come from 'Armenian Radio':

Q. What would happen if they build socialism in the Sahara desert?

A. Nothing initially, but soon terrible shortages of sand will occur...

Q. What is the difference between democracy and socialist democracy?

A. It is like the difference between a normal chair and an electric chair...

Q. Who invented socialism—scientists or politicians?

A. It must have been politicians, for scientists would have tried it on dogs first...

Q. What's the world's shortest joke?

A. Communism.

And so on. It is important to remember that one could easily end up in prison for telling any of the above in public. And that was probably their main distinction from similarly toned Irish jokes.

'What's all that noise in the street, Pat,' a gentleman asks his servant.

'Oh, nothing, sir,'—he replies. 'They are only forcing a man to join the Volunteers.'

The last repartee is a good example of one of the most admirable, to my mind, varieties of Irish humour known as 'The Bull' (from the proverbial 'Irish bull' who is always pregnant). Sean McCann, the compiler of the anthology *Irish Wit*, defines it as 'the saying that contradicts itself, in a manner palpably absurd to listeners but unperceived by the person who makes it.' I would describe it simply as a verbal four-angled triangle. 'If you don't come to your friends' funerals, they won't come to yours' is another illustration. Oscar Wilde was the master of 'The Bull' ('Do I know George Moore? Of course! I know him so well I haven't spoken to him for ten years!'), and so was Peter Ustinov ('The speech was so boring that I had to look at my watch every hour to realise that only five minutes had passed.'). Interestingly, Soviet humour was as paradoxical and absurdist as its Irish counterpart. This last similarity must have something to do with the level of oppression in a society, for all tyrannies—religious, military or political—are absurd by their very nature.

When I worked for the popular satirical page of Moscow's *Literaturnaya Gazeta* in the 1980s, we invented a spoof satirical hero—writer Evgeny Sazonov, whose most famous aphorism was 'When something is forbidden, but desperately desired, then it is allowed'—another classic incarnation of the expectant Irish 'Bull'.

To me, one of the most delightful qualities of present-day Ireland is the all-permeating casual humour of its everyday life, to which I was frequently (and more than willingly) exposed during my fifteen months in the country. I liked the laconic tongue-in-cheek way in which Dubliners described some of the city's landmarks: 'Dead Zoo', for Natural History Museum; 'Stiletto in the Ghetto' (or—even better—'Pole in the Hole') for the unfortunate O'Connell Street Spire; 'She-Doesn't-Understand-Me-Street', for Leeson Street, with all its dodgy night-clubs.

A Dublin taxi-driver once told me that he himself grew up in the notoriously rough Northside of the capital, whereas his wife was from the plush Southside. 'She only married me because she wanted her handbag back,' he concluded. And a driver-cum-guide of a Dublin City Tour bus, having branded O'Connell Street 'by far the widest main street in Europe', paused and added: 'Although the Champs Elysées, of course, is slightly wider…'

It is not just in Dublin that the cheek-impregnated 'Irish Bull' has his pastures.

During my flying visit to Limerick city, I was taken by the fact that its two main newspapers were the *Limerick Leader* and the *Limerick Dealer*—a spoonerism that would make Spooner himself green with envy. In the city's train/bus station I spotted a huge, brightly lit sign with a biblical quote: I AM THE DOOR, AND ANY MAN WHO ENTERS ME WILL BE SAVED. The sign wouldn't have been particularly funny, had it not been placed (deliberately, I am sure) right above the door of the men's toilet!

And although the true origins of the world's wittiest poetic five-liner are still disputed, I want to believe that limericks as a genre originated from the early-19th-century Irish-language satirical verses of the Poets of the Maige from Co. Limerick. Here's my favourite limerick of all time:

> There was an old man in Spain
> Who felt terribly sick on a train—
> Not once, but again
> And again, and again,
> And again, and again, and again.

But I've digressed.

To me, everyday life in Ireland is so full of practical humour that I am often led to think that all of it is but one protracted joke. See for yourselves. The very first Christmas card I received in Ireland wishing me, among other things, 'a peaceful New Year' was from…Sinn Féin.

The second one came from Dublin City Council, and its real purpose was to announce that from 1 January 2005 the Council would introduce 'a new pay-by-use/volume system for household waste-collection services'. I thought that was the very best example of 'The Irish Bull' I had come across so far. Next morning, I discovered a couple of someone else's rubbish bags dumped at my doorstep. One of them was crowned with a rather soiled, as if already semi-recycled, red-and-white Santa hat. Happy Irish Christmas!

The Santa hat did its trick, however. Instead of getting angry, I smiled uneasily and dragged the rubbish bags away from my door. Towards my neighbour's (only joking).

Not all modern Irish humour, however, is as black as a rubbish bag, planted at one's door under cover of darkness.

While in Northern Ireland, I heard the story of a US-born nine-year-old Irish-American boy, brought for holidays to Belfast last year—for the first time in his life. After several days in the city, he asked his father: 'Dad, who was that Jewish man, called Ira, who has written his name on all the city walls and fences?'

Compare it to the dark one-or-two-week-holiday-in-Belfast joke of the not-so-distant past. A differently charged sort of humour. Could it also be a sign of changing times? I'd seriously like to hope that it is…

What's the shortest Irish joke then? Dublin? The Dáil? Celtic Tiger? Or, possibly, the smoking ban? 'From next year the Irish government is going to introduce a ban on fun and smiles,' a poker-faced Dublin woman told me as we stood puffing away for all we were worth outside a restaurant.

I cackled uneasily and thought that I wouldn't be surprised if Bertie Ahern, who—unlike his *Thomas-the-Tank-Engine* name-sake *Bertie the Bus*—always struck me as one of the most unsmiling creatures in existence, indeed decreed laughter in public places socially dangerous and subject to fines (to help balance the next annual Budget).

But even if he did, the Irish people would still keep laughing—at their life, at their government and, most importantly, at themselves.

For, as Elizabeth Bowen put it, where would the Irish be without someone to be Irish at?

# References

1. By 'Baedeker' I mean not one person but a dynasty (and a large team of writers) that included: Karl Baedeker I (1801–1859), Ernst Baedeker (1833–1861), Karl Baedeker II (1837–1911), Fritz Baedeker (1844–1925) and Hans Baedeker (1874–1959).
2. John Murray, a prominent British publisher of the 19th and early 20th centuries, was simultaneously Baedeker's 'esteemed' friend and his bitter rival/competitor.
3. As in the 'Skeleton Routes' section of Murray's *A Handbook for Travellers in Ireland*, 1912.
4. According to an omniscient Dublin friend, it was also a popular spot for secret summer trysts of 'celibate' Roman Catholic clergymen from all over Ireland with their clandestine sweethearts: male and female.
5. As you have noticed, Ostap Bender and his creators Ilf and Petrov will be joining my team of time-travelling companions.
6. *The coachman is drunk* (German).
7. That particular plastic moaner meant the 1798 rebellion, ruthlessly suppressed by the British army.
8. Russian for 'Do you speak Russian?'
9. James Hardiman, an Irish historian, who published his book *History Galway* in 1820. There are a number of references to it in W.M Thackeray's *Irish Sketch Book* as well as in Murray's *Ireland*. Hardiman once referred to Galway as 'Connaught's Rome'.
10. Contrary to what you might think, traditional Galway fishing boats.
11. One of the funeral parlours in N. was called 'Do Us the Honour Funeral Home'.
12. The paper was then officially called *Cork County Eagle & Munster Advertiser*. Each issue had four editions!
13. The brackets here are NOT mine.
14. Having passed through Waterford several weeks before, I was impressed most of all by how ethnically mixed it was. Approaching Sherkin, I couldn't help conjuring up an image of those Vietnamese, Turkish, Polish etc., 'citizens of Waterford' attacking the tiny island…
15. I found the echoes of that joke in the modern, hundred-per-cent-serious 2005 *Belfast Visitor's Guide* published by Tourism Ireland. On its front cover the guide-book comes up with the following city logo: 'BELFAST…better believe it.' It felt like the barrel of a gun aimed at my head: better believe it, or else…
16. Collins Dictionary, HarperCollins Publishers, 1990.
17. *Champagne, I am dying* (German).
18. According to Murray, it was James I who changed the name of the city from

Derry to Londonderry and granted it a new 'charter of incorporation' in 1613. By then, 'over 200 acres' of Derry's territory belonged to 'the citizens of London'.

19. I deliberately choose to refer to the city as 'London/Derry'—or for brevity 'L/D'—not to take a stand (for I don't have any) in the continuing dispute over its name. My 2004 *Rough Guide*, incidentally, mentions the nickname 'Stroke City', an attempt to placate both Nationalists and Unionists. I will resort to the latter occasionally, too.

20. Later I learn that Northern Ireland has the UK's lowest rate of car theft and vandalism (albeit the highest car insurance cost!), and Belfast is the safest place to leave your vehicle overnight. Are the reasons the same? Fear as a deterrent of road rage and street crime?

21. '...whose apostolic fervour and simple bravery will long be the theme of admiration'. (Murray, 1912)

22. In his essay on the city's history, preceding the Londonderry entry of his 1912 *Handbook*, Murray has a splendid literary passage on the Monument and the Walls: 'On the summit is the statue of Walker, such as when, in the last and most terrible emergency, his eloquence roused the fainting courage of his brethren. In one hand he grasps a Bible; the other, pointing down the river seems to direct the eyes of his famished audience to the English top-masts in the distant bay. Such a monument was well deserved; yet it was scarcely needed; for, in truth, the whole city is to this day a monument of the great deliverance. The wall is carefully preserved, nor would any plea of health or convenience be held by the inhabitants sufficient to justify the demolition of that sacred enclosure which, in evil time, gave shelter to their race and religion.' The IRA, it seems, was willing to forsake the 'pleas' and had no qualms about demolishing the 'sacred' city sites.

23. This exchange comes from Baedeker's *Traveller's Manual of Conversation* (1886).

24. 'The City Hall is a palatial structure built of Portland stone in the classical Renaissance style.' (Murray's *Ireland*, 1912)

25. Commenting on the White Star line vessels the *Olympic* and 'the ill-fated *Titanic*', Murray notes that they 'cost the enormous sum of £1.5 million each'.

26. And I did.

27. 'Armagh strongly challenges Downpatrick's claim to be the burial place of St Patrick; locals argue that since the relics of Patrick's book, bell and staff are here, his body must be too (although the burial site is not identified).' (*Rough Guide to Ireland*, 2004)

28. There is a popular Soviet joke about a factory which made a triple marital bed called 'Lenin is always with us'.

29. 'Trian' (tree-an) refers to the division of ancient Armagh into districts, or Trians as they were called.